THE GREAT BIG
BOOK *OF*
HOW TO STUDY

BY
RON FRY

CAREER PRESS
FRANKLIN LAKES, NJ

THE GREAT BIG BOOK OF HOW TO STUDY
Cover design by Lu Rossman
Printed in the U.S.A. by Book-mart Press

To order this title, please call toll-free 1-800-CAREER-1 (NJ and Canada: 201-848-0310) to order using VISA or Master Card, or for further information on books from Career Press.

The Career Press, Inc., 3 Tice Road, PO Box 687, Franklin Lakes, NJ 07417

Library of Congress Cataloging-in-Publication Data

Fry, Ronald W.
    The great big book of how to study / by Ron Fry.
      p.   cm.
    Includes index.
    ISBN 1-56414-423-2 (pbk.)
    1. Study skills. 2. Note-taking. 3. Students--Time management. 4. Test-taking skills.   I. Title.
    LB1049.F7353   1999
    370.3'028'1--dc21

                               99-15099
                                 CIP

CONTENTS

PREFACE   7

BOOK 1: HOW TO STUDY

Introduction: 13
How to use this book

Chapter 1:   23
How to start out right

Chapter 2:   34
How to organize your studying

Chapter 3:   56
How to read and remember

Chapter 4:   92
How to use your library

Chapter 5:   103
How to use your computer

Chapter 6:   120
How to write terrific papers

Epilogue   151

BOOK 2: MANAGE YOUR TIME

Introduction: 155
Make time to study smarter

Chapter 1:   162
Take the time to plan

Chapter 2:   173
Spend time to save time

Chapter 3:   179
Set the stage for success

Chapter 4:   201
Get the big picture

Chapter 5:   212
Add the detailed brush strokes

Chapter 6:   220
Help! Tips, tips, and more tips

Chapter 7:   232
It's time to deal with ADD

Chapter 8:   240
Time management forms

BOOK 3: TAKE NOTES

Introduction: 247
There is a right way to take notes

Chapter 1:   252
Gather your note-taking equipment

Chapter 2:   254
Class notes: Learning to listen

Chapter 3:   264
Class notes: Successful strategies

Chapter 4:   278
Making short work of class notes

Chapter 5:   291
Texts: Read first, then write

Chapter 6:   298
Texts: Now get out your pen

Chapter 7:   310
Outlines and other tools

Chapter 8:   317
Taking great notes for oral reports

Chapter 9:   324
Let's practice what we've preached

BOOK 4: ACE ANY TEST

Chapter 1:   343
So, what are you afraid of?

Chapter 2:   352
Creating the time to study

Chapter 3:   370
When should you *really* start studying?

Chapter 4:   380
Study smarter, not harder

Chapter 5:   388
Essay tests: Write on!

Chapter 6:   397
Objective tests: Discriminate and eliminate

Chapter 7:   416
The day of the exam: Psyching up

Chapter 8:   425
Post-test: Survival and review

Chapter 9:   432
How teachers make up tests

INDEX   439

PREFACE

Ten years ago, I wrote and published a small book called **How to Study.** I was surprised at the time that I couldn't find any book like it. Nothing about how to organize homework, reports, or projects. Nothing about how to do better on tests (except for those phone book-sized volumes with hints for all the alphabet tests). Nothing about improving reading (unless you just wanted to read very, very fast). Little on helping students learn memory techniques. Nothing on taking better notes.

You get the idea. There was seemingly one heck of a need out there!

History has proven that the need was *overwhelming.* **How to Study** has gone through four editions, which, combined, have sold more than one million copies.

As helpful as this single volume quickly became, many students, teachers, and parents called or wrote and asked for even more help. *More* examples. *More* practice. *More* quizzes. Pretty much more *everything.* Because I didn't want to create a 1,000-page book, I wrote a series of smaller volumes covering specific aspects of studying—**"Ace" Any Test, Get Organized, Improve Your Memory, Improve Your Reading, Improve Your Writing, Manage Your Time, Take Notes, Use Your Computer**—many

BOOK 1

HOW TO STUDY

HOW TO USE THIS BOOK

"What one knows is, in youth, of little moment;
they know enough who know how to learn."
—Henry Adams

Learning how to study *is* learning how to *learn*. And that is, to me, the greatest gift you can ever give yourself.

Having stated that so boldly, I suspect I still have to convince some of you that spending any time trying to master this stuff—studying, learning, reading, note-taking, writing, whatever you call it—is worth your while.

Believe it or not, there are some terrific reasons why you *should* learn how to study, why you *must* learn how to study. But before I start convincing you that developing proper study skills really *is* important, and why, let's figure out exactly what we mean by "study skills," so we're all on the same wavelength.

Yes, **How to Study** includes hints, advice, and techniques for taking notes in class, while you're reading your textbooks, in the library, or even online, how to prepare for tests and how to organize your study schedule to get the best results in the shortest amount of time. But that's the *last* half of the book. There are essential skills you may think don't even have anything to do with studying, and important steps you need to take right from the start.

Here's where to start

Developing great study habits is like a race between you and all your friends around a track. Before you can declare a winner, you have to agree on where the finish line is. In other words, how do you measure your ability to use these skills? What's good? What's poor?

But you can't even start the race until you know where the *starting* line is—especially if it's drawn at a different spot for each of you!

Chapter 1 starts by explaining each study skill and clarifying how each can and should function in your life. Then you have the chance to find your own starting line.

In Chapter 2, you'll learn the importance of where, how, and when you study and start building the study environment that's perfect for *you*. Why is this important? If you've spent three hours reading *Ulysses* with Everlast shaking the walls, it's not surprising you're still on page three. Reading about and understanding Bloom's day might have little to do with increasing reading comprehension, rescheduling your time, or changing books...and a lot more to do with just turning down the volume.

There is no magic elixir in the study habit regimen. If math and science are not your strong suits, memorizing *How to Study* will not transform you into a Nobel Prize-winning physicist. Nobody is great at *every*thing, but everybody is great at *some*thing. So you'll also get a chance to rate the subjects you like and dislike, as well as those classes you do best and worst in.

Chapter 2 also introduces some of the "intangibles" in the study equation: your home environment, attitude, motivation, etc. If you are dedicated to studying and motivated to achieve certain goals, all the other factors that affect your study habits will fall more naturally into place. A belief in the study ethic is one of the keys to success.

Finally, some generalities about the study process—learning to "read" teachers, developing mentors, dealing with perfectionism, the importance of flexibility—will help you get off to the right start.

Reading and comprehension

Chapter 3 introduces the skills basic to any study process: reading and comprehension. No matter how well you learn to take notes, how familiar you become with your library, how doggedly you study for tests, if you are reading poorly (or not enough) and not understanding what you read, life will be difficult.

Becoming a good reader is a skill, one usually acquired early in life. If it's a skill you haven't acquired yet, now is the time! Chapter 3 also points out how your ability to recall ideas, facts, and figures can be significantly increased (quantitatively and qualitatively) with the right practice.

Learning your library

Chapter 4 introduces you to the single most important resource in your study career—your library. You'll learn about the books, periodicals, newspapers, magazines, computer software, video and audio tapes, and other reference materials available to you, and suggestions for how to find and use them, including an explanation of the Dewey Decimal Classification and Library of Congress systems.

Surfing now, surfing now...

You may already be computer literate, perhaps even a frequent Net surfer. If you don't know a bit from a byte, you'll learn in Chapter 5 how vital it is to master the computer, plus how to find the Net and what to do when you get there.

So you're not the next Hemingway

I'm convinced that too many of you place the emphasis in "writing papers" on the word "writing." In Chapter 6, I'll introduce you to a remarkably easy way to gather research, take notes, and organize your information. By breaking down any paper, no matter how complex, into easy-to-follow steps, I think you'll find that you create papers infinitely better than before—even if you're still no threat to Hemingway (or anybody else) when it comes to writing.

(As I mentioned in the Preface, three chapters in this book have been eliminated: "How to organize your time," "How to excel in class," and "How to study for tests." The topics they covered are contained in much greater detail in the other three books in this compilation: *Manage Your Time, Take Notes,* and *"Ace" Any Test.)*

How smart do *you* study?

How to Study is the most comprehensive study guide ever written—a fundamental, step-by-step approach that *you* can follow to develop and sharpen your study skills.

If you're struggling through college or graduate school, here's your life raft.

If you're a high school student planning to attend college, *now*'s your chance to hone your study skills.

If you're heading for trade school, planning to dance, write, paint, etc., not considering college, even if you're ready to drop out of high school at the earliest possible instant, you need *How to Study*.

If you're an adult returning to the classroom after a lengthy absence, there's no substitute for the tips and techniques you will learn in this helpful collection.

So what if you're a really poor student? How smart you are is not the point. *What counts is how smart you study.*

With the possible exception of those few of you who qualify as truly "gifted," the effective study habits *How to Study* teaches will help students of any age.

If your grades are average to good, you will see a definite improvement. If you are on the borderline of the pass/fail range, you will benefit considerably. If good study habits are in place but rusty as a result of years away from the classroom, *How to Study* will be the perfect refresher for you.

And if you *are* one of those lucky "gifted" ones, I *still* think you'll find many helpful techniques in these pages.

Who is this book really for?

Although I originally wrote *How to Study* for high school students, I've discovered over the years that I could probably count on only a couple of hands the number of such students who actually bought a copy of the book.

The surprise was that so many of the people buying *How to Study* (and writing me reams of letters along the way) were adults. Yes, a number of them were returning to school and saw *How to Study* as a great refresher. And some were long out of school but had figured out that if they could learn *now* the study skills their teachers never taught them, they'd do better in their careers.

All too many were parents who had the same lament: "How do I get Jack (or Jill) to read (study, do better on tests, remember more, get better grades, etc.)?"

So I want to briefly take the time to address every one of the audiences for this book and discuss some of the factors particular to each of you.

If you're a high school student

You should be particularly comfortable with the format of the book—its relatively short sentences and paragraphs, occasionally humorous (hopefully) headings and subheadings, and the language used. I wrote it with you in mind!

But you should also be *un*comfortable with the fact that you're already in the middle of your school years—the period that will drastically affect, one way or the other, all the *rest* of your school years—*and you still don't know how to study!* Don't lose another minute. Make learning how to study and mastering *all* of the study skills in this book your *absolute priority.*

If you're a junior high school student

Congratulations! You're learning how to study at *precisely* the right time. Sixth, 7th, and 8th grades—before that cosmic leap to high school—is without a doubt the period in which all these study skills should be mastered, because doing so will make high school not just easier, but a far more positive and successful experience.

If you're a "traditional" college student...

...somewhere in the 18 to 25 age range, I hope you are tackling one or two of the study skills you failed to master in high school (in which case I highly recommend you also study the appropriate title(s) of the other eight books in my

How to Study Program). Otherwise, I can't see how you're ever going to succeed in college. If you are starting from scratch, my advice is the same as to the high school students reading this book: Drop everything and make it your number one priority. Do not pass Go. Do not order pizza.

If you're the parent of a student of any age

Your child's school is probably doing little if anything to teach him or her how to study. Which means he or she is not learning how to *learn*. And that means he or she is not learning how to *succeed*.

Should the schools be accomplishing that? Absolutely. After all, we spend $275 billion on elementary and secondary education in this country, *an average of $6,000 per student per year*. We ought to be getting more for that money than possible graduation, some football cheers, and a rotten entry-level job market.

What can parents do?

There are probably even more dedicated parents out there than dedicated students, because the first phone call at any of my radio or TV appearances comes from a sincere and worried parent asking, "What can I do to help my kid do better in school?" Okay, here they are, the rules for parents of students of any age:

1. **Set up a homework area.** Free of distraction, well lit, all necessary supplies handy.
2. **Set up a homework routine.** When and where it gets done. Same bat-time every day.
3. **Set homework priorities**. Make the point that homework *is* the priority—before a date, before TV, before going out to play, whatever.

4. **Make reading a habit**—for them, certainly, but also for yourselves, if it isn't already. Kids will inevitably do what you *do*, not what you *say* (even if you say *not* to do what you *do*).

5. **Turn off the TV.** Or at the very least, severely limit the amount of TV-watching you do.

6. **Talk to the teachers.** Find out what your kids are supposed to be learning.

7. **Encourage and motivate**, but don't nag them to do their homework. It doesn't work.

8. **Supervise their work**, but don't fall into the trap of *doing* their homework.

9. **Praise them to succeed**, but don't overpraise them for mediocre work.

10. **Convince older students of reality.** Learning and believing that the real world won't care about their grades, but measure them solely by what they know and what they can do is a lesson that will save many tears (probably yours).

11. **If you can afford it, get your kid(s) a computer** and all the software they can handle. Your kids, whatever their age, absolutely must master technology (computers) in order to survive, let alone succeed, in and after school.

The importance of your involvement

Don't for a minute underestimate the importance of *your* commitment: Your involvement in your child's education is absolutely essential to his or her eventual success.

So please, take the time to read this book (and all of the others in the series). Learn what your kids *should* be learning (and which of the other subject-specific books in the series your child needs the most).

And you can help tremendously, *even if you were not a great student yourself, even if you never learned great study skills.* You can learn now with your child—not only will it help him or her in school, it will help *you* on the job, whatever your field.

If you're a nontraditional student

If you're going back to high school, college, or graduate school at age 25, 45, 65, or 85—you probably need the help in *How to Study* more than anyone! Why? Because the longer you've been out of school, the more likely you don't remember what you've forgotten. And you've forgotten what you're supposed to remember! As much as I emphasize that it's rarely too early to learn good study habits, I must also emphasize that it's never too *late*.

What you won't find in *How to Study*

I've seen so-called study books spend chapters on proper nutrition, how to dress, how to exercise, and a number of other topics that are *not* covered *at all* in *How to Study,* except for this briefest of all acknowledgments (right here): It is an absolute given that diet, sleep, exercise, use of drugs (including nicotine and caffeine), and alcohol all affect studying, perhaps significantly.

Having said that, I see little reason to waste your time detailing what should be obvious: Anything—including studying—is more difficult if you're tired, hungry, unhealthy, drunk, stoned, etc. So please use common sense. Eat as healthy as you can, get whatever sleep your body requires, stay reasonably fit, and avoid alcohol and drugs. If your lack of success is in any way due to one of these other factors and you're unable to deal with it alone, find a good book or a professional to help you.

There are other study guides

Though I immodestly maintain my *How to Study Program* to be the most helpful to the most people, there are certainly lots of other purported study books out there. Unfortunately, I don't think many of them deliver what they promise. In fact, I'm actually getting angry at the growing number of study guides out there claiming to be "the sure way to straight A's" or something of the sort. These are also the books that dismiss reasonable alternative ways to study and learn with: "Well, that never worked for me," as if that is a valid reason to dismiss it, as if we should *care* that it didn't work for the author.

There are very few "rights" and "wrongs" out there in the study world. There is certainly no absolute "right" way to attack a multiple choice test or single "right" way to take notes. So don't be fooled into thinking there *is*, especially if what you're doing seems to be working for you. Don't change what "ain't broke" just because some self-proclaimed study guru claims what you're doing is all wet. Maybe he's all wet.

Needless to say, don't read *my* books looking for the Truth—that single, inestimable system of "rules" that works for everyone. You won't find it, 'cause there's no such bird. You *will* find a plethora of techniques, tips, tricks, gimmicks, and what-have-you, some or all of which may work for you, some of which won't. Pick and choose, change and adapt, figure out what works for you. Because *you* are responsible for creating *your* study system, *not me.*

I think we've spent enough time talking about what you're *going* to learn. Let's get on with the learning.

CHAPTER 1

HOW TO START OUT RIGHT

Taking a good, honest look at yourself is not the easiest thing in the world to do. In the next two chapters, I'm going to help you evaluate the current level of all your study skills, a necessary step to identify the areas in which you need to concentrate your efforts; identify the study environment and learning style that suit you; and categorize all of your school subjects according to how well you *like* them and how well you *do* in them.

How to keep score

In the next few pages, I'll explain the 11 primary study skills covered in this book: reading and comprehension, memory development, time management, library skills, computer skills, textbook note-taking, classroom note-taking, library note-taking, classroom participation, writing papers, and test preparation. Then I'll ask you to rate yourself on your current level of achievement and understanding of these skills: A for mastery or near mastery of a particular skill; B for some mastery; C for little or none.

Remember: There are no right or wrong answers in this assessment. It's only a place to start, a jumping-off point from which you can measure your progress and rate those areas in which your skills need improvement.

To simplify the process, I've listed the primary study skills on page 23 of this chapter. Take a separate piece of paper and rate yourself on each of the 11 skills (from reading to test preparation) *before you read the rest of this chapter.* After you've rated yourself in each area, give yourself two points for every A, one point for every B, zero points for every C. If your overall rating is 18 or more, excellent (give yourself an A); 13 to 17, good (give yourself a B); and if 12 or less, fair (give yourself a C). Mark this rating under Initial Study Skills Evaluation in the chart that follows.

Now, let's review each of these areas, giving you insight as to what "fair," "good," and "excellent" really mean. As you read each section, fill in your score on the "Your Starting Point" chart—and be honest with yourself. This evaluation will give you a benchmark from which to measure your improvement after you've completed the book. File it away and make the comparison when you've completed reading.

Your Starting Point

Initial Study Skills Evaluation	A ( )	B ( )	C ( )
Reading	A ( )	B ( )	C ( )
Memory development	A ( )	B ( )	C ( )
Time management	A ( )	B ( )	C ( )
Textbook note-taking	A ( )	B ( )	C ( )
Classroom note-taking	A ( )	B ( )	C ( )
Classroom participation	A ( )	B ( )	C ( )
Basic library skills	A ( )	B ( )	C ( )

Computer skills	A ( )	B ( )	C ( )
Library note-taking	A ( )	B ( )	C ( )
Writing papers	A ( )	B ( )	C ( )
Test preparation	A ( )	B ( )	C ( )
Overall study skill level	A ( )	B ( )	C ( )

Reading

Speed, comprehension and recall are the three important components of reading. Comprehension and recall are especially interrelated—better to sacrifice some speed to increase these two factors. To test your reading and comprehension skills, read the passage that follows, close the book, and jot down the key points made in the selection you read, then review the text and compare your notes with the reading selection. You will get a good idea of how well you understood what you read and just how good your top-of-the-mind recall is.

Five major scandals tainted the administration of President Ulysses S. Grant. Although the hero of Vicksburg was the first president to encounter charges of substantial wrongdoing during his administration, it was never proved that he was directly involved in any criminal acts nor that he profited from any of the acts of others.

The first incident occurred in 1869, the first year of his presidency. Known as Black Friday, it involved speculators James Fisk and Jay Gould and their attempt to corner the gold market. President Grant was not directly involved in Fisk's and Gould's machinations, but he gave the appearance of complicity, allowing himself to be entertained lavishly and publicly on Fisk's yacht.

The second major scandal involved the embezzlement of massive amounts of money by the Credit Mobilier holding company, which was involved with the construction of the Union Pacific railway. To avoid being discovered, the conspirators heavily bribed Congressmen and officials of the Republican Party, of which Grant was the nominal head.

Two other scandals involved taxes and officials appointed to collect them. One tax collector, John Sanborn, managed to keep nearly half of the delinquent taxes he collected, a total exceeding $200,000. That paled in comparison to the fraud discovered by Treasury Secretary Benjamin H. Bristow among liquor distillers and the officials charged with collecting taxes from them. Although Grant called for swift action against the conspirators, his fervor flagged when his trusted personal secretary, Orville Babcock, was implicated in the scheme. Grant then slowed the investigation, but 110 conspirators were eventually found guilty.

In the final year of Grant's second term, evidence mounted that Secretary of War W.W. Belknap had been taking bribes from white traders at Indian trading posts. Faced with certain impeachment, Belknap resigned.

Score: If you can read the material straight through and accurately summarize what you've read, all in less than two minutes, give yourself an A. If you have some problems reading and understanding the text but are able to complete the assignment in less than four minutes, give yourself a B. If you are unable to complete the assignment in that time, remember what you read, or produce accurate notes at all, give yourself a C.

Retention and memory development

There are specific methods to help you recall when you must remember a lot of specific facts. One of these is memorization—committing information to word-for-word recall. Memorize only when you are required to remember something for a relatively short periods of time.

Test #1: Look at the number following this paragraph for 10 seconds. Then cover the page and write down as much of it as you can remember:

762049582049736

Test #2: Below are 12 nonsense words from a language I just made up and their "definitions." Study the list for 60 seconds in an attempt to remember each word, how it's spelled, and its definition:

Bruhe	Arm	**Trouch**	Vomit
Imbor	Worry	**Laved**	Woman
Timp	Brother	**Yout**	Toe
Batoe	Walker	**Frewie**	Closet
Plitter	Chin	**Slecum**	Pants
Kruk	Bathroom	**Preb**	Shout

Done? Close the book and write down each of the 12 words and its definition. They do not need to be in the order in which they were listed.

Score: *Test # 1:* If you remembered 12 or more digits in the correct order, give yourself an A; eight to 12, a B; seven or less, a C.

Score: *Test # 2:* If you accurately listed eight or more words and definitions (and that includes spelling my new words correctly), give yourself an A. If you listed from five to seven words and their definitions, or correctly listed and spelled more than eight words but mixed up their definitions, give yourself a B. If you were unable to remember at least four words and their definitions, give yourself a C.

Time management

Your effective use of available study time can be measured by two yardsticks: 1) your ability to break down your assignments into component parts (for example, reading, note-taking, outlining, writing); and 2) your ability to complete each task in an efficient manner.

Score: If you feel you use your time wisely and efficiently, give yourself an A. If you know there *are* times you simply run out of time, give yourself a B. If you can't *tell* time, give yourself a C.

Basic library skills

Making the most of the library is a function of understanding its organization—and *using* it! The more time you spend there—studying, reading, researching—the more productive you'll be. You'll become adept at tracking down reference materials and finding the information you need quickly.

Virtually all libraries follow the same organization—once you understand it, you'll be "library literate," no matter which library you use. In this book, you'll discover what kinds of resources are available (books, periodicals, directories, encyclopedias, dictionaries, magazines, newspapers, documents, microfilm files), you'll learn how to select and find books (learning the Dewey Decimal and Library of Congress systems), and you'll find out about the functions of the library staff.

To better evaluate your library skills, answer the following questions:

1. What collections are restricted in your local library?
2. Where would you find a biography of Herbert Hoover in your library?
3. Where is the reference section in your local library?

4. Given the Dewey number for a book, could you find it in less than five minutes? The Library of Congress number?

5. How often have you been to the library in the past six months? The past month?

Score: If the answers to these questions are all obvious to you, indicating a steady pattern of library use, then you can claim to have the library habit—give yourself an A. If you can't answer one or more of the questions or will freely own up to a spotty record of library use, give yourself a B. If you don't have the faintest clue of where the closest library is, give yourself a C.

Computer skills

It's virtually impossible now to succeed at almost any level of education without complete mastery of the computer. But knowing how to use a computer and modem and scanner is just the beginning. You have to know how to use them to study both more efficiently and effectively. That includes learning how to write better papers and keep your schedules and taking advantage of the almost limitless research possibilities available online.

Score: If you are capable of doing just about anything online short of hacking into the Pentagon and have made your computer equipment a key tool in your quest for more efficient studying and better grades, give yourself an A. If you are adept at word processing and playing games and at least can get online, but have never used 75 percent of the other tools on your computer and "wipe out" more often than surf, give yourself a B. If you don't even know what "being online" means and need four minutes to figure out how to turn your computer on, give yourself a C.

Note-taking

Three different arenas—at home with your textbooks, in the classroom, at the library—require different methods of note-taking.

From your textbooks: Working from your books at home, you should identify the main ideas, rephrasing information in your own words, as well as capturing the details with which you were unfamiliar. Take brief, concise notes in a separate notebook as you read. You should write down questions and answers to ensure your mastery of the material, starring those questions to which you *don't* have answers so you can ask them in class.

In class: Class *preparation* is the key to class *participation*. By reading material to be covered before you come to class, you will be able to concentrate and absorb the teacher's interpretations and points. Using a topical, short sentence approach or your own shorthand or symbols, take notes on those items that will trigger thematic comprehension of the subject matter. Your notes should be sequential, following the teacher's lecture pattern. When class is completed, review your notes at the first opportunity. Fill in any blanks and your own thoughts.

In the library: What's the difference between taking notes at the library or working at home with library books vs. your own textbooks? Sooner or later you'll have to return library books (if you're allowed to take them out at all), and librarians tend to frown on highlighting them, so you need an effective system for library note-taking. In *Take Notes*, I'll show you mine.

Score: If you feel that your note-taking skills are sufficient to summarize the necessary data from your textbooks and capture the key points from classroom lectures and discussions and they allow you to prepare detailed outlines and write good papers, give yourself an A. If you feel any one of these three areas is deficient, give yourself a B. If notes are what you pass to your friends in class, give yourself a C.

Participating in class

I don't know too many teachers who don't take each student's class participation into account when giving grades, no matter how many spot quizzes they pull or how many term papers they assign. And, you may have discovered, there are teachers out there who will mark down students who "ace" every paper and quiz if they seem to disappear in the classroom.

Score: If you are always prepared for class (which means, at the very least, reading all assigned material, preparing assigned homework and projects, and turning them in when due), actively participate in discussions, and ask frequent and pertinent questions as a way of both trumpeting what you already know and filling in the gaps in that knowledge, give yourself an A. If you fail in any of these criteria, give yourself a B. If you aren't sure where the classroom is, give yourself a C.

Writing papers

Preparing any sort of report, written or oral, is 90 percent perspiration (research) and 10 percent inspiration (writing). In other words, the ability to write a good paper is more dependent on your mastery of the other skills we've already discussed than your mastery of *writing.* If you are an avid reader, familiar with your local library, a good note-taker, and capable of breaking down the most complex topic into the manageable steps necessary to write a paper, you probably turn in superior papers.

Score: If you have already given yourself an A in library skills, library note-taking, time management, and reading, give yourself an A. If you feel you turn in relatively good papers but definitely lack in any of these areas, give yourself a B. If your idea of writing a paper is photocopying the pertinent *Cliff's Notes* and recopying the summary in your own handwriting, give yourself a C.

Test preparation

The key to proper test preparation is an accurate assessment of what material will be covered and what form the test will take. Weekly class quizzes usually cover the most recent material. Midterm and final examinations cover a much broader area—usually all the subject matter to date. Multiple-choice tests, essays, lists of math problems, science lab tests all require different preparation and different test-taking skills. Knowing the kind of test you're facing will make your preparation much easier.

So will creating your own list of questions you think your teacher will most likely ask. Through periodic review of your text and class notes, the areas in which your teacher appears most interested—and on which he or she is most likely to test you—should begin to stand out. As a final trick, prepare a list of 10 or more questions *you* would ask if the roles were reversed and *you* were the teacher.

Score: If you are able to construct tests that are harder than the ones your teacher gives you—and you perform well on those, give yourself an A. If you feel you know the material, but somehow don't perform as well as you think you should at test time, give yourself a B. If you didn't pass your driver's test, let alone algebra, give yourself a C.

Your overall score

Once again, after you've rated yourself in each area, give yourself two points for every A, one point for every B, zero points for every C. If your overall rating is 18 or more, excellent (give yourself an A); 13 to 17, good (give yourself a B); and if 12 or less, fair (give yourself a C). Put your new score in the section "Overall study skills level" in the chart on page 25 of this chapter.

Now what?

The fact that you have been honest with yourself in evaluating those talents you bring into the study game is a big plus in your favor. Knowing where you are strong and where you need to improve makes everything else a good deal easier. Now, based on your test results, draw up a list of your assets and liabilities—your areas of strength and weakness. This will focus your attention on those areas that will require the most work to improve.

Although I would strongly recommend you read the entire book, this simple test has enabled you to identify the chapters you really need to work on and the specific skills that may require work long after you finish reading this book.

CHAPTER 2

HOW TO ORGANIZE YOUR STUDYING

What effect can good study habits have? Certainly native-born talents and skills—the basic abilities you're born with—have the most to do with success in school. Fifty percent. Maybe 60. And the environment in which you're trying to learn, your health, and other factors may be another 10 percent, maybe 15. That leaves 25 to 40 percent for study skills.

Don't believe that learning how to study can have such a monstrous effect? Two comments: One, try me. Read *How to Study*, practice the skills, watch the results. I think you'll discover I'm right. Second, if you don't believe study skills are so important, you must be giving more weight to ability, kind of a "smart kids do well because they're smart" approach. Well, a lot of smart kids *don't* do well. At *all.* Others do well in school but test poorly. And many are great in some subjects and not so great in others. I don't have to prove this. Look at your friends, at others in your school. I guarantee you'll prove it to yourself.

What kind of effort are we talking about here? Another hour a night? Two hours a night? *More???* And what about that "Study Smarter, Not Harder" slogan that's plastered all over the bookstore display for the ***How to Study Program***. "If I'm studying longer," you might reasonably contend, "I'm sure as heck studying harder, at least by my definition."

Let's take the latter point first. You *can* study smarter. You *can* put in less time and get better results. But learning how to do so *is* hard, because learning of *any* kind takes discipline. And learning self-discipline is, to many of us, the most difficult task of all. So don't kid yourself: You aren't going to sit down, read ***How to Study***, and miraculously transform yourself from a C student to an A student. But you absolutely can if you put in the time to learn the lessons it contains and, more importantly, practice and use them every day.

If you're currently doing little or nothing in the way of schoolwork, then you *are* going to have to put in more time and effort. How much more? Or even more generally, how long should you study, period? Until you get the results you want to achieve. The smarter you are and the more easily you learn and adapt the techniques in ***How to Study***, the more likely you will be spending less time on your homework than before. But the further you need to go—from Ds to As rather than Bs to As—the more you need to learn and the longer you need to give yourself to learn it.

Don't get discouraged. You will see results very quickly.

Making study habit-forming

If you're doing poorly in school and you're actually putting in a reasonable amount of study time, you've got poor study habits. Lord knows where or when you acquired them, but failure has, to some extent, become a habit.

This is good news! Not only can *bad* habits be broken, but they can be replaced by *good* habits relatively easily. Here's your battle plan:

☞ It is much easier to *replace* one of your habits than to break it entirely. So don't attempt to stop poor study habits, just learn the good ones that substitute for them.

☞ Practice, practice, practice. There is just no way around it, practice is the motor oil that lubricates any habit's engine. The more you do something, the more ingrained it becomes. Just ask any smoker—if you can still find one—how many times he or she lit a cigarette just today without even noticing that he or she had done so!

☞ Tell your friends and family of your decision to do better in school by honing your study skills. This is a trick that works for *some* people, who find that the added pressure is a good motivator.

☞ Smokers are notorious for doing this, hoping that the fear of embarrassment (of disappointing all those friends and family if they light up again) will serve as one more strong motivation to quit. For some of you, however, such a strategy simply adds *too much* pressure and is more likely to backfire instead, encouraging failure. My advice would be to use such a strategy if you know it will help you personally, avoid it if you know it will actually hurt.

☞ You don't have to grind it out from Ds to As with no feedback. Obviously, there's a lot of distance you're traveling and you'll be seeing the effects of better study habits all along the way. And each effect you see just strengthens your resolve and makes it even easier to keep on going. To make sure you get a "motivational jolt" from every accomplishment, resolve to chart every inch of your progress, even if, like Robert Frost, you have miles to go before you sleep. You may want to set up a chart on your wall on which you list "Today's Successes" *every day*. And remember the small steps you're taking—saving five minutes on a reading assignment, finding the books you need at the library more quickly, feeling that you took good notes in a lecture, raising your hand to actually answer a professor's question in a class discussion, and so on.

Get ready to become a "lifer"

Learning how to study is really a long-term process. Once you undertake the journey, you will be surprised at the number of landmarks, pathways, side streets, and road signs you'll find. Even after you've transformed yourself into a better student than you'd ever hoped to be, you'll inevitably find one more signpost that offers new information, one more pathway that leads you in an interesting new direction. Consider learning how to study a *lifelong process* and be ready to modify anything you're doing as you learn another method.

This is especially important right from the start when you consider your overall study strategies. How long you study per night, how long you work on a particular subject, and how often you schedule breaks are going to vary considerably depending on how well you were doing before you read this book, how far you have to go, how interested you are in getting there, how involved you are in other activities, the time of day, your health, etc. Are you getting the idea?

It gets more complicated: What's your study sequence? Hardest assignments first? Easiest? Longest? Shortest?

Are you comfortable switching back and forth from one to another or do you need to focus on a single assignment from start to finish?

This gets even more difficult (believe it or not!) when you consider that the tasks themselves may have a great effect on your schedule. When I sit down to plan out the chapter of a book, for example, I need a relatively long period of uninterrupted time—at least an hour, perhaps as long as three hours—in order to get my notes in the order I want them and to think through the entire chapter, writing transitions in my head, noting problem areas, figuring out where I need an example or illustration. If I only have half an hour before a meeting or appointment, I wouldn't even attempt to start such a project, because I'd just have to start all over again when I had the right amount of time.

You may find yourself to be the same way, and, therefore, need to ensure your schedule is flexible enough to adapt to the demands of the specific task. Fifteen-minute study unit increments might work well for you most of the time (though I suspect half an hour is an ideal unit for most of you, an hour only for those of you who can work that long without a break and who have assignments that traditionally take that long to complete).

On the other hand, you may have no problem at all working on a long project in fits and starts, 15 or 20 minutes at a time, without needing to retrace your steps each time you pick it up again.

What's the lesson in all of this? There is no ideal, no answer, certainly no "right" answer, to many of the questions I've posed. It's a message you'll read in these pages over and over again: Figure out what works for you and keep on doing it. If it later stops working or doesn't seem to be working as well, change it.

None of the study techniques discussed at such length in this book is carved in stone. You not only should feel free to adapt and shape and bend them to your own needs, you *must* do so.

Follow the Yellow Brick Road

When I talk about test-taking, one of the key bits of advice is to read the instructions before you start the test. This helps you avoid the poor grade (not to mention the frustration and embarrassment) that results from trying to answer all six essay questions in an hour when you were only supposed to pick three.

Tests aren't the only time "reading the instructions" is important. Many teachers have their own rules and regulations about turning in homework assignments, preparing papers or projects, reporting lab results, etc. And it's just as important to follow these instructions—and just as devastating if you *don't*.

I really did have a teacher in 10th grade—when none of us had access to personal computers and few of us had learned to type—who failed a student because her paper was handwritten (when the instructor required it be typewritten). What bothered me then was that the paper was really *good*...and it didn't mean a hill of beans to that teacher. Isn't it ridiculous to get a low grade for such a lousy reason?

Be proud of your work...and show it

Do you know any students who make sure they count every word on their 500-word assignment and head to a conclusion as fast as they can as soon as they reach that magic number?

How about the student who is convinced his chicken scratch is perfectly decipherable, even when the teacher has to wade through several cross-outs on every page and follow arrows from one page to another because the student thought the order should be changed after the fact?

Or those who only spell one thing correctly per paper—their name—or, even worse, spell a word correctly two or three times and incorrectly four or five others, all on the same page?

Teachers are human. They respond to presentation. Although I am not advocating—and most teachers will not buy—an emphasis on form over substance, one should certainly consider that if the substance of two papers or tests or projects is relatively equal, the form in which they're presented may well affect the grade, perhaps significantly.

Besides, there are a lot of teachers who make it a point to decrease grades because of poor grammar, spelling, presentation, etc. (Luckily, there are others who may subconsciously increase grades—or give a better grade than the work really warrants—because the presentation was done with care and a sense of pride.)

Know thy teachers

Teachers are different, too, in their approach to their subjects, their expectations, standards, flexibility, etc. It certainly is worth the effort to compile a "profile" of each of your teachers: What do each of them want to see in terms of notes, level of participation, papers, projects? What are their individual likes and dislikes? Their methods of grading and testing?

Knowing these various traits should certainly lead you to some adaptation of your approach to each class. Let's say—not that it would ever *really* happen to *you*, of course—that you have managed to dig yourself a very deep hole. It's 11 p.m., you're well past your study prime, and you still have reading assignments to complete for English and history tomorrow morning.

Your English teacher demands maximum class participation and makes it a large part of your grade—and your test scores be damned. Her hobby seems to be calling on the unprepared, and she has an uncanny and unerring knack for ferreting them out.

Your history teacher discourages discussion, preferring to lecture and answer a couple of questions at the end of the class. He never calls on anyone for anything. Given this situation, and knowing you can stay awake long enough to read only *one* of the two assignments, which would it be?

In fact, presuming you care at all about your studies and grades, would there *ever* be a time, barring a simultaneous typhoon, eclipse, and national holiday, that you would show up for that English class unprepared?

I'll show you later how to ensure that poor scheduling does not become a habit that leads to such choices, but I suspect far too many of you do not take the natural differences among your various teachers into account when scheduling homework, preparing papers, or studying for tests.

Likewise, I suspect far too few of you try to create a bond with one special teacher—a mentoring relationship—that could well help you avoid some of the bumps and swerves and reach your goal with far less trouble. Why should you go out of your way to find a mentor? Because you probably need more help—in life, not just in school—than your friends or parents can provide. A mentor can give you that perspective, advice, and help.

Intrinsic and extrinsic motivation

Motivators are either intrinsic or extrinsic. What's the difference? You sign up for a voice class. Although the hours certainly apply to your graduating requirements, you attend class because you love singing.

You also signed up for biology. You hate the thought of dissecting frogs, and you couldn't care less whether they have exoskeletons, endoskeletons, hydroskeletons, or no skeletons at all, but the class is required.

In the first case, you're motivated by *intrinsic* factors—you are taking the voice class simply because you truly enjoy it.

The second scenario is an example of *extrinsic* motivation. You have no interest in biology, but your reward for taking the class is external—you'll be able to graduate.

Extrinsic motivation can help you make it through boring or unpleasant tasks that are part of the process of reaching your goals. A vivid image of your final goal can be a powerful motivating force. One student thought about what his job as a computer programmer would be like whenever he needed some help getting through class.

Try imagining what a day in *your* life will be like five or 10 years down the road. If you haven't the faintest clue, no *wonder* you're having a hard time motivating yourself to work toward that career as a final goal!

The goal pyramid

One way to easily visualize all your goals—and their relation to each other—is to construct what I call a *goal pyramid*. Here's how to do it:

1. Centered at the top of a piece of paper, write down what you hope to ultimately gain from your education. This is your long-range goal and the pinnacle of your pyramid. Example: Become a successful advertising copywriter.

2. Below your long-range goal(s), list mid-range goals—milestones or steps that will lead you to your eventual target. For example, if your long-range goal is to become an advertising copywriter, your mid-range goals might include getting into college, "acing" all your writing courses, completing all required courses, and getting a summer internship at a major ad agency.

3. Below the mid-range goals, list as many short-range goals as you can—smaller steps that can be completed in a relatively short period of time. For example, if your long-range goal is to become a travel writer for a widely read magazine, your mid-range goal may be to earn a journalism degree. Short-range goals may include writing a travel article to submit to the school paper, registering for magazine writing courses, or getting an excellent grade in a related class.

Change your goal pyramid as you progress through school. You may eventually decide on a different career. Or your mid-range goals may change as you decide on a different path leading to the long-range goal. The short-range goals will undoubtedly change, even daily.

The process of creating your own goal pyramid allows you to see *how* all those little daily and weekly steps you take can lead to your mid-range and long-term goals, and will thereby motivate you to work on your daily and weekly tasks with more energy and enthusiasm.

Make goal-setting a part of your life

The development of good study skills is the highway to your goals, whatever they are. And no matter how hard you have to work or how much adversity you have to over-come along the way, the journey will indeed be worth it.

How do you make setting goals a part of your life? Here are some hints I think will help:

1. **Be realistic when you set goals.** Don't aim too high or too low and don't be particularly con-cerned when (*not* if) you have to make adjust-ments along the way.

2. **Be realistic about your expectations.** An improved understanding of a subject for which you have little natural aptitude is preferable to getting hopelessly bogged down if mastering the subject is just not in the cards.

3. **Don't give up too easily.** You can be *overly* re-alistic—too ready to give up just because some-thing is a trifle harder than you'd like. Don't aim too high and feel miserable when you don't come close, or aim too low and never achieve your poten-tial. Find the path that's right for you.

4. **Concentrate on areas that offer the best chance for improvement.** Unexpected suc-cesses can do wonders for your confidence and might make it possible for you to achieve more than you thought you could even in other areas.

5. **Monitor your achievements and keep re-setting your goals.** Daily, weekly, monthly, yearly—ask yourself how you've done and where you'd like to go *now*.

Use rewards as artificial motivators

The way you decide to use a reward system all depends on how much help you need getting motivated to study. As we've observed, tasks that are intrinsically interesting require little outside motivation. However, most schoolwork can be spurred along by the promise of little rewards along the way. If the task is especially tedious or difficult, make the rewards more frequent so that motivation doesn't sag.

As a general rule, the size of the reward should match the difficulty of the task. For an hour of reading, promise yourself a 10-minute walk. For completion of a rough draft for a big assignment, treat yourself to a movie. When you finish the paper, add popcorn for the movie!

Success begets success

Students often think they should be able to complete tasks out of sheer willpower. Many fear that if their willpower is not strong enough, offering themselves rewards for something they should be doing anyway will further weaken their resolve.

Rewarding yourself can actually be a way of *strengthening* your self-discipline. If you consistently set goals that are unreachable, all you are doing is practicing to fail. Practice makes perfect. Fail you will.

On the other hand, shooting to achieve smaller goals and rewarding yourself every time you reach them will build your list of *successes*. As you work on these study goals—and *reach* them—you will begin to believe in yourself more and more, and your performance will continue to improve.

Remember, your purpose is not to suffer through school like a martyr. There's nothing wrong with making it as enjoyable as possible.

Are you Bugs Bunny or Elmer Fudd?

In trying to motivate yourself, do you tend to use the carrot or the stick? Positive and negative thoughts can both motivate.

The following are examples of *negative* thoughts that students have used to motivate themselves:

1. "If I don't get a good mark on this test, there goes my grade."
2. "If I don't finish this assignment, I'll have to miss the party."
3. "If I blow this college entrance exam, my future is shot."
4. "If I don't do well in this class, I'll be forced to go to summer school."

Now here are some examples of *positive* thoughts that students have used to motivate themselves:

1. "For every hour of solid study, I get to listen to two songs on my new CD."
2. "If I get this assignment done early, I will be able to go skiing Friday."
3. "If I earn an A in this class, I'll reward myself with a weekend at the beach."
4. "If I do well in these courses, my chances for grad school are excellent."

Which do you tend to use to motivate yourself, the carrot or the stick? If you're not sure, try the following exercise. Look at pages 53 and 54 of this chapter. On the lines beneath the heading, "This Year's Successes," on page 53 list as many successes over the past year as you can think of. Examples might be getting a good grade on a term paper, getting a terrific grade for the semester, landing on the honor roll or dean's list, making a sports team, landing a part in a play, or committing yourself to a fitness routine.

Then, on page 54 beneath the heading, "This Year's Failures," list as many failures as you can think of. All done? Okay, now ask yourself, which list was the easiest to fill out? Look them over again. Which has the most items?

Before you did this exercise, which items (positive or negative) did you tend to dwell on the most?

Chances are, many of you found it easier to list your failures than your successes. In fact, you may have discovered you didn't have enough *room* for all your failures, while you struggled to list even a few successes.

Turn your failures into successes

Well, I have something to say about success and failure. Failures are just as valuable experiences as successes—in fact, they may well be *more* valuable. What was one of the first lessons you learned in life? Not to touch a hot stove? Not to stick a fork into the toaster when it's plugged in? Not to leave your talking doll out in the rain? And how did you discover these profound truths? Probably the hard way. Yet, you learned from these experiences, these "failures." Likewise, you can learn from *every* failure, and then turn it into a success.

Review your list of failures. Think about what you learned from each experience, then reword it so that it is a success story. For example, let's pretend that one of your recent failures was that you turned in a paper late, and, as a direct result of your lateness, received a lower grade.

What did this failure teach you? You learned that getting projects done on time is as important as doing them well. You realized that you had to learn to manage your time better, so you picked up this book and you've committed yourself to implementing a good time-management system. You're now taking control of your life.

Congratulations!

You've just turned your failure into a success story!

There is no rule against using the stick to motivate yourself. But learn to turn your failures into successes—this will keep your attitude positive and keep the wind in your sails. Focusing on the positive helps you feel good about yourself and provides excitement to keep you motivated.

How perfect are you?

What is a perfectionist, and are you one? And if you are, why is it a problem?

Perfectionists care perhaps too much, finding it impossible to be satisfied with anything less than "perfect" work (as they define it), presuming for a moment that such an ideal can actually be attained.

It is possible, of course, to score a "perfect" 100 on a test or to get an A+ on a paper the teacher calls "Perfect!" in the margin. But in reality, doing anything "perfectly" impossible.

What does all this have to do with you? Nothing, unless you find yourself spending two hours polishing an already A+ paper or half an hour searching for that one "perfect" word or an hour rewriting great notes to make them "absolutely perfect." In other words, although striving for perfection may well be a noble trait, it can very easily, perhaps inevitably, become a major problem if it becomes an uncontrollable and unstoppable urge that seriously inhibits your enjoyment of your work and your life.

Take it from a perfectionist. It's easy (though still not necessarily great) to "be a perfectionist" when you're in the elementary grades. But just try to attend class and labs (as I did) 38 hours a week, work nearly full-time, and, of course, do 50-plus hours of homework per week, all while wasting *days* searching for that perfect word! There comes a time—I hope, for your sake, sooner rather than later—when you must simply conclude that you cannot *afford* to be a perfectionist. That taking two hours to make a paper "perfect" when the three word changes you decided upon made absolutely no difference to your grade (or, for that matter, the caliber of your work or your understanding of the subject) is a *big waste of time*.

I'm convinced that there aren't too many of you out there nodding your head and thinking, "Oh, yeah, that's me!" But I'm equally convinced that those of you to whom this all makes sense are making your lives incredibly tough. If you are starting to lean towards the obsessive-compulsive side of the fence, recognize what you're doing and take the necessary steps to rein yourself in. If you really would prefer spending another couple of hours polishing that A+ paper to taking in a movie, reading a book, or getting some *other* assignment done, be my guest.

Staying focused on your studies

If you find yourself doodling and dawdling more than reading and remembering, try these solutions:

Create a work environment in which you're comfortable. The size, style, and placement of your desk, chair and lighting may all affect whether or not you're distracted from the work at hand. Take the time to design the area that's perfect for you. Needless to say, anything that you know will distract you—a girlfriend's picture, a radio or TV, whatever, should disappear from your study area.

Turn up the lights. Experiment with the placement and intensity of lighting in your study area until you find what works for you, both in terms of comfort and as a means of staying awake and focused.

Set some rules. Let family, relatives, and especially friends know how important your studying is and that specific hours are inviolate.

Take the breaks you need. Don't just follow well-intentioned but bogus advice about how long you should study before taking a break. Break when *you* need to.

Fighting tiredness and boredom

If you've chosen the best study spot and no one could fault you on its setup, but you're still using pencils to prop up your eyelids, try one or more of the following:

Take a nap. What a concept! When you're too tired to study, take a short nap to revive yourself. Maximize that nap's effect by keeping it short—20 minutes is ideal, 40 minutes absolute maximum. After that, you go into another phase of sleep and you may wake even more tired than before. If you can't take such short naps, train yourself to do so. I did during college out of necessity; my ability to nap virtually anywhere, anytime, and automatically wake after 20 minutes is one of my more useful talents.

Have a drink. A little caffeine won't harm you—a cup of coffee or tea, a glass of soda. Just be careful not to mainline it—caffeine's "wake-up" properties seem to reverse when you reach a certain level, making you far more tired than you were!

Turn down the heat. You needn't build an igloo out back, but too warm a room will inevitably leave you dreaming of sugarplums...while your paper remains unwritten on your desk.

Shake a leg. Go for a walk, high step around the kitchen, do a few jumping jacks—even mild physical exertion will give you an immediate lift.

Change your study schedule. Presuming you have some choice here, find a way to study when *you* are normally more awake and/or most efficient.

Find out where you shine

It is the rare individual who is superior, or even good, in *every* subject. If you are, count your blessings. Most of us are a little better in one subject or another. Some of us simply *like* one subject more than another—and don't think *that* doesn't change your attitude toward it. Others are naturally gifted in one area, average in others.

For example, skill with numbers and spatial relations may come easily to you, but you may have absolutely no ear for music or languages. Or you may find learning a language to be a piece of cake, but not have the faintest clue why Pythagoras came up with his Theorem—or why you should care. Some students are good with their hands. Others (again, like me) may find making the simplest item in industrial arts class akin to torture.

The reasons for such unequal distribution of native-born talents rest somewhere in the area between karma and God, depending on your philosophy.

My advice is to be thankful for whatever native-born talents you possess and use their gift as a two-edged sword. Shift some study time from easily achieved tasks to those you find more difficult. The balance you will see in your development will be well worth the effort.

And if you've never really thought about the subjects you like and dislike, use the chart on page 55 of this chapter to identify them. You'll also be asked to identify those in which you perform well or poorly. (Your report card should confirm those!) Use this list to organize your own schedule to take advantage of your natural talents and give added time to the subject areas that need the most work.

And if you have a choice...

All college students—and some high school students—are able to pick and choose courses according to their own schedules, likes, dislikes, goals, etc. The headiness of such freedom should be tempered with the commonsense approach you're trying to develop through reading this book. Here are a few hints to help you along:

51

1. Whenever possible, consider each professor's reputation as you decide whether to select a particular course (especially if it is an overview or introductory course that is offered in two or three sections). Word soon gets around as to which professors' lectures are stimulating and rewarding—an environment in which learning is a joy, even if it isn't a subject you like!

2. Attempt to select classes so your schedule is balanced on a weekly, even daily, basis, though this will not always be possible or advisable. (Don't change your major just to fit your schedule!) Try to leave an open hour or half-hour between classes—it's ideal for review, post-class note-taking, quick trips to the library, and so on.

3. Try to alternate challenging classes with those that come more easily to you. Studying is a process of positive reinforcement. You'll need encouragement along the way.

4. Avoid late-evening or early-morning classes, especially if such scheduling provides you with large gaps of "down time."

5. Set a personal study pace and follow it. Place yourself on a study diet, the key rule of which is: *Don't overeat.*

The landscape is littered with the shades of unsuccessful students who have failed in their pursuits—*not* because they lacked the talent or motivation, but because they just overloaded on information and pressure.

You *can* be successful without killing yourself!

This year's successes

_____

_____

_____

_____

_____

_____

_____

_____

_____

_____

_____

_____

_____

_____

_____

_____

_____

_____

_____

_____

_____

_____

_____

_____

_____

_____

_____

_____

_____

This year's failures

_____
_____
_____
_____
_____
_____
_____
_____
_____
_____
_____
_____
_____
_____
_____
_____
_____
_____
_____
_____
_____
_____
_____
_____
_____
_____
_____
_____

Evaluation of subject areas

List the subject areas/courses you like most:

_____

_____

_____

_____

_____

List those you like least:

_____

_____

_____

_____

_____

List the courses in which you get the best grades:

_____

_____

_____

_____

_____

And those in which you get the worst grades:

_____

_____

_____

_____

_____

CHAPTER 3

HOW TO READ AND REMEMBER

Reading transforms and transports us through times past, present, and future. Nothing you will do as you pursue your studies will be as valuable as the reading skills you develop—they are your ultimate long-term learning tool.

Define your purpose for reading

What is your purpose in reading? If the best answer you can come up with is, "Because my teacher said so," we need some better reasons. According to reading experts, there are six fundamental purposes for reading:

1. To grasp a certain message.
2. To find important details.
3. To answer a specific question.
4. To evaluate what you are reading.
5. To apply what you are reading.
6. To be entertained.

Using the clues in your textbooks

There are special sections found in nearly all textbooks and technical materials (in fact, in almost all books except novels) that contain a wealth of information and can help you glean more from your reading. Becoming familiar with this data will enrich your reading experience and often make it easier. Here's what to look for:

The first page after the title page is usually the *table of contents*—a chapter-by-chapter list of the book's contents. Some are surprisingly detailed, listing every major point or topic covered in each chapter.

The first prose section is the *preface*, which can usually be found after the title page, table of contents, and, perhaps, acknowledgments page, in which the author thanks other authors and his or her editor, typist, researcher, friends, relatives, teachers, etc.—most of which can be ignored by the reader). It is usually a description of what information you will find in the book. Authors may also use the preface to point out unique aspects of their books.

The *introduction* may be in place of or in addition to the preface and is written by the author or some "name" the author has recruited to lend additional prestige to his or her work. Most introductions are an even more detailed overview of the book—chapter-by-chapter summaries are often included to give the reader a feel for the material to be covered.

Footnotes may be found throughout the text (a slightly elevated number following a sentence, quote, etc., for example, "jim dandy"[24]) and either explained at the bottom of the page on which they appear or in a special section at the back of the text. Footnotes may be used to cite sources of direct quotes or ideas and/or to further explain a point, add information, etc., outside of the text. You may make it a habit to ferret out sources cited in this way for further reading.

If a text tends to use an alarmingly high number of terms with which you may be unfamiliar, the considerate author will include a *glossary*—essentially an abridged dictionary that defines all such terms.

The *bibliography*, usually at the end of the book, may include the source material the author used to research the textbook, a list of "recommended reading," or both. It is usually organized alphabetically by subject, making it easy for you to go to your library and find more information on a specific topic.

Appendices containing supplementary data or examples relating to subject matter covered in the text may also appear at the back of the book.

The last thing in a book is usually the *index*, an alphabetical listing that references, by page number, every mention of a particular name, subject, topic, etc., in the text.

Making it a habit to utilize all of these tools in your textbooks can only make your studying easier.

Find other textbooks if necessary

Although the authors and editors of most textbooks might well be experts, even legends, in a particular subject, writing in jargon-free, easy-to-grasp prose is probably not their strong suit. You will occasionally be assigned a textbook that is so obtuse you aren't even sure whether to read it front to back, upside down, or inside out.

If you find a particular chapter, section, or entire textbook as tough to read as getting your baby brother to do you a favor, get to the library or the bookstore and find *another* book covering the *same* subject area that you *can* understand.

If you just don't get it, maybe it's because the *author* just doesn't know how to *explain* it. *Maybe it's not your fault!* Too many students have sweated, moaned, dropped classes, even changed majors because they thought they were dumb, when it's possible it's the darned textbook that's dense, not you.

Use the clues in each chapter

Begin with a very quick overview of the assignment, looking for questions that you'd like answered. Consider the following elements of your reading assignment *before* you begin your reading.

Chapter titles and bold-faced subheads announce the detail about the main topic. And in some textbooks, paragraph headings or bold-face "lead-ins" announce that the author is about to provide finer details.

So start each reading assignment by going through the chapter, beginning to end, *reading* only *the bold-faced heads and subheads.*

Look for end-of-chapter summaries. Knowing what the author is driving at in a textbook will help you look for the important building blocks for his conclusions while you're reading.

Most textbooks, particularly those in the sciences, will have charts, graphs, numerical tables, maps, and other illustrations. Be sure to observe how they supplement the text and what points they emphasize, and make note of them.

In some textbooks, you'll find that key terms and information are highlighted within the body text. To find the definitions of these terms may then be your purpose for reading.

Some textbook publishers use a format in which key points are emphasized by questions, either within the body of or at the end of the chapter. If you read these questions *before* reading the chapter, you'll have a better idea of the material on which to concentrate.

If you begin your reading assignment by seeking out these heads, subheads, and other purpose-finding elements of the chapter, you'll have completed your prereading. I advise that you *always* preread every assignment!

3 ways to read

Depending on what you're trying to accomplish in a particular reading assignment and the kind of book involved, there are three different ways to read. Knowing when to use each will make any assignment easier:

1. **Quick reference reading** focuses on seeking specific information that addresses a particular question or concern we might have.
2. **Critical reading** is used to discern ideas and concepts that require a thorough analysis.
3. **Aesthetic or pleasure reading** is for sheer entertainment or to appreciate an author's style and ability.

Skim first

Let me repeat this: The best way to begin any reading assignment is to skim the pages to get an overall view of what information is included. Then read the text carefully, word-for-word, and highlight the text and/or take notes in your notebook. (A brief digression: Most everyone I know confuses "skim" and "scan." Let me set the record straight. *Skim is to read quickly and superficially. Scan is to read carefully but for a specific item.* So when you skim a reading selection, you are reading it in its entirety, though you're only hitting the "highlights." When you scan a selection, you are reading it in detail but only until you find what you're looking for. Scanning is the *fastest* reading rate of all—although you are reading in detail, you are *not* seeking to comprehend or remember anything that you see until you find the bit of information you're looking for. I now trust none of you will ever confuse these words again!)

Newspapers make reading simple—gleaning the key news stories is as easy as reading the headlines and the first two or three paragraphs of each.

Your textbooks are not always written to facilitate such an approach, but most of the authors probably make their key point of any paragraph in the first sentence of that paragraph. Succeeding sentences add details. In addition, most of your textbooks include helpful "call outs"—those brief notes or headings in the outside margins of each page that summarize the topic covered in the paragraph or section. Or, like this book, include headings and subheadings to organize the material.

These standard organizational tools should make your reading job simpler. The next time you have to read a history, geography, or similar text, try skimming the assigned pages first. Read the heads, the subheads, and the call outs. Read the first sentence of each paragraph. Then go back and start reading the details.

By beginning your reading with a 20-minute skim of the text, you should be ready to answer three questions:

1. What is the text's principal message or viewpoint?
2. Is an obvious chain of thought or reasoning revealed?
3. What major points are addressed?

While the heads, subheads, first sentences and other author-provided hints we've talked about will help you get a quick read on what a chapter's about, some of the *words* in that chapter will help you concentrate on the important points and ignore the unimportant. Knowing when to speed up, slow down, ignore, or really concentrate will help you read both faster *and* more effectively.

When you see words like "likewise," "in addition," "moreover," "furthermore," and the like, you should know nothing new is being introduced. If you already know what's going on, speed up or skip what's coming entirely.

On the other hand, when you see words like "on the other hand," "nevertheless," "however," "rather," "but," and their ilk, slow down—you're getting information that adds a new perspective or contradicts what you've just read.

Lastly, watch out for "payoff" words such as, "in conclusion," "therefore," "thus," "consequently," "to summarize," especially if you only have time to "hit the high points" of a chapter or if you're reviewing for a test. Here's where the real meat is. Slow down and pay attention!

Now go back for detail

If a more thorough reading is then required, turn back to the beginning. *Read one section (chapter, etc.) at a time.*

As you read, make sure you know what's going on by asking yourself if the passage is written to address one of these questions:

1. **Who?** The paragraph focuses on a particular person or group of people. The topic sentence tells you *who* this is.

2. **When?** The paragraph is primarily concerned with *time*. The topic sentence may even begin with the word "when."

3. **Where?** The paragraph is oriented around a particular place or location. The topic sentence states *where* you are reading about.

4. **Why?** A paragraph that states reasons for some belief or happening usually addresses this question. The topic sentence answers *why* something is true or *why* an event happened.

5. **How?** A paragraph that identifies the way something works or the means by which something is done. The topic sentence explains the *how* of what is described.

Do not go on to the next chapter or section of your textbook until you've completed the following exercise:

1. Write definitions of any key terms you feel are essential to understanding the topic.

2. Write questions and answers you feel clarify the topic.

3. Write any questions for which you *don't* have answers—then make sure you find them through rereading, further research, or asking another student or your teacher.

4. Even if you still have unanswered questions, move on to the next section and complete numbers one to three for that section. (And so on, until your reading assignment is complete.)

The challenge of technical texts

You've already learned a lot of ways to improve your reading. It's time to examine the unique challenges posed by highly technical texts—physics, trigonometry, chemistry, calculus—you know, subjects that three-fourths of all students avoid like the plague. More than any other kind of reading, these subjects demand a logical, organized approach, a step-by-step reading method. And they require a detection of the text's *organizational devices*.

Developing the skill to identify the basic sequence of the text will enable you to follow the progression of thought, a progression that is vital to your comprehension and retention.

In most technical writing, each concept is like a building block of understanding—if you don't understand a particular section or concept, you won't be able to understand the *next* section, either.

Most technical books are saturated with ideas, terms, formulas, and theories. The chapters are dense with information, compressing a great wealth of ideas into a small space. They demand to be read very carefully.

In order to get as much as possible from such reading assignments, you can take advantage of some devices to make sense of the organization. Here are five basics to watch for:

1. Definitions and terms.
2. Examples.
3. Classifications and listings.
4. Use of contrast.
5. Cause-effect relationships.

In reading any specialized text, you must begin at the beginning—understanding the terms particular to that discipline. Familiar, everyday words have very precise definitions in technical writing. Everyday words can have a variety of meanings, some of them even contradictory, depending on the context in which they're used.

In contrast, in the sciences, terminology has fixed and specific meanings. For example, the definition of elasticity *(the ability of a solid to regain its shape after a deforming force has been applied)* is the same in Bangkok or Brooklyn.

Another communication tool is the example. Technical writing often is filled with new or foreign ideas, many of which are not readily digestible. They are difficult in part because they are abstract. Examples work to clarify these concepts, hopefully in terms more easily understood.

A third tool frequently utilized in texts is classification and listings. Classifying is the process by which common subjects are categorized under a general heading. Especially in technical writing, authors use classification to categorize extensive lists of detail. Such writings may have several categories and subcategories that organize these details into some manageable fashion.

A fourth tool used in communicating difficult information is that of comparing and contrasting. Texts use this tool to bring complicated material into focus by offering a similar or opposing picture. Through comparison, a text relates a concept to one that has been previously defined— or to one a reader may readily understand. Through contrast, the text concentrates on the differences and distinctions between two ideas. By focusing on distinguishing features, these ideas become clearer as one idea is held up against another.

A final tool that texts employ to communicate is the cause-effect relationship. This device is best defined in the context of science, where it is the fundamental quest of most scientific research. Science begins with the observation of the effect—what is happening? It is snowing. The next step is to conduct research into the cause: *Why* is it snowing? Detailing this cause-effect relationship is often the essence of scientific and technical writing.

Read with a plan

More than any other type of writing, highly specialized, technical writing must be read with a plan.

Your plan should incorporate the following guidelines:

1. **Learn the terms** that are essential to understanding the concepts presented.

2. **Determine the structure of the text.** Most chapters have a pattern that forms the skeleton for the material. Often it can be discerned through the contents page or titles and subtitles.

3. **Skim the chapter** to get a sense of the author's viewpoint. Ask questions to define your purpose in reading. Use any summaries or review questions to guide your reading.

4. **Do a thorough analytical reading** of the text. Do not proceed from one section to the next until you have a clear understanding of the section you are reading—the concepts generally build upon each other.

5. **Immediately upon concluding your thorough reading, review!** Write a summary of the concepts and theories you need to remember. Answer any questions raised when you skimmed the text. Do the problems. If possible, apply the formulas.

Whether math and science come easily to you or make you want to find the nearest pencil-pocketed computer nerd and throttle him, there are some ways you can do better at such technical subjects:

☞ Whenever you can, "translate" formulas and numbers into words. To test your understanding, try to put your translation into *different* words.

☞ Try translating a particularly vexing math problem into a drawing or diagram.

☞ Before you even get down to solving a problem, try to estimate the answer.

☞ Play around. There are often different paths to the same solution, or even equally valid solutions. If you find one, try to find others.

☞ When you are checking your calculations, try working *backwards*.

☞ Try to figure out what is being asked, what principles are involved, what information is important, what's not.

☞ Teach someone else. Trying to explain mathematical concepts to someone will very quickly pinpoint what you really know or don't know.

Reading foreign language texts

Foreign language texts should be approached in the same way, especially basic ones teaching vocabulary. If you haven't mastered the words you're supposed to in the first section, you'll have trouble reading the story at the end of section three, even if you've learned all the words in sections two and three. So take it one step at a time and make sure you have mastered one concept, vocabulary list, lesson, etc., before jumping ahead.

Aesthetic (pleasure) reading

Most fiction is an attempt to tell a story. There is a beginning, in which characters and setting are introduced. There is a conflict or struggle that advances the story to a climax—where the conflict is resolved. A final *denouement* or "winding up" unravels the conclusion of the story. Your literature class will address these parts using terms that are often more confusing than helpful. The following are brief definitions of some of the more important ones:

Plot. The order or sequence of the story—how it proceeds from opening through climax. Your ability to understand and appreciate literature depends upon how well you follow the plot—the *story.*

Characterization. The personalities or characters central to the story—the heroes, heroines, and villains. You will want to identify the main characters of the story and their relationship to the struggle or conflict.

Theme. The controlling message or subject of the story, the moral or idea that the author is using the plot and characters to communicate.

Setting. The time and place in which the story occurs. This is especially important when reading a historical novel or one that takes you to another culture.

Point of view. Who is telling the story? Is it one of the central characters giving you flashbacks or a first-person perspective? Or is it a third-person narrator offering commentary and observations on the characters, the setting and the plot?

The first step in reading literature is to familiarize yourself with these concepts, then try to recognize them in the novel or short story. As you begin your reading, approach it first from an aesthetic standpoint: How does it make you feel? What do you think of the characters? Do you like them? Hate them? Relate to them?

Second, make sure you know what's going on—this involves the plot or story line and the development of the characters. On a chapter-by-chapter basis, you may find it helpful to keep a sheet of paper on which you can write a sentence or two of the plot development (and, if you wish, characters introduced, etc.).

How fast can you understand?

Are you worried that you read too slowly? You probably shouldn't be—less-rapid readers are not necessarily less able. What counts is what you comprehend and remember. And like anything else, practice will probably increase your speed levels. If you must have a ranking, read the 500-word selection below from start to finish, noting the elapsed time on your watch. Score yourself as follows:

Under 30 seconds	very fast
31-45 seconds	fast
46-60 seconds	high average
61-89 seconds	average
90-119 seconds	slow
120 seconds or more	very slow

If you're like most members of the third estate, you wonder if there are any real differences between politicians who say they're liberal Democrats and those who say they're conservative Republicans. Aren't they all just slick-talking, vote-seeking, pocket-lining, power-hungry egomaniacs bent on getting elected? Maybe they are, but they also tend to have basic philosophical differences guiding their slick-talking, vote-seeking, pocket-lining, power-hungry pursuit of office.

Let's look at some fundamental political, social, and economic differences between these groups.

Conservatives tend to champion free enterprise, or limited governmental control of the economy. They make the argument that people should be rewarded for their hard work and shouldn't expect government hand-outs through the welfare system. They are also heavily into national defense, law enforcement, and promotion of the fundamental values of family, God, and country. (Makes you want to break out into several verses of "The Star Spangled Banner," doesn't it?)

Liberals take a more paternalistic view of government. It is the last and only hope for many members of society who have suffered at the unscrupulous or uncaring hands of others. They contend that business would run amuck, exploiting workers and consumers in every market exchange, if not for government oversight. They also tend to be more concerned that everyone in society has equal access to a fair share of the economic pie, regardless of race, creed, sex, religion, shoe size, bank account, eye color, or planet of birth. Their hearts bleed for all.

These differences often place Republicans and Democrats on different sides of issues such as school prayer, environmental quality, welfare reform, worker safety, abortion, the death penalty, business regulation, sex education, and, well, just about every other newsworthy topic over the past 10 gadzillion years.

Some of you might claim to be registered Democrats, yet you support school prayer and welfare reform, or contend you're Republican but sure as heck want clean air and water and are willing to fight for them. Does this make you schizophrenic or hypocritical? Not necessarily. In fact, there are few *truly* liberal Democrats or *absolutely* conservative Republicans who support the "straight" party line. Many members of the third estate have a combination of liberal and conservative views...just like you.

Now answer the following questions *without referring back to the text:*

1. According to the author, which of the following do traditional Republicans *not* favor?

A. School prayer
B. Sex education
C. Welfare reform
D. Banning abortion

2. Republicans favor:
A. Limited governmental control of the economy
B. Free enterprise
C. Both
D. Neither

3. Democrats favor:
A. Less stringent environmental laws
B. Lower taxes
C. Both
D. Neither

4. The author is probably:
A. A Democrat
B. A Republican
C. An independent
D. A smart aleck

A good reader should be reading fast or very fast and have gotten at least three of the four questions correct. (Answers are at the end of the chapter.)

What decreases reading speed/comprehension?

1. Reading aloud or moving your lips when you read.
2. Reading mechanically—using your finger to follow words, and moving your head along as you read.
3. Applying the wrong *kind* of reading to the material.
4. Lacking sufficient vocabulary.

There are several things you can do to improve these reading mechanics.

To increase your reading speed:

1. Focus your attention and concentration.
2. Eliminate outside distractions.
3. Provide yourself with an uncluttered, comfortable environment.
4. Don't get hung up on single words or sentences, but *do* look up in the dictionary key words that you must understand in order to grasp an entire concept.
5. Try to grasp overall concepts rather than attempting to understand every detail.
6. If you find yourself moving your lips when you read (vocalization), practice reading with a pen or some other (nontoxic, nonsugary) object in your mouth. If it falls out while you're reading, you know you have to keep working!

To increase comprehension:

1. Try to make the act of learning sequential—comprehension is built by adding new knowledge to existing knowledge.
2. Review and rethink at designated points in your reading. Test yourself to see if the importance of the material is getting through.
3. If things don't add up, discard your conclusions. Go back, reread, and try to find an alternate conclusion.
4. Summarize what you've read in your notes, rephrasing it in your own words.

Most importantly, read at the speed that's comfortable for you. Though I *can* read extremely fast, I *choose* to read novels much more slowly so I can appreciate the author's word play. Likewise, any material that I find particularly difficult to grasp slows me right down.

Should you take some sort of speed reading course, especially if your current speed level is slow? I can't see that it could particularly hurt you in any way. I can also, however, recommend that you simply keep practicing reading, which will increase your speed naturally.

Remembering what you read

In a world where the ability to master and remember a growing explosion of data is critical for individual success, too little attention is paid to the dynamics of memory and systems for improving it. Developing your memory is probably the most effective way to increase your efficiency, in reading and in virtually everything else.

There are some basic tools that will help you remember what you read:

☞ **Understanding.** You will remember only what you understand. When you read something and grasp the message, you have begun the process of retention.

☞ **Desire.** You remember what you *choose* to remember. To remember the material, you must *want* to remember it and be convinced that you *will* remember it.

☞ **Overlearn.** To really remember what you learn, you should learn material thoroughly, or *over*learn. This involves prereading the text, doing a critical read, and having some definite means of review that reinforces what you should have learned.

☞ **Systematize.** It's more difficult to remember random thoughts or numbers than those organized in some pattern. For example, which phone number is easier to remember: 538-6284 or 678-1234? Have a system to help you recall how information is organized and connected.

☞ **Association.** Mentally link new material to existing knowledge so that you are giving this new thought some context in your mind.

Retention

Retention is the process by which we keep imprints of past experiences in our minds, the "storage depot." Subject to other actions of the mind, what is retained can be recalled when needed. Things are retained in the same order in which they are learned. So your studying should build one fact, one idea, one concept upon another.

Broad concepts can be retained more easily than details. Master generalities, and details will fall into place.

If you think something is important, you will retain it more easily. So convincing yourself that what you are studying is something you must retain (and recall) increases your chances of adding it to your storehouse.

Retention is primarily a product of what you understand. It has little to do with how *fast* you read, how great an outline you can construct or how many fluorescent colors you can find to mark your textbooks. Reading a text, grasping the message and remembering it are the fundamentals that make for high-level retention. Reading at a 1,000-word-per-minute clip does not necessarily mean that you have a clue as to what a text really says.

As you work toward improving your reading, realize that speed is secondary to comprehension. If you can read an assignment faster than anyone in class, but can't give a one-sentence synopsis of what you read, you lose. If you really get the author's message—even if it takes you an hour or two longer than some of your friends—the extra investment of time will pay huge dividends in class and later in life.

Recall

This is the process by which we are able to bring forth those things that we have retained. Recall is subject to strengthening through the process of repetition. *Recall is least effective immediately after a first reading,* emphasizing the importance of review. The dynamics of our ability to recall are affected by several factors.

☞ We most easily recall those things that are of interest to us.

☞ Be selective in determining what you need to recall. All information is not of equal importance —focus your attention on being able to recall the most *important* pieces of information.

☞ Allow yourself to react to what you're studying. Associating new information with what you already know will make it easier to recall.

☞ Repeat, out loud or just in your mind, what you want to remember. Find new ways of saying those things that you want to recall.

☞ Try to recall broad concepts vs. isolated facts.

☞ Use the new data you have managed to recall in a meaningful way—it will help you recall it the next time.

Recognition

This is the ability to see new material and recognize it for what it is and what it means. Familiarity is the key aspect of recognition—you will feel that you have "met" this information before, associate it with other data or circumstances, and then recall the framework in which it logically fits.

If you've ever envied a friend's seemingly wondrous ability to recall facts, dates, and telephone numbers virtually at will, take solace that, in most cases, *this skill is a result of study and practice*, not something he was born with.

There are certain fundamental memory systems that, when mastered, can significantly expand your capability. It is beyond the scope of this book to teach you these detailed techniques, but if you feel you need help, I recommend my own ***Improve Your Memory***. You'll probably find a number of helpful titles at your library, as well.

Why we forget

As you think about the elements of developing good memory, you can use them to address why you *forget*. The root of poor memory is usually found in one of these areas:

1. We fail to make the material meaningful.
2. We did not learn prerequisite material.
3. We fail to grasp what is to be remembered.
4. We do not have the desire to remember.
5. We allow apathy or boredom to dictate how we learn.
6. We have no set habit for learning.
7. We are disorganized and inefficient in our use of study time.
8. We do not use the knowledge we have gained.

You must remember this

There are dozens of sophisticated memory tricks and techniques, some of which are so sophisticated that no one can remember how to use them. Let me help you learn the *simplest* technique, which will probably solve 90 percent of your problems posed by lost keys, forgotten appointments or assignments, and the names of those people you just met.

The "chain link" method will help you remember items that appear in sequence, whether it's the association of a date with an event, a scientific term with its meaning, or other facts or objects that are supposed to "go together."

The basis for the chain-link system is that memory works best when you associate the unfamiliar with the familiar, though sometimes the association may be very odd. But to really make it effective, the odder the better.

One of the simplest methods is to try to remember just the first letter of a sequence. That's how "Roy G. Biv" (the colors of the spectrum, in order from left to right—red, orange, yellow, green, blue, indigo, violet) got famous. Or "Every Good Boy Does Fine," to remember the notes on a musical staff. Or, perhaps the simplest of all, "FACE," to remember the notes in between. (The latter two work opposite of old Roy—using *words* to remember *letters.*) Of course, not many sequences work out so nicely. If you tried to memorize the signs of the zodiac with this method, you'd wind up with (A)ries, (T)aurus, (G)emini, (C)ancer, (L)eo, (V)irgo, (L)ibra, (S)corpio, (S)agittarius, (C)apricorn, (A)quarius, (P)isces. Now maybe you can make a name or a place or something out of ATGCLVLSSCAP, but I can't!

One solution is to make up a simple sentence that uses the first letters of the list you're trying to remember as the first letters of each word. For example, "**A** **T**all **G**uy **C**an **L**oom **V**ery **L**usciously, **S**ome **S**irens **C**an **A**ttack **P**latters." (I *told* you to "think odd"!)

Wait a minute! It's the same number of words. Why not just figure out some way to memorize the first set of words? What's better about the second set? A couple of things. First of all, it's easier to picture the guy, alarms and platters and what they're doing. As we'll soon see, creating such mental images is a very powerful way to remember almost anything. Second, because the words in our sentence bear some relationship to each other, they're much easier to remember. Go ahead, try it. See how long it takes you to memorize the sentence vs. all the signs. This method is especially easy when you remember some or all of the items but *don't* remember their *order.*

Remember: Make your sentence(s) memorable to *you.* *Any* sentence or series of words that helps you remember these letters will do. Here are just two more I created in a few seconds: "**A Tall Girl Called Lively Vera Loved to Sip Sodas from Cans And Plates. Any Tiny Gerbil Could Love Venus. Long Silly Snakes Could All Pray.**" Isn't it easy to make up memorably silly pictures in your head for these?

The rain in Spain

Let's say that I was a literature major who wanted to remember that Vladimir Nabakov published *Lolita*, his most famous novel, in 1958.

The usual way for me to do this would be to repeat over and over again, "*Lolita*, 1958, *Lolita*, 1958..." *ad nauseam.* How much easier it would be to just say, "Lolita was my date in '58"! I've established a link between Lolita, the coquettish girl of Nabakov's novel, the date of publication, and some imaginary Saturday night special date.

In addition, I was able to use another terrific memory technique—rhyming. Rhyme schemes, no matter how silly or banal they seem, can help us remember things for years.

For instance, who can forget that it's "*i* before *e* except after *c*, or when it sounds like *a* as in *neighbor* and *weigh*"?

The stranger the better

Let's step away from schoolwork for a moment to consider the case of a woman who can't remember where she puts anything—car keys, wallet, her month-old baby (just kidding!).

Using the chain-link method would ensure that she would never forget. For instance, let's say she puts her car keys down on her kitchen counter and, as she does, thinks of a car plowing right into the kitchen and through the countertop. Will that woman be able to forget what she did with her keys? Would you?

Or, to pick an example more germane to academic life, let's say that you wanted to remember that *mitosis* is the process whereby one cell divides itself into two. Instead of repeating word and definition countless times, why not just think, "My toes is dividing," and form a mental picture of two of your toes separating? Much easier, isn't it?

Where in the world is...?

The best way to teach this technique is by example, so let's take another one. Suppose you wanted to remember the following list of 10 relatively obscure world capitals (and, of course, the countries they go with): Tirana (Algeria), Belmopan (Belize), Thimphu (Bhutan), Suva (Fiji), Brazzaville (Congo), Moroni (The Comoros), Accra (Ghana), Muscat (Oman), Valletta (Malta), Funafuti (Tuvalu).

Study the list for no more than two minutes, cover up the page, and try to write down as many combinations as you remember. Heck, you don't even have to do them in order (but you get serious extra credit if you do!).

Time's up

How did you do? Did you get them all right? How long do you think you'd have to study this list to be able to recite it perfectly? I guarantee you it would take a lot less time if you established a chain link that you could just withdraw from your memory bank.

Here are the associations and pictures I would use to remember this list (and remember, make your pictures memorable to *you*!):

Tirana (Algeria): Being a New Yorker, the thing that immediately came to mind was the *Tawana* Brawley case in which Rev. *Al* Sharpton was involved. I'd remember a picture of the Reverend being *jeered* when it was discovered the whole thing was a hoax.

Belmopan (Belize): Picture *Elmo* from *Sesame Street* wearing a big *B* on his chest (hence *Belmo*) while holding a pan and begging you to take it (*Puleeze!*).

Thimphu (Bhutan): Thimphu is a *thimble* trying on a *tan boot*. Picture it on the pan Elmo is holding to make it really memorable!

Suva (Fiji): I'd remember the Indian god *Siva* being very nervous (*fidgeting*).

Brazzaville (Congo): So happens I once worked with an author named Jerry *Braza*. I'd picture him in his *villa* playing his *bongo*.

Moroni (The Comoros): The *Commodores* (an old singing group, for those of you under 30!) eating *macaroni*.

Accra (Ghana): "The water (*agua*) is *gone*."

Muscat (Oman): *Muskrat! Oh, my!* You can always combine these last two, picturing yourself looking for water, finding none, then seeing a fat muskrat grinning with water rolling down his cheeks. (Remember, I *said* strange.)

Valetta (Malta)—To make it really weird, the musk-rat's *valet, Walter* is standing at attention, waiting to dress him. (See the next one; it's gets better.)

Funafuti (Tuvalu)—That's right, he's dressing him in that *fun* and *fruity* vest from *True Value* hardware stores!

Got all that? Okay, let's put it all together into a single string. Now it really gets strange:

So you're standing on a street corner watching Reverend Al getting jeered while he talks about Tawana. Elmo runs in front of him, carrying a pan that holds a thimble trying on a tan boot. To the right, there's Siva fidgeting in front of Jerry Braza's villa, where he's playing the bongos to accompany the Commodores while they sing and eat macaroni. (This has all made me very thirsty, so...) I look for some water, only to find it's gone. The muskrat drank it. And there he is (oh my!) while his valet, Walter, stands by, waiting to dress him in his fun and fruity vest from True Value.

Is this efficient?

You're probably wondering just how much time it took me to construct these ridiculous associations and the even more bizarre story to go with them. The answer: about three minutes. I'll bet it will take you a lot longer to memorize the list of capitals and countries. And my way of doing this is so much more fun! Not only that, but I'd be willing to bet that you'll remember "that muskrat and his valet" a lot longer than "Muscat" and "Valetta."

The reason is that you use so much more of your brain when you employ techniques like this. Reciting a list of facts over and over to yourself uses only three of your faculties—sight (as you read them from the page), speech, and hearing—in carving the memory trail. Constructing a bizarre story like the one we just did also puts to work your imagination, perhaps the most powerful of your mind's many powers.

How the French do it

Let's try another example, one with which I doubt you are at all familiar—the French Revolutionary calendar: Brumaire, Floréal, Frimaire, Fructidore, Germinal, Messidor, Nivôse, Pluviôse, Prairiel, Thermidor, Vendémiaire, Ventôse.

Here's the way I would remember: There'd be a big *broom* sweeping through the *air* across a field of *flowers*. That's the first picture—two down (Brumaire, Floréal).

Now the broom would turn into a *frying pan* flying through the *air* (Frimaire).

Suddenly a refrigerator (naturally a Frigidaire) would open (Fructidore) and out would pop my friends Germ and Al (Germinal). They'd yell at me, "Hey, why have you got such a *messy door?*" (Messidor).

Well, people yelling at me make me *nervous* (Nivôse) so I'd stammer, "*Please, you've toast*ed me!" (Pluviôse).

So I got down on some *rail*road tracks to *pray* (Prairiel) until a giant Lobster *Thermidor* came tumbling down in a *vend*ing machine, right out of the *air* (Vendémiaire).

The smell went right to my nose (Ventôse).

Immediately after making up this story, I turned away from the computer and, without even trying, recited the words I was supposed to have just memorized. It's actually that easy.

Now you try. How would you remember another obscure list, like this longer one of alphabets? Chalcidan, cuneiform, Cyrillic, devanagari, entrangelo, futhark, Glagol, Glossic, Greek, Gurmukhi, hieroglyphs, hiragana, ideograph, kana, katakanam Kuffic, linear A, linear B, logograph, nagari, naskhi, ogham, pictograph, Roman, runic, syllabary.

Time yourself. When you can construct a series of pictures to remember a list like this—and remember it—all in less than five minutes, you are well on your way to mastering this powerful memory technique.

Hear my song

Observations of people who have been in accidents or suffered other types of severe brain trauma have yielded many interesting insights into the ways our minds and memories work. For instance, people who have had the left side of their brains damaged might lose their ability to speak and remember words and facts, but often are still able to sing songs perfectly.

Current thinking on this is that the faculty for speech resides in the left hemisphere of the brain, while the ability to sing can be found in the right.

Because it is my feeling that the more of your mind's power you put behind the job of remembering, the better you'll do, I'd like to suggest song as another great way to remember strings of information.

For instance, I remember few things from chemistry class in my junior year of high school (not having had memory training at that time). But one thing I'll never forget is that ionization is a dissociative reaction; it is the result of electrons becoming separated from their nuclei.

The reason I remember this is that Mr. Scott, my crazy chemistry teacher, came into class singing (to the main theme from the opera *Grenada*) "I-, I-, I-onization. I-, I-, I-onization. Oh, this is, oh, this is a dissociative reaction in chemistry."

Or there's the case of one of Robert Frost's most loved poems, "Stopping by Woods On a Snowy Evening." Did you ever realize that you could sing the entire poem to the music of "Hernando's Hideaway" by Xavier Cugat?

Try it with the last four lines—"The woods are lovely dark and deep, but I have promises to keep, and miles to go before I sleep. And miles to go before I sleep." Trust me: It works for the whole poem. Unfortunately, that beautiful poem, one of my favorites, may now be ruined forever!

Just do it

Music is just one of the ways that you can create a chain link to improve your memory. As the examples we've already discussed show, there are many others:

Unusual. To the extent possible, make the chain-link scenarios you construct highly unusual.

Active. Don't think of an object just sitting there. Have it do something! Remember Mom and her car smashing through the kitchen counter earlier in the chapter? How can such an image be forgotten?

Emotional. Conjure up a scenario in establishing your chain link that elicits an emotional reaction—joy, sorrow, physical pain, whatever.

Rhyming. Many lessons for preschoolers and those just in 1st and 2nd grade are done with rhymes. If it works for them, it should work for you, right?

Acronyms. If you've taken trigonometry, you've probably come across good old Chief *SOH-CAH-TOA.* If you've been lucky enough to evade trig (or didn't have Mr. Oldehoff in 7th grade), you've missed one of the easiest ways to remember trigonometric functions: *S*ine equals *O*pposite/*H*ypotenuse; *C*osine equals *A*djacent/*H*ypotenuse; *T*angent equals *O*pposite/*A*djacent.

Relax and have fun

You're probably thinking that all of this doesn't sound like it will make your life any easier. I know it *seems* like a lot of work to think of the sound-alikes and construct crazy scenarios or songs using them. Trust me: If you start applying these tips *routinely*, they will quickly become second nature and make you a more efficient student.

There's the rub

The only problem with this method is that you might occasionally have trouble remembering what your sound-alike signified in the first place. But the process of forming the link will, more often than not, obviate the problem because the link to the original item is made stronger by the act of forming these crazy associations. Again, the crazier they are, the more *memorable* they are.

Build a library

If you are ever to become an active, avid reader, access to books will do much to cultivate the habit. I suggest you "build" your own library. Your selections can and should reflect your own tastes and interests, but try to make them wide and varied. Include some of the classics, contemporary fiction, poetry, and biography.

Save your high school and college texts—you'll be amazed at how some of the material retains its relevance. And try to read a good newspaper every day to keep current and informed.

Your local librarian can refer you to any number of lists of the "great books," most of which are available in inexpensive paperback editions. Here are four more lists—compiled by yours truly—of the "great" classical authors;

"great" not-so-classical authors, poets and playwrights; some contemporary "pretty greats;" and a selection of "great" works. You may want to put these on your buy list, especially if you're planning a summer reading program.

I'm sure that I have left off someone's favorite author or "important" title from these lists. They are not meant to be comprehensive, just representative. I doubt anyone would disagree that a person familiar with the majority of authors and works listed would be considered well-read!

Some "great" classical authors

Boccaccio	Chaucer	Confucius	Goethe
Emerson	Aristotle	Kant	Dewey
Aesop	J. Caesar	Dante	Erasmus
Aquinas	Balzac	Descartes	Hegel
Cervantes	Cicero	Machiavelli	Aristophanes
S. Johnson	Plato	Flaubert	Ovid
Spinoza	Aeschylus	Rousseau	Santayana
Homer	Milton	Voltaire	Swift
Horace	Montaigne	Shakespeare	Pindar
Nietzsche	Plutarch	Vergil	Burke

Some "great" not-so-classical authors

Sherwood Anderson	Lord Byron
W.H. Auden	Albert Camus
Samuel Beckett	Lewis Carroll
Brandan Behan	Joseph Conrad
William Blake	e.e. cummings
Bertolt Brecht	Daniel Defoe
Charlotte Bronte	Charles Dickens
Emily Bronte	Emily Dickinson
Pearl Buck	Feodor Dostoevski

Arthur Conan Doyle
Theodore Dreiser
Alexandre Dumas
George Eliot
T.S. Eliot
William Faulkner
Edna Ferber
F. Scott Fitzgerald
E.M. Forster
Robert Frost
John Galsworthy
Jose Ortega y Gasset
Nikolai Gogol
Maxim Gorki
Thomas Hardy
Nathaniel Hawthorne
Ernest Hemingway
Hermann Hesse
Victor Hugo
Aldous Huxley
Washington Irving
William James
James Joyce
Franz Kafka
John Keats
Rudyard Kipling
D.H. Lawrence
H.W. Longfellow
James Russell Lowell
Thomas Mann
W. Somerset Maugham
Herman Melville
H.L. Mencken

Henry Miller
H.H. Munro (Saki)
Vladimir Nabokov
O. Henry
Eugene O'Neill
George Orwell
Dorothy Parker
Edgar Allan Poe
Ezra Pound
Marcel Proust
Ellery Queen
Ayn Rand
Erich Maria Remarque
Bertrand Russell
J.D. Salinger
George Sand
Carl Sandburg
William Saroyan
Jean Paul Sartre
George Bernard Shaw
Percy Bysshe Shelley
Upton Sinclair
Aleksandr I. Solzhenitsyn
Gertrude Stein
Robert Louis Stevenson
Dylan Thomas
James Thurber
J.R.R. Tolkien
Leo Tolstoy
Ivan Turgenev
Mark Twain
Robert Penn Warren
Evelyn Waugh

H.G. Wells	P.G. Wodehouse
Walt Whitman	Thomas Wolfe
Oscar Wilde	William Wordsworth
Thornton Wilder	William Butler Yeats
Tennessee Williams	Emile Zola

Some "pretty great" contemporary authors

Edward Albee	Norman Mailer
Isaac Asimov	Bernard Malamud
John Barth	Gabriel Garcia Marquez
Saul Bellow	Cormac McCarthy
T. Coraghessan Boyle	Toni Morrison
Anthony Burgess	Joyce Carol Oates
Truman Capote	Flannery O'Connor
John Cheever	Thomas Pynchon
Don DeLillo	Philip Roth
Pete Dexter	Isaac Bashevis Singer
E. L. Doctorow	Jane Smiley
William Gaddis	Wallace Stegner
William Golding	Rex Stout
Robert Heinlein	William Styron
Joseph Heller	Anne Tyler
Lillian Hellman	John Updike
John Hersey	Alice Walker
Oscar Hijuelos	Eudora Welty
Jerzy Kozinski	

Some "great" works

The Adventures of Huckleberry Finn	*The Aeneid*
	Aesop's Fables
The Adventures of Tom Sawyer	*Alice In Wonderland*

All Quiet On the Western Front
An American Tragedy
Animal Farm
Anna Karenina
Arrowsmith
Atlas Shrugged
As I Lay Dying
Babbitt
The Bell Jar
Beloved
The Bonfire of the Vanities
Brave New World
The Brothers Karamazov
The Canterbury Tales
Catch-22
The Catcher In the Rye
Chimera
Confessions of an English Opium Eater
The Confessions of Nat Turner
The Count of Monte Cristo
Crime and Punishment
David Copperfield
Death Crimes for the Archbishop
Death of a Salesman
The Deerslayer
Demian
Don Juan
Don Quixote
Ethan Fromme

Far From the Maddening Crowd
A Farewell to Arms
The Federalist Papers
The Fixer
For Whom the Bell Tolls
The Foundation
A Good Scent From a Strange Mountain
The Good Earth
The Grapes of Wrath
Gravity's Rainbow
The Great Gatsby
Gulliver's Travels
Hamlet
Heart of Darkness
The Hound of Baskervilles
I, Claudius
The Idiot
The Iliad
The Immortalist
The Invisible Man
Jane Eyre
JR
Julius Caesar
Kim
King Lear
Lady Chatterley's Lover
"Leaves of Grass"
The Legend of Sleepy Hollow
Les Miserables
A Lesson Before Dying

*A Long Day's Journey Into
  Night*
Look Homeward, Angel
Lord Jim
The Lord of the Rings
MacBeth
The Magic Mountain
Main Street
Man and Superman
The Merchant of Venice
The Metamorphosis
Moby Dick
Mother Courage
Native Son
1984
Of Human Bondage
Of Mice and Men
The Old Man and the Sea
Oliver Twist
*One Flew Over the
  Cuckoo's Nest*
The Optimist's Daughter
Othello
Our Town
Paradise Lost
The Pickwick Papers
The Picture of Dorian Gray
*A Portrait of the Artist as a
  Young Man*
Portrait of a Lady
Pride and Prejudice
The Prophet
Ragtime

"The Raven"
The Red Badge of Courage
*The Remembrance of
  Things Past*
The Return of the Native
"The Road Not Taken"
Robinson Crusoe
Romeo and Juliet
The Scarlet Letter
The Shipping News
Siddhartha
Silas Marner
Sister Carrie
Sophie's Choice
The Sound and the Fury
Steppenwolf
A Streetcar Named Desire
The Sun Also Rises
The Tale of Genji
A Tale of Two Cities
Tender Is the Night
The Thin Red Line
The Time Machine
A Thousand Acres
Tom Jones
The Trial
Ulysses
Vanity Fair
Walden
War and Peace
"The Wasteland"
Winesburg, Ohio
Wuthering Heights

Reading every one of these books will probably make you a better reader; it will certainly make you more well-read. That is the extra added bonus to establishing such a reading program—an appreciation of certain authors, certain books, certain cultural events, and the like is what separates the cultured from the merely educated and the undereducated.

Read on

Insofar as one can in a single chapter, I've tried to sum up the essentials of reading. It is not a finite science, but rather a skill and appreciation that one can develop over time. Good grade-school training is essential. And for those of you who have been able to identify problem areas, there are always remedial classes.

If you feel you need more help with your reading comprehension, I urge you to consult *Improve Your Reading* and *Improve Your Memory* (available separately or in the companion to this new volume—*Ron Fry's Big Book of Personal Productivity.*

Answers to quiz: B, C, D, D.

CHAPTER 4

HOW TO USE YOUR LIBRARY

Libraries contain the written record of humankind's brief stay on Planet Earth. They stand unparalleled as one of our finest accomplishments and unchallenged as reference and research sources. In your attempt to develop life-long study skills, you will find yourself using the library constantly. It presents a single well from which we can draw knowledge and material throughout our lifetimes... without ever worrying about coming up dry.

Libraries are a staple in cities large and small across the United States and represent an amazingly democratic aspect of our culture. Rules and restrictions vary from library to library—public vs. college, large vs. small— but high school and college students usually have access to virtually all library materials. Don't forget the best part: These services are *free*. A library card is your ticket to the world of knowledge that could keep you busy for the rest of your life.

Where to find a library

Start with your local phone directory. I can virtually guarantee there is a library within minutes of your home, because there are more than 15,000 public and nearly 5,000 academic (high school, college, university, and graduate school) libraries in the United States. These are the ones you would most likely be using.

If for some reason you don't think the resources of these nearly 20,000 libraries are sufficient, there are also nearly 500 libraries on military bases throughout the country, plus more than 10,000 government and special (law, medical, religious, art, etc.) libraries nationwide.

And, of course, as we'll discuss in the next chapter, you can access nearly any library in the world from the comfort of your own home. All you need is a computer, a modem, and some Net-surfing smarts.

Many major university libraries dwarf all but the largest public library systems. Harvard, Yale, Princeton, and similar bastions of learning offer tremendous resources even the major public libraries can't. If you have access to a major university library, consider it your good fortune and take advantage of it.

How libraries work

Most libraries are divided into reading rooms, restricted collections, and unrestricted book stacks. Unrestricted book stacks are those through which anyone using the library can wander, choosing books to use while in the library or, if allowed, to take home. Restricted areas generally include any special collections of rare books, those open only to scholars or to those with particular credentials, either by library rule or by order of whoever donated the collection (and often the room housing it). In some libraries, *all* book stacks are closed, and *all* books must be obtained from a librarian.

Most libraries contain both *circulating materials*—those books and other items you may check out and take home with you—and *noncirculating materials*—those that must be used only in the library. All fiction, general nonfiction, and even most scholarly titles will usually be found in the first group. Reference material, periodicals, and books in special collections are usually in the second.

A look at a major library

How extensive is the collection of information at a major institution like the New York Public Library? You'd be amazed.

Let's look only at the main library on Fifth Avenue, which stands like a monument at the dividing line between the East and West sides of Manhattan.

The first thing you discover is that no books can be taken out of this building. Because there are 82 branches throughout the five boroughs of New York (which together house more than 13,000,000 volumes) that *will* let you take out many of their holdings, this is not exactly a problem.

So you can't take anything with you. What can you study while you're there? In addition to an extensive collection of the fiction and nonfiction works you'd expect to find in such a library, shelves of books on every conceivable topic from airplanes to zoology, back issues of more periodicals than you could probably name and more recordings than your local record store stocks, there are separate rooms—that's right, *rooms* (large ones, too!)—for prints and photographs, art, microfilm, U.S. and local history and genealogy, rare books, manuscripts, archives, maps, a Science and Technology Research Center, Economic and

Public Affairs Center, Slavonic and Oriental Divisions. (In the system as a whole there's also an extensive African-American collection and a separate Library for the Blind and Physically Handicapped.) Although a few of the more specialized collections (rare books, manuscripts, prints and photographs) require a special card just to enter the area that houses the collection, most of this amazing storehouse of knowledge is open to the public!

But the New York Public Library also demonstrates through its many programs that the library is much more than just a repository for books. It offers daily programs of films, lectures, book discussion groups, plays, poetry readings, concerts, and exhibits for adults; films, story telling and preschool programs for children; and is a meeting place for a wide variety of community, consumer, educational, health, social service, religious, and cultural groups.

You could live at the New York Public Library and *never* get bored!

How your library is organized

To provide organization and to facilitate access, most libraries utilize the Dewey Decimal Classification System, which uses numbers from 000 to 999 to classify all material by subject matter. It begins by organizing all books into 10 major groupings:

000 - 099	General	500 - 599	Science
100 - 199	Philosophy	600 - 699	Useful Arts
200 - 299	Religion	700 - 799	Fine Arts
300 - 399	Social Sciences	800 - 899	Literature
400 - 499	Language	900 - 999	History

Given the millions of books available in major libraries, just dividing them into these 10 groups would still make it quite difficult to find a specific title. So each of the 10 major groupings is further divided into 10 and each of these 100 groups is assigned to more specific subjects within each large group. For example, within the Philosophy classification (100), 150 is psychology and 170 is ethics. Within the history classification (900), 910 is travel and 930 is ancient history.

There is even further subdivision. Mathematics is given its own number in the 500 (Science) series—510. But specific subjects within mathematics are further classified: 511 is arithmetic; 512, algebra, and so on.

Finally, to simplify your search for materials even more, the last two digits in the Dewey Decimal code signify the type of book:

01 Philosophy of

02 Outlines of

03 Dictionary of

04 Essays about

05 Periodicals on

06 Society transactions and proceedings

07 Study or teaching of

08 Collections

09 History of

If your library doesn't use the Dewey system, it probably is organized according to the Library of Congress System, which uses letters instead of numbers to denote major categories:

A General works (encyclopedias and other reference)

B Philosophy, Psychology and Religion

C   History: Auxiliary sciences (archeology, genealogy, etc.)
D   History: General, non-American
E   American history (general)
F   American history (local)
G   Geography/Anthropology
H   Social sciences (sociology, business, economics)
J   Political sciences
K   Law
L   Education
M   Music
N   Fine arts (art and architecture)
P   Language/Literature
Q   Sciences
R   Medicine
S   Agriculture
T   Technology
U   Military science
V   Naval science
Z   Bibliography/Library science

There are more than 50,000 new books published each year, and your library probably buys a number of these. Books arrive almost daily and are sent to the cataloging section for classification, special bindings (if needed), and shelf placement. Once entered into the system, books are indexed in the card catalog (or, as is more and more often the case, in the computer) by author, title, and subject matter. Finding a biography of Tolstoy, for example, is as easy as looking up Tolstoy in the card catalog and copying down the appropriate codes for the particular one you want. (Yes, your library probably has more than one!)

In a closed-shelf environment, you would give the appropriate numbers to a librarian and the books would be delivered to you. If the shelves are open, you have merely to learn the way they are organized and go search for your own books. Open shelf areas are often designated by letters of the alphabet (for fiction), by subject matter (in smaller libraries), or, in virtually all major libraries, according to the Dewey or Library of Congress codes.

You may go to your local library and not even find a card catalog, which might confuse you. Computers are taking over the world of business, so it's no surprise that a record-intensive "business," such as the library, is in the forefront of computerization. A majority of all libraries—maybe yours—already are online.

Today, you don't even have to leave home to access some of the greatest libraries in the world via the Internet, including, within the next few years, the entire Library of Congress. Yep. All 110 million items currently housed on 500 miles of shelves will be available on the Internet. A lot of information is already on the Net, including early films of New York, hundreds of Mathew Brady's Civil War photos, special exhibitions from the Vatican Library and Dead Sea Scrolls, and much, much more. (I'd still recommend a trip to the nonvirtual Library of Congress. How else can you view—especially up close and personal—a Gutenberg bible, Lincoln's handwritten draft of the Gettysburg Address, and, most important of all—to my daughter anyway—the very first Barbie doll, among hundreds of other treasures?)

Where to start

Feeling overwhelmed by the stacks of volumes, classification systems, card catalogs, and computers? You still have no excuse for not taking advantage of your library. All you have to do—if at all confused about tracking down the information you need—is ask the librarian.

Where to look for materials

You should review as wide a variety of reference materials as possible.

But how do you find out whether anyone has written a magazine or newspaper article about your topic? How do you know if there are any government documents or pamphlets that might be of help? How do you locate those written-by-the-experts reference books?

Look in your library's publication indexes. These indexes list all of the articles, books, and other materials that have been published and/or are available in your library.

I've listed some of the major publication indexes below. There are many, many others, so remember to ask your librarian for additional suggestions.

1. **The card catalog.** This is a list of all the books in your library. (Stored on computer at most libraries these days, it's still often called a card catalog because it used to be kept on index cards.) Books are indexed in three different ways: by subject, author, and title.

2. **Newspaper indexes.** Several large-city newspapers provide an indexed list of all articles they have published.

3. **Periodical indexes.** To find out if any magazine articles have been published on your subject, go to a periodical index. *The Readers' Guide to Periodical Literature,* which indexes articles published in the most popular American magazines, may be one with which you're familiar.

4. **Vertical file.** Here's where you'll find pamphlets and brochures.

5. *U.S. Documents* **monthly catalog.** Useful for locating government publications.

Many libraries print lists of their resources and maps of where they can be found. What if yours doesn't? That's right...just ask your librarian for help—that's what he or she is there for!

Your approach to research

All of us who have become familiar with the wonders of the library have probably developed our own approach to enjoying its amenities and using them most efficiently.

My own experience emphasizes what may already be obvious: Getting the right start is all-important. Because I try to keep from becoming overwhelmed with material, I start any research working with the broadest outlines or topics (and the broadest resources) and wend my way down the ladder, getting more and more specific in topic and sources as I go.

Let's assume your assignment is to prepare a report on the current state of affairs in Bosnia. Here's how you might approach the task:

1. Consult any one of the numerous leading **encyclopedias** you will find in your local library— *Britannica, Americana, Collier's, World Book,* etc. Here you will find an overview and historical perspective on the area. Encyclopedic entries are usually the most comprehensive and concise you will find. They cover so much territory and are so (relatively) up-to-date that they are an ideal "big-picture" resource. Of course, when you're dealing with a relatively late-breaking news

story such as that of Bosnia, you may find *any* encyclopedia woefully out-of-date. (Did you guess to look up "Yugoslavia" instead to get some historical perspective? Good for you!)

2. With overview in hand, you can start consulting the **major indexes and directories** your library has to develop a list of more specific resources. Obviously, the entries in these major resources can then be directly consulted—specific issues of *The New York Times* on microfilm, periodicals at the periodicals desk, etc. In no time at all, you'll develop a long list of names and places to check out, leading you to a number of potential topics and sources.

   Here's just a brief list of those you could cull from a single magazine or newspaper article, all relating to Bosnia: Alija Izaetbegovic, Bosnia and Herzegovina, Croatia, Franjo Tudjman, Serbia, Slobodan Milosevic, Montenegro, Radovan Karadzic, Bosnian Serbs, Bosnian Croats, Ratko Mladic, Posavina Corridor, Eastern Slavonia, Muslims, Sarajevo, Belgrade, and Dayton, Ohio. Think you'll run out of research materials?

In one brief tour of your library's resources, you'll easily discover and know how to obtain more material than you would need to write a book on virtually any one of the subtopics, let alone a report encompassing all of them.

What if you're uncomfortable in the library? An infrequent user? Or simply find it a confusing place that's more trouble than it's worth? As I've emphasized, developing *any* habit is just a matter of practice. The more you use the library, the more comfortable you will become using it, and the more books you'll become comfortable with. In a very short time, you will have your own list of resources that you start with whenever you receive an assignment.

Many of you might not use the library as much as you should (or even would like) because it seems like a confusing series of catacombs. The more comfortable you are—the more you know about the materials it contains and how to locate and use them—the more you will *want* to be there.

And the more help you will be able to obtain from this great resource that's just waiting to welcome you!

CHAPTER 5

HOW TO USE YOUR COMPUTER

Using a computer is like having a dialogue. It's a one-way dialogue, with you asking questions and issuing orders, and your talking partner responding without complaint. It's a great way of communicating except for two small drawbacks: You and your partner speak totally different languages, and neither of you hears what the other is saying. It's these little problems that make computers seem so mysterious and difficult to use. But remember: Operating your computer is just like having a chat with a friend. All that hardware—those boxes, hard drives, chips, ports, busses, expansion slots, the screen, the keyboard, and the mouse—is only there to make that simple little conversation possible.

Whether you have the latest high-tech equipment or an old clunker balancing precariously on your desk, you can use your computer to increase your skills, expand your knowledge, and make research simple. Your computer can help you to:

☞ Increase and test your knowledge of mathematics, including algebra and geometry.

☞ Brush up your English skills.

☞ Listen to native speakers pronouncing words in the language you are studying.

☞ Research issues in numerous encyclopedias, dictionaries, and other reference sources.

☞ Get information on abortion, civil rights, and other issues from organizations involved.

☞ Travel down the Amazon River, visit ancient Greek ruins, or the site of a concentration camp.

☞ Read classical literature and philosophy in its original language or in English.

☞ "Dissect" the human body or watch as a virus invades a body cell.

☞ Pose questions to other students or professionals in the field you are studying.

☞ Study paintings in the Louvre and many other museums around the world.

☞ Read abstracts and complete articles from professional journals published around the world.

☞ Study the Declaration of Independence, the text of Dr. Martin Luther King's "I Have a Dream" speech, or all of the presidential inauguration speeches.

☞ View blueprints of significant buildings.

☞ Practice for the SAT, GRE, and other tests.

☞ Leave messages for and get information from the President of the United States, senators, congressmen, Supreme Court justices, and other government officials.

☞ See the stars and the planets through the "eyes" of spacecraft, satellites, and probes.

☞ Study time lines of history, literature, physics, and just about any other subject.

Once you've gathered all that information, you can use word processing programs such as Microsoft Word or WordPerfect to correct your spelling and grammar, to help you find more interesting words to use and to prepare professional-looking documents complete with italicized and boldfaced type, columns, and inserts.

For math or accounting projects, you can use spreadsheet programs such as Excel or Lotus 1-2-3 to organize and manipulate data, and to prepare charts and graphs that illustrate the main points you want to make.

Database programs, which help you keep track of large bodies of information, can make gathering and organizing information for a paper a breeze. Graphics programs help even the artistically challenged sketch out drawings and plans. Multimedia programs that combine text, video, sound, and pictures can help you present what you've learned in a dynamic, compelling manner.

With various word processing, spreadsheet, database, graphics, and multimedia programs, with educational and special-topic programs, with access to online and Internet services, the computer-aided student has a definite leg up in the race to educational success.

Computers won't study for you or make you smarter, but they can make learning much more enjoyable, efficient, and productive.

Buying the right computer

You might have thought mastering computer lingo and developing a general understanding of computers and what they can do for you was the hard part. As many of you know, actually buying the machine is often more difficult. With so many types of computers and peripherals available, made by many manufacturers, it can be difficult to decide which is best for you.

The countless different computers, screens, printers, hard drives, and other devices lining the shelves can make a trip to the computer store both baffling and intimidating. There are so many things to consider: Do you want to become part of the Macintosh world or the IBM world? If it's IBM, do you want an actual IBM machine, a Packard Bell, a Compaq, a Dell, or one of any number of other IBM-clones? Should you buy a black and white monitor, a color monitor, a VGA color monitor or a super VGA? Is a 500 MG hard drive enough? What about the Pentium?

Asking yourself the right questions

Begin the buying process by deciding what you want your computer to do, then finding the software that will do it. Only then should you look for the hardware to run that software. Long before thinking about which brand of computer or how many megs of RAM you need, ask yourself these 11 questions:

1. What are you going to use the computer for?
2. What software will you likely be using?
3. What kind of hardware does it take to run that software?
4. How much memory do you need to run your software?
5. What kind of hardware does your school use?
6. Where will you be using the computer?
7. How are you going to protect your files?
8. How much can you afford to spend?

9. Will you pay more for a recognizable brand name, or do you want to save money with a lesser-known company?

10. How much time do you want to spend setting up and configuring your computer?

11. Does the manufacturer of the computer you're considering offer service and support?

Some final tips before you buy

☞ Shop around. You'll find computers in computer stores, computer "super" stores, electronic stores, department stores, large discount warehouses, and, of course, online.

☞ Get written quotes, and make sure that everything you want is included in that quote.

☞ Don't be afraid to haggle. Prices are rarely fixed, and you can often negotiate a better deal.

☞ Find out if the computer you want is in stock, or if you have to wait for delivery.

☞ Ask whether or not the store stands behind what it sells, or if you have to go to the manufacturer in case of a problem.

☞ Tell the salesperson that you want your system software and other key programs pre-installed by the store—especially if you're a computer novice.

☞ Go elsewhere if the salespeople don't answer your questions. If they're not helpful *before* they get your money, how helpful will they be once they do?

Finding the right software

Software is the key to computers; without it, all of that expensive hardware can't do anything.

The programs (software) that you purchase and plug into your hardware are really just directions to the computer, nothing more than "instruction books" written in code that the computer can understand.

Ah, but what those instruction books can make a computer do! They can fill your screen with the complete works of many authors, along with pictures and commentary. They can ask you hundreds of questions, then give you the answers, to help you prepare for tests such as the SAT or GRE. They can "speak" to you in French and many other foreign languages so that you can hear how the language is supposed to sound. They can take you on tours of foreign countries, lands under the seas, battlefields, and the inner workings of the human body. They can play music, show you great artwork, and recite poetry. They can, in short, be superb educational assistants.

When deciding whether to buy educational software, remember that:

☞ There is no such thing as the "best" program in any educational category. Some are stuffed with complex information, while others focus on a few simplified concepts. Some rely heavily on text, while others delight you with sounds, pictures, videos, and games. Some are geared for younger students, while others are for the more advanced. Some are plain looking and bare-bones, others high tech and glitzy. Which one is best? The one that best serves *your* needs.

☞ You can find much of this same information on the Internet or through the online services, and information on a computer disk can quickly become dated. However, there's nothing like having what you need, right at hand, when you need it.

☞ Your school may already have software you like in the classrooms or computer lab. See what your school has to offer before buying your own.

☞ It's best not to rely solely on the advertising copy you read on software boxes. Talk with your friends and read software reviews before parting with your money.

☞ You must check the side of the software box for hardware requirements to make sure your computer can run the software. Be wary of "minimum" and "suggested" RAM requirements. In most cases, the suggestion is really a requirement.

Going online

Going online is easy, right? All you have to do is master a few concepts and techniques, and learn the difference between the *Information Superhighway, the Internet, Mosaic, Gopher, the Web, WAIS, BBSes, servers, browsers, online services* and *ISPs.*

Going online puts a tremendous amount of information at your fingertips. It's especially helpful to students, for it gives them access to a mind-boggling array of educational and research facilities, including:

☞ Thousands of journals and magazines.

☞ Newspapers from around the country.

☞ Encyclopedias.

☞ Bulletin boards.

☞ Homework Helper and similar "answer finders."

☞ Online "teachers" who personally answer questions.

☞ Internet access to information sites filled with documents, statistics, lists, and bibliographies on just about subject you can think of.

☞ Minicourses in math, English, physics, American history, and most other subjects.

☞ Information about the SAT, GRE, and other tests, plus practice tests.

☞ Information about hundreds of colleges, their admission requirements, student demographics, and costs.

☞ Information on financial aid.

☞ An opportunity to "chat" with other students.

☞ The ability to contact experts in every field, many of whom will take the time to answer questions or engage in debates.

...and much, much more. New online features make it possible for you to request information on any subject. Think of all the time and effort you'll save!

Before you begin surfing

Going online simply means hooking your computer up to another computer—or to many others—and allowing them to communicate with each other. You've "lined up" your computer with another so that the information can flow. You can go online by:

☞ Physically running a cable between your computer and someone else's.

☞ Connecting computers via the telephone. If you connect over the phone wires, you'll need a *modem* to convert the computers' signals into a form that can travel through the phone system.

Once online, you can begin cruising the Information Superhighway, also known as the Global Information Highway, the Information Highway, the info highway, The Highway, and cyberspace.

What kind of information is on the Information Super-highway? Almost everything. Universities and research centers are online. So are federal, state and local governments, libraries, planetariums, newspapers, magazines, museums, political parties, sports teams, gardening clubs, and Grateful Dead fan clubs, just to mention a few.

The amount of information on the superhighway is literally limitless, because you can use the highway to "speak" to millions of other people via computer. Countless experts and amateurs in all fields are online, and many will allow you to take information out of their computers, or will answer your questions.

"Road maps"

Many "road maps" to the Internet and other parts of the information highway have been developed, making it easy even for a novice to zip from information site to information site. For example, the *World Wide Web,* also known as the *Web,* or *WWW,* was developed as a navigational "map" of the Internet, helping people find what they were looking for. Other programs, such as *Netscape, Lycos, Excite, Yahoo!,* etc., also help you *browse* (search) the Net.

Linking up to the Internet is easy. You simply go online through an *Internet Service Provider (ISP),* a company that puts your computer in touch with the others (for a fee). Students may be able to tap into the Internet via their school computers.

You can also plug into the Internet by way of commercial (for-profit) *online services* such as America Online.

Getting answers with AOL

Need help finding information? Have a question that has to be answered right now? Want to take some practice tests to see how much you know? America Online (AOL), one of the major national online services, offers a smorgasbord of information in its Education section. Resources range from the Academic Assistance Center to the *Library of Congress Online* to the *Writer's Club*. There's also *Barron's BookNotes*, the *Columbia Encyclopedia*, the *National Academy of Sciences Online*, *Classical Music Online*, the *Nature Conservancy*, *Compton's Encyclopedia & Forum*, the *National Space Society*, information on college and financial aid, an online campus, and a teacher's network.

Let's take a look at some of the many ways students can test their knowledge, find answers and hone their learning skills through AOL. Go to the main screen and click on "Education." Then, to get the quickest and most direct answers to your questions, click on the Academic Assistance Center.

Academic assistance

The Academic Assistance Center helps students sharpen their skills and complete their homework. The Center is divided into several areas, including Teacher Pager, Academic Message Board, Academic Assistance Classrooms, Study Skills Center, Exam Prep Center.

You'll also find Mini-Lesson Libraries, academic contests, *Simon & Schuster's College Online, College Board Online, Kaplan Online,* and other resources. Let's take a closer look at some of the key resources, beginning with the Teacher Pager, the Academic Message Board, and the Academic Assistance Classrooms, the three choices on the right side of the Academic Assistance Center screen.

Teacher Pager

Have you ever wished that you had a teacher on call, 24 hours a day, who was just dying to answer your questions? The Teacher Pager is probably the closest most of us will get to that fantasy. You can ask any question you like, on topics ranging from anatomy to zoology.

After clicking on the Teacher Pager button, you select the general area in which your question lies: math, science or technology, English or foreign language, history and social science, or other. Then type in your question, and indicate whether you want the answer to be geared for an elementary school, middle school, high school, or college student. Your answer will be e-mailed to you within 30 minutes to 24 hours, although 48 hours may be required to answer more complex questions.

Academic Message Board

For less pressing problems, and for an opportunity to hear from other students as well as from teachers, you can post a question on the Academic Message Board. The message boards are similar to chat rooms, but tend to be more focused and academically oriented—it's like asking your study group for help. Some questions receive one or just a few answers, while others provoke an ongoing dialogue. America Online's teachers reply to many of the questions, often pointing out resources to explore.

Just as you do when asking classmates for help, you have to carefully consider the replies you receive on the Message Board. Just because an answer has been posted doesn't mean it's right!

Academic Assistance Classrooms

The third way to get answers is to go "back to class" in the Academic Assistance Classrooms—live chat areas with teachers on hand to answer questions. There are five areas, covering:

☞ Math.

☞ History, plus the social sciences and law.

☞ Science and medicine.

☞ English, literature, and foreign languages.

☞ All other subjects, including help preparing for tests.

"Teachers" are on duty in the Academic Assistance Center from 4 p.m. to 2 a.m. Eastern time, and may be available at other times of the day. Simply go to the right room and ask your question. (Unfortunately, the "right" teacher may not be in the classroom when you are. But it's worth a try.)

After you've tried "live" help...

The Teacher Pager, Academic Message Board, and Academic Assistance Classrooms give live, rapid (maybe even instant), feedback. But there are plenty of other ways to get information.

After you've tried the pager, board, and classrooms, check into the choices listed in the scrollable menu to the left of the Academic Assistance screen. You'll find Homework Helpers, Mini-Lessons and much more.

Homework Helpers

Homework Helpers are mini-essays on a variety of topics, including chemistry, physics, biology, math, Greek and Roman gods, the American Revolution, Shakespeare, and European history.

To get to Homework Helpers, click on "AAC News." A new window, titled AAC News and Information will appear. Homework Helpers are the second item in the new window. Scroll through the subjects listed and choose the one that will help you. You'll find information on topics ranging from adding negative and positive integers to the speed of sound in water to what is beyond space and much more.

Mini-Lesson Libraries

Here you can download numerous minilessons on a variety of subjects including: algebraic equations, American Gothic, arches in architecture, Battle of Gettysburg, beta decay, black holes, city life in the Middle Ages, famous composers, General John Burgoyne, graphing linear equations, gravity, Greek/Roman gods, hemophilia, Iran in the Cold War, kinetic energy, King Henry I, logarithms and statistics, lunar eclipses, Mayan Indians, NeoNazism, personal hygiene in outer space, physics, Romanticism and Impressionism, Salvador Dali's childhood, The Milky Way, theater trends in the 1980s, Thomas Alva Edison, World War I, and British classes.

Barron's BookNotes

Although it's best to read the entire book, condensed versions with commentary, such as Barron's BookNotes, can be helpful study aids. The brief summaries and questions they pose can stimulate your thinking.

A typical guide looks at many aspects of a work. For example, the guide to *Macbeth* covers the plot, Macbeth himself, Lady Macbeth (his wife and partner in crime), Banquo (his fellow general and friend upon whom he turns), the witches who set the action in motion by foretelling the future, Malcolm and Duncan (sons of the king he slays), the setting and themes, form and structure, Shakespeare's sources, changes in the meanings of words since *Macbeth* was written, and more.

Each BookNote includes a biography of the author whose work is under discussion, literary criticism of the work, plus an analysis of the work's characters, plot, and other qualities. AOL has many of the BookNotes, including *The Aeneid, A Farewell to Arms, Anna Karenina, Beowulf, Brave New World, Canterbury Tales, Crime and Punishment, The Crucible, Death of a Salesman, Don Quixote, Grapes of Wrath, Great Expectations, Hamlet, The Iliad, Jane Eyre, Lord Jim, Lord of the Flies, Moby Dick, The Red Badge of Courage, The Scarlet Letter, Slaughterhouse-Five, The Sun Also Rises, A Tale of Two Cities,* and others—more than enough to get you through any English literature class!

The Odyssey Project

If you want to get information on a "visual" topic, the kind you might see in *National Geographic,* investigate The Odyssey Project. The Odyssey Project puts pictures above the words to describe what it's like to hold a baby chimpanzee while floating down the Zaire River, to enter into a shark's cave near the Yucatan Peninsula, or clamber up and down Andean mountains looking for dinosaur footprints.

You can take a computer odyssey to study Kenya, the great white shark, the Mississippi River, Bali, Christmas in New York, or take a special trip back to 1627.

Putting it all together

How do you draw these resources together to find what you need, quickly? Let's say you were doing a report on the heart. You could work your way through the Reference Newsstand and Education sections, looking at the encyclopedias, health magazines, and other references. Or you could type in the keyword "Health" and be taken right to the Health screen, where you find AOL's health resources gathered together.

Now you can investigate the Community Forum, the Better Health & Medical Forum, References, Magazines and News or move into the Internet.

If you open the Heart & Circulatory selection under the scrollable Community Forum list, you'll find a wealth of information on heart and circulatory system disorders, including: aneurysms, glaucoma, heart attack, and more.

You can also read the messages and replies posted, or post one of your own.

The Better Health and Medicine Forum allows you to search the online Health Forum and participate in chats on mental health, addiction, sexuality, health reform, and other topics. The Forum also has a section on Alternative Medicine Information where you can research a large number of heart-related topics, including acupressure, acupuncture, aromatherapy, the Alexander Technique, biological rhythms, chiropractic, holistic medicine, homeopathy, naturopathy, and vegetarian diets.

The Forum also includes a library of health and heart-related software you can download into your computer, a chat room devoted to heart disease, message boards, and other information.

The Heart Message Board is an excellent way to gather information by asking questions and exchanging information in discussion and support groups covering a wide variety of topics, from angina to strokes and surgery.

Speaking to others who share your interest can help you cut through a lot of preliminary research and get right to the "heart" of the matter.

Studying how to study online

Learning how to study more effectively, finding answers and getting help with problem areas can smooth the way for any student. Those who need a little extra, well-focused help can find that, too, by looking in the Study Skills Service. For example, if you're in an English class, you'll find lots of appropriate help with choosing between "who" and "whom," linking independent clauses, comma placement, and more.

Testing your knowledge

AOL presents "How Much Do You Know?" quizzes in the form of contests, with winners receiving free computer time. They're good for two reasons: You get to test your knowledge, and you learn as you play. You'll find the quizzes in the Brain Bowl.

Those are just some of the resources available on America Online. AOL also has an exam preparation center and fee-charging online courses in a variety of subjects. (For a fee, you can hook up with Kaplan and other test-preparation services.)

Surf's up on the Internet

The Internet—that vast, mysterious collection of computer networks linking every corner of the globe—is a cornucopia of facts, statistics, documents, opinions, arguments, lists, video and sound clips. The answer to most any question is on the Internet—somewhere. The trick is to find it. There's no room in this book to list even a smattering of pertinent Internet sites (though I have included an extensive list in Chapter 7 of *Use Your Computer*). Wherever you go on the Net, just remember:

☞ Some of the sites are informative and well-organized, some are quirky and skimpy.

☞ Some are well-researched and trustworthy, and some are the rantings of a mad person. Just because you see it on your computer screen doesn't mean that it's the truth.

☞ Some provide unbiased information with no ulterior motive, some slant their information to sell you on their cause. Some are just offering enough information to entice you to buy something.

☞ Some are easy to use, some require you to search through listings to find what you need.

☞ Some have the information, some link you to other sites, and some are simply listings of sites.

☞ Some may be gone when you look for them again. That happens.

☞ Some are free, but some cost, and cost a lot. Be sure to check out cost before going online.

The final word

Your computer and the world it can open for you is a wondrous tool and a fabulous adventure. Just remember that it *is* only a tool, one that works much better if you've already developed all the *other* study skills in this book.

CHAPTER 6

HOW TO
WRITE
TERRIFIC PAPERS

It's going to happen. Whether you like it or not. Sooner or later, you'll have to prepare written and/or oral reports for virtually every one of your classes. And if you're like most students, your reaction will be the same every time: "Why me? What do I do? Where do I start?"

Reading this chapter will probably not make you such a good writer that you can quit school and start visiting bookstores to preen in front of the window displays featuring your latest bestseller.

But there is absolutely no reason to fear a written paper or oral report, once you know the simple steps to take and rules to follow to complete it satisfactorily. Once you realize that 90 percent of preparing a paper has *nothing* to do with writing...or even being *able* to write. And once you're confident that preparing papers by following my suggestions will probably get you a grade or two higher than you've gotten before...even if you think you are the world's poorest excuse for a writer.

Doing a research paper requires a lot of work. But the payoff is great, too. You will learn, for example:

1. How to track down information about *any* subject.
2. How to sort through that information and come to a conclusion about your subject.
3. How to prepare an organized, in-depth report.
4. How to communicate your ideas clearly and effectively.

Once you develop these skills, you *own* them.

You'll be able to apply them in *all* your high-school or college classes, not only when you prepare other research papers, but also when you tackle smaller writing assignments, such as essays and oral reports.

When you graduate, these same skills will help you get ahead in the work world; the ability to analyze a subject and communicate through the written word are keys to success, no matter what career you choose.

Of all the things you'll learn in school, the skills you acquire as we produce your research paper will be among the most valuable.

5 basic rules of paper-writing

Let's start with the fundamental rules that need to be emblazoned on your wall:

1. **Always** follow your teacher's directions to the letter.
2. **Always** hand in your paper on time.
3. **Always** hand in a clean and clear copy of your paper.

4. **Never** allow a spelling or grammatical error in your paper.

5. **Always** keep at least one copy of every paper you write.

You wanted it *type*written?

Your teacher's directions may include:

☞ A general subject area from which topics should be chosen—"some aspect of Lincoln's presidency," "a 19th-century invention," "a poem by Wordsworth," etc.

☞ Specific requirements regarding format—typed, double-spaced, include title page, do not include title page, etc.

☞ Suggested length—for example, 10 to 15 typewritten pages.

☞ Other requirements—turn in general outline before topic is approved; get verbal okay on topic before proceeding; don't include quotes (from other works) longer than a single paragraph; other idiosyncrasies of your own teachers.

Whatever his or her directions, follow them *to the letter*. High school teachers may be somewhat forgiving, but I have known college professors who simply refused to accept a paper that was not prepared *exactly* as they instructed—and gave the poor but wiser student an F for it (without even *reading* it).

If you are unsure of a specific requirement or if the suggested area of topics is unclear, it is *your* responsibility to talk to your teacher and clarify whatever points are confusing you.

It is also not a bad idea to choose two or three topics you'd like to write about and seek his or her preliminary approval if the assignment seems particularly vague—this way, you'll *know* for sure that you are fulfilling the topic requirement.

So then my dog chewed the paper...

If you've skipped ahead and read ***Manage Your Time***, there is certainly no reason, short of catastrophic illness or life-threatening emergency, for you to *ever* be late with an assignment. Again, some teachers will refuse to accept a paper that is late. At best, they will mark you down for your lateness, perhaps turning an A paper into a B...or worse.

Presuming you have no choice but to be late, for reasons good or bad, you might want to find a copy of my newest book—*Last Minute Study Tips*—to figure out how to write a good paper when there's little or no time to spare!

Is that jelly stain worth a B?

Teachers have to read a lot of papers and shouldn't be faulted for being human if, after hundreds of pages, they come upon your jelly-stained, pencil-written tome and get a bit discouraged. Nor should you be surprised if they give you a lower grade than the content might merit just because the presentation is so poor.

I'm not advocating "form over substance." Far from it—the content is what the teacher is looking for, and he or she will primarily be basing your grade on *what* you write. But presentation is important. So please follow these simple rules:

☞ Never handwrite your paper.

☞ If you're using a word processor or word-processing program on your computer, use a new ribbon in your dot matrix printer and/or check the toner cartridge in your laser printer. If you type (or have someone else type) your paper, use clean white bond and (preferably) a new carbon ribbon so the images are crisp and clear.

☞ Unless otherwise instructed, always double space a typewritten paper.

☞ Use a simple typeface that is clear and easy-to-read; avoid those that are too big—stretching a five-page paper to 10—or too small and hard to read.

☞ Never use a fancy italic, modern, or other ornate or hard-to-read typeface for the entire paper.

Use your old papers as maps

There should be a number of helpful messages in your returned papers, which is why it's so important to retain them. What did your teacher have to say? Are there comments applicable to the paper you're writing now—poor writing, lack of organization, lack of research, bad transitions between paragraphs, poor grammar or punctuation, misspellings? The more such comments—and, one would expect, the lower the grade—the more extensive the "map" your teacher has given you for your *next* paper, showing you right where to "locate" your A.

If you got a low grade but there aren't any comments, shouldn't you have asked the teacher why you got such a poor grade? You may get the comments you need to make the next paper better. You'll also be showing the teacher you actually care, which could help your grade the next time around.

Many employers merrily use resumes and cover letters with grammatical and/or spelling errors for hoops practice. Don't expect your teachers to be any more forgiving—there are definitely a few out there who will award an F without even noticing that the rest of the paper is great; too bad you misspelled "Constantinople" or left a participle twisting slowly in the wind.

The Fry paper-writing system

The more complex a task or the longer you need to complete it, the more important your organization becomes. By breaking down any paper-writing project into a series of manageable steps, you'll start to feel less chaotic, hectic, and afraid right away.

Here are the steps that, with some minor variations along the way, are common to virtually any written report or paper:

1. Research potential topics.
2. Finalize topic.
3. Carry out initial library research.
4. Prepare general outline.
5. Do detailed library research.
6. Prepare detailed outline (from note cards).
7. Write first draft.
8. Do additional research (if necessary).
9. Write second draft.
10. Spell-check and proofread.
11. Have someone *else* proofread.
12. Produce final draft.
13. Proofread one last time.
14. Turn it in and collect your A+.

Create a work schedule

Get out your calendar. Find the date on which your paper is due. How many weeks do you have till then? Plan to spend at least half of that time on research, the other half on writing.

Now, block out set periods of time during each week to work on your paper. Schedule two- or three-hour chunks of work time, rather than many short periods, so you can really immerse yourself in your work.

As you make up your work schedule, set deadlines for completing various steps of your paper. For example:

Week 1:   Decide on topic and "angle" of your paper.

Week 2:   Make list of references.

Weeks 3/4:   Read reference materials; take notes.

Weeks 5/6:   Do detailed outline; write first draft.

Week 7:   Edit paper; prepare bibliography.

Week 8:   Proofread paper; type final copy.

You should probably plan on consulting and/or taking notes from at least 10 different books, articles, or other reference materials. (Your teacher or subject may demand more.) And you should plan on writing two or three drafts of your paper before you arrive at the final copy.

Refer to your work schedule often, and adjust your speed if you find yourself lagging behind.

Steps 1 & 2: Consider and choose topic options

In some cases, your teacher will assign your topic. In others, your teacher will assign a general area of study, but you will have the freedom to pick a specific topic within that general area.

There are some pitfalls you must avoid. Let's say you need to write a 15-page paper for your American history class, and you decide your topic will be The Industrial Revolution. Can you really cover that in *15* pages? Not unless you simply rehash the high points, *à la* your third-grade history book. You could write *volumes* on the subject (many people have!) and have plenty left to say.

Instead, you need to focus on a particular, limited angle of your subject, such as, "The Effect of Eli Whitney's Cotton Gin on the Industrialization of the South."

By the same token, you must not get too narrow in your focus. Choose a subject that's too limited, and you might run out of things to say on the second page of your paper. "How a Cotton Gin Works" might make an interesting one- or two-page story. It certainly won't fill 10 or 15 pages.

Pick a topic that's too obscure, and you may find that little or no information has been written about it. In which case, you will have to conduct your own experiments, interview your own research subjects, and come up with your own original data. Hint: If you can't find a single *book* on your supposed topic, rethink it! While you could choose a topic that can be researched via magazine articles, the newspaper, monographs, and the like, why make your life so difficult if you don't have to?

Make sure there is enough research material available about your topic. And make sure that there are enough *different* sources of material—different authors, different books, etc.—so you can get a well-rounded view of your subject (and not be forced for lack of other material to find ways to make somebody else's points sound like your own).

Taking all of the above into consideration, do a little brainstorming now about possible topics for your paper.

Don't stop with the first idea—come up with several different possibilities. Put this book down until you have a list of three or four potential topics.

How about trying to get two or more papers for two or more classes *out of the same research?* You may not be able to simply produce one paper for two classes, but with a little extra research—*not* what you would need to do for an entirely different paper—you may well utilize a good portion of the first paper as the basis for a second. What a great way to maximize your library time!

Step 3: Begin initial library research

Got your list? Then get thee to a library. You need to do a little advance research. Scan your library's card-catalog index and *Readers' Guide to Periodical Literature* or other publication indexes. See how many books and articles have been written about each topic on your "possibilities" list. Next, read a short background article or encyclopedia entry about each topic.

With any luck at all, you should be left with at least one topic that looks like a good research subject. If two or more topics passed your preliminary-research test, pick the one that interests you most. You're going to spend a lot of time learning about your subject. There's no rule that says you can't enjoy it!

Develop a temporary thesis

Once you have chosen the topic for your paper, you must develop a temporary thesis. (The word "thesis" is a relative of "hypothesis" and means about the same thing— the central argument you will attempt to prove or disprove in your paper. A thesis is not the same thing as a *topic.* Your topic is what you study; your thesis is the conclusion you draw from that study.)

A "thesis statement" is a one-sentence summary of your thesis. It sums up the main point of your paper.

Note that I said *temporary* thesis. It may not wind up being your final thesis. Because you haven't completed all your research yet, you can only come up with a "best-guess" thesis at this point.

If a temporary thesis doesn't spring easily to mind—and it probably won't—sit back, and do some more brainstorming. Ask yourself questions like:

☞ What's special or unusual about ___? (Fill in the blank with your topic.)

☞ How is ___ related to events in the past?

☞ What impact has ___ made on society?

☞ What do I want the world to know about ___?

☞ What questions do I have about ___?

Step 4: Create a temporary outline

Once you have developed your temporary thesis, give some thought as to how you might approach the subject in your paper. Jot down the various issues you plan to investigate. Then, come up with a brief, temporary outline of your paper, showing the order in which you might discuss those issues.

Don't worry too much about this outline—it will be brief, at best. It's simply a starting point for your research, a plan of attack. But don't skip this step, either—it will be a big help in organizing your research findings.

Step 5: Do detailed library research

We've already reviewed the library and how to take advantage of its resources. Now, let's talk about exactly how you'll keep track of all the resources and information you'll gather for your paper.

To create your working bibliography, you'll need a supply of 3 x 5 index cards. You'll also use index cards when you take notes for your paper, so buy a big batch now. About 300 cards ought to suffice. While you're at it, pick up one of those little envelope files designed to hold the cards. Put your name, address, and phone number on the file. If you lose it, some kind stranger can return it.

Before you do anything else, send away for anything you want to review that isn't available in your library. If you want a brochure from a particular association, for example, order it now. It may take a few weeks for such materials to arrive. (Check the online services and Internet to see if any needed material can be easily downloaded. The more skilled Web browsers among you may spend little on postage, even for obscure material from Zimbabwe.)

Start a systematic search for any materials that might have information related to your paper. Look through the indexes we covered in Chapter 4 and any other indexes your librarian recommends. (And don't overlook the extensive resources available online.)

When you find a book, article, or other resource that looks promising, take out a blank note card. On the front of the card, write down the following information:

In the upper right-hand corner of the card: The library call number (Dewey decimal number or Library of Congress number), if there is one. Add any other details that will help you locate the material on the library shelves ("Science Reading Room," "Reference Room").

On the main part of the card: The author's name, if given—last name first, first name, middle name/initial. Then the title of the article, if applicable, in quotation marks.

Then the name of the book, magazine, newspaper, or other publication—underlined.

Add any details you will need if you have to find the book or article again, such as the date of publication, edition, volume number, and page numbers on which the article or information appears.

In the upper left-hand corner of the card: Number it. The first card you write will be #1, the second, #2, and so on. If you happen to mess up and skip a number somewhere along the line, don't worry. It's only important that you assign a different number to each card (and, therefore, to each *book*).

At the bottom of the card: If you're going to be researching in more than one library, write the library's name. Also write down the name of the index in which you found the resource, in case you need to refer to it again.

Do this for *each* potential source of information you find. *And put only one resource on each card.*

Sample Bibliography Card for a Book

(1)	315.6
	Main Reading Room

Jones, Karen A.

The Life and Times of Bob Smith.
(see esp. pp. 43-48)

Card Catalog
Main Street Library

Sample Bibliography Card for a Magazine Article

---

(2)   Periodical Room

Perkins, Stan

"The Life and Times of Bob Smith"
<u>Smith Magazine</u>
(April 24, 1989; pp. 22-26)

Readers' Guide
University Library

Sample Bibliography Card for a Newspaper Article

---

(3)   Microfiche Room

Black, Bill

"Bob Smith: The New Widget Spinner"
<u>The New York Times</u>
(June 16, 1976, late edition, p. A12)

New York Times Index
Main Street Library

Citing online information

Because students are increasingly using online sources, the MLA, which publishes style guides for research papers, has integrated electronic citations into its latest edition. Xia Li's and Nancy Crane's guide, *Electronic Style: A Guide to Citing Electronic Information* (Meckler Media) is another good reference. Sample online citation:

Terhune, Alan J. "Sensationalism." <u>Reporting News</u>.
http://www.ccs.syr.edu/home/lbp/reporting-news.html
(22 May 1995)

Now hit the books

Set aside solid blocks of time for your library work. It's much better to schedule a handful of extended trips to the library than 15 or 20 brief visits. When you go to the library, take your bibliography cards, a good supply of blank index cards, your preliminary outline, and several pens or pencils.

Your bibliography cards serve as the map for your information treasure hunt. Get out a stack of five or six cards, and locate the materials listed on those cards. Set up camp at a secluded desk or table and get to work.

When you write your paper, you'll get all the information you need from your notes, rather than from the original sources. Therefore, it's vital that you take careful and complete notes. What sort of information should you put in your notes? Anything related to your subject and especially to your thesis. This includes:

1. General background information (names, dates, historical data, etc.).
2. Research statistics.
3. Quotes by experts.
4. Definitions of technical terms.

You may be used to keeping your notes in a three-ring binder or notepad. I'm going to show you a better way—recording all of your notes on index cards.

Let's say that you have found a reference book that contains some information about your subject. Before you begin taking notes, get out the bibliography card for that book.

Check that all of the information on your card is correct. Is the title exactly as printed on the book? Is the author's name spelled correctly? Add any other information you'll need to include in your final bibliography. (For more information on exactly what you need to include, be sure to refer to *Improve Your Writing, 3rd Ed*. It includes details on bibliographic and source note formats.)

Note-taking guidelines

☞ **Write one thought, idea, quote, or fact on each card.** If you encounter a very long quote or string of data, you can write on both the front and back of a card, if necessary. *But never carry a note to a second card.*

☞ **Write in your own words.** Summarize key points about a paragraph or section. Avoid copying things word for word.

☞ **Put quotation marks around any material copied verbatim.** It's okay to include in your paper a sentence or paragraph written by someone else to emphasize a particular point (providing you do so on a limited basis). But you must copy such statements *exactly as written* in the original source—every word, every comma, every period.

Adding detail to your note cards

As you finish each note card, do the following:

☞ **In the upper left-hand corner of the card**, write down the resource number of the corresponding bibliography card (from its left-hand corner). This will remind you where you got the information.

☞ **Below the resource number**, write the page number(s) on which the information appeared.

☞ **Get out your preliminary outline.** Under which outline topic heading does the information on your card seem to fit? Jot the appropriate topic letter in the upper right-hand corner of your note card.

☞ **Put an asterisk instead of a topic letter** if you're not sure where the information fits into your outline,. Later, when you do a more detailed outline, you can try to fit these "miscellaneous" note cards into specific areas.

☞ **Next to the topic letter**, jot down a one- or two-word "headline" that describes the information on the card.

☞ **When you have finished taking notes from a particular resource**, put a check mark on the bibliography card. This will let you know that you're done with that resource, at least for now.

Be sure that you transfer information accurately to your note cards. Double-check names, dates, and other statistics. As with your bibliography cards, it's not so important that you put each of these elements in the exact places I've outlined above. You just need to be consistent. Always put the page number in the same place, in the same manner. Ditto with the resource number, the topic heading, and the headline.

This is the key note-taking system I learned from Mr. Carl in 9th grade. It is the same system I use today to write every article, report, proposal, and book (including this one). It is absolutely the simplest and best system I've found-and it is the easiest to learn, even for elementary school kids. Even though my 4th grader has been assigned written reports for more than a year, no one (but me, of course) ever gave her any advice whatsoever on how to take notes, create a bibliography, organize her notes for a first draft, etc. This is the system *she* now uses. If Lindsay can do it, *you* can do it.

Add your personal notes

Throughout your note-taking process, you may want to make some "personal" note cards. On these cards, jot down any thoughts, ideas, or impressions you may have about your subject or your thesis.

Write each thought on a separate note card, as you have with information you've taken from other resources. Assign your note card a topic heading and mini-headline, too. In the space where you would normally put the number of the resource, put your own initials.

Step 6: Prepare a detailed outline

Your research is done.

This means that at least *one-half* of your *paper*—perhaps as much as *three-quarters* of it—is done, even though you've yet to write one word of the first draft.

It's time to organize your data. You need to decide if your temporary thesis is still on target, determine how you will organize your paper, and create a detailed outline.

This is where the note-card system really pays off. Your note cards give you a great tool for organizing your paper. Get out all of your note cards, then:

1. Group together all of the cards that share the same outline topic letter (the letter in the right-hand corner of each card).

2. Put those different groups in order, according to your temporary outline. (Put all of your topic A cards at the front of the stack of cards, followed by topic B cards, then topic C cards, etc.)

3. Within each topic group, sort the cards further. Group the cards that share the same "headline" (the two-word title in the upper-right corner).

4. Go through your miscellaneous topic cards, the ones you marked with an asterisk. Can you fit any of them into your existing topic groups? If so, replace the asterisk with the topic letter. If not, put the card at the very back of your stack.

Your note cards now should be organized according to your preliminary outline. Take a few minutes to read through your note cards, beginning at the front of the stack and moving through to the back. What you're reading is actually a rough sketch of your paper—the information you've collected in the order you plan to present it in your paper. Does that order make sense? Would another arrangement work better?

Here are some of the different organizational approaches you might consider for your paper:

1. **Chronological.** Discuss events in the order in which they happened (by time of occurrence).

2. **Spatial.** Present information in geographical or physical order (from north to south, largest to smallest, etc.).

3. **Cause/effect.** One by one, discuss the effects of a series of individual events or actions.

4. **Problem/solution.** Present a series of problems and possible solutions.

5. **Compare/contrast.** Discuss similarities and differences between people, things, or events.

6. **Order of importance.** Discuss the most important aspects of an issue first and continue through to the least important.

If necessary, revise your general outline according to the organizational decision you have made. Next, go through each group of cards that share the same topic letter. Rearrange them so that they, too, follow the organizational pattern you chose.

After you sort all the cards that have been assigned a specific topic heading (A, B, C, etc.), review cards that are marked with an asterisk. Try to figure out where they fit in your stack of cards.

Now flip through your note cards from front to back. See that? You've created a detailed outline without even knowing it. The topic letters on your note cards match the main topics of your outline. And those headlines on your note cards are the subtopics for your outline.

Simply transfer your note-card headlines to paper. They appear on your outline in the same order as they appear in your stack of cards.

Step 7: Write the first draft

You may not have realized it, but you've already *done* a lot of the hard work that goes into the writing stage. You have thought about how your paper will flow, you have organized your notes and you have prepared a detailed outline. All that's left is to transfer your information and ideas from note cards to paper.

Good writing takes concentration and thought. And concentration and thought require quiet—lots of it! You also need to have plenty of desk space so you can spread out your note cards in front of you. Your work area should be well lit and you should have a dictionary and thesaurus close at hand. If possible, work on a computer, so you can add, delete, and rearrange your words at the touch of a button.

Remember: At this point, your goal is to produce a rough draft—with the emphasis on the word "rough." Your first draft isn't supposed to be perfect. It's *supposed* to need revision.

But your thoughts, ideas and logic are the foundation of your paper. And you need to build a foundation before you worry about hanging the front door. So, for now, just concentrate on getting your thoughts on paper. Don't worry about using exactly the "right" word. Don't worry about getting commas in all the right places. We'll take care of all that polishing later.

Your note cards helped you come up with a detailed outline. Now, they're going to help you plot out the actual paragraphs and sentences of your paper.

1. Your note cards should be arranged in the same order as your detailed outline. Take out all of the note cards labeled with the letter of the first topic on your outline.
2. Out of that stack, take out all the cards marked with the same "headline" as the first subheading in your outline.
3. Look at the information on those cards. Think about how the various pieces of information might fit together in a paragraph.
4. Rearrange those cards so they fall in the order you have determined is best for the paragraph.

5. Do this for each group of cards, until you reach the end of the deck.

Each paragraph in your paper is like a mini-essay. It should have a topic sentence—a statement of the key point or fact you will discuss in the paragraph—and contain the evidence to support it. This evidence can come in different forms, such as quotes from experts, research statistics, examples from research or from your own experience, detailed descriptions or other background information.

Construct each paragraph carefully, and your readers will have no choice but to agree with your final conclusion.

Now put it all on paper

Turn your note-card draft into a written rough draft. Using your cards as your guide, sit down and write.

Double- or triple-space your draft, so that it will be easy to edit later on. After you are finished with a note card, put a check mark at the bottom of the card.

If you decide that you won't include information from a particular card, don't throw the card away...yet. Keep it in a separate stack. You may decide to fit in that piece of information in another part of your paper. Or you may change your mind after you read your rough draft and decide to include the information after all.

Help for when you get stuck

Got writer's block already? Here are a few tricks to get you unstuck.

☞ Pretend you're writing a letter to a good friend, and tell him or her everything you have learned about your subject and why you believe your thesis is correct.

☞ Use everyday language. Too many people get so hung up on using fancy words and phrases that they forget that their goal is communication. Simpler is better. Drop the "dollar" words and settle for the "25-centers."

☞ Type *something*. Once you have written that first sentence—even if it's really *bad*—your brain will start to generate spontaneous ideas.

☞ Don't edit yourself! As you write your rough draft, don't keep beating yourself up with negatives. Remember, your goal at this point is just a *rough* draft.

☞ Keep moving. If you get hung up on a particular section, don't sit there stewing over it. Just write a quick note about what you plan to cover in that section, and go on.

☞ If you can't get even that much out, skip the section altogether and come back to it later. Force yourself to make it all the way through your paper, with as few stops as possible.

Document your sources

To avoid plagiarism, you must document the source when you put any of the following in your paper:

☞ Quotations taken from a published source.

☞ Someone else's theories or ideas.

☞ Someone else's sentences, phrases or special expressions.

☞ Facts, figures and research data compiled by someone else.

☞ Graphs, pictures and charts designed by someone else.

There are some exceptions. You don't need to document the source of a fact, theory or expression that is common knowledge.

And you also do not need a source note when you use a phrase or expression for which there is no known author.

For a test of whether a statement needs a source note, ask yourself whether readers would otherwise think that you had come up with the information or idea all by yourself. If the answer is yes, you need a source note. If you're in doubt, include a source note anyway.

Footnotes

For many years, the preferred way to credit sources was the footnote. Two other forms of documentation, endnotes and parenthetical notes, are popular now as well.

A footnote is a source note that appears at the bottom of a page of text. You put a raised (superscript) number at the end of the statement or fact you need to document, which tells your readers to look at the bottom of the page for a note about the source of the data.

What goes in a footnote? The same information that's in the bibliography listing. *And* the exact page number the information appears on.

In front of that source note, you put the same superscript number as you put next to the statement or fact in your text.

There is no limit to the number of footnotes you may have in your paper. Number each footnote consecutively, starting with the number 1. For every footnote "flag" in your paper, be sure there is a corresponding source note at the bottom of the page.

Like bibliography listings, different authorities cite different rules for setting up footnotes. Ask your teacher whose rules you are to follow.

If your teacher doesn't have a preference, you might as well use the Modern Language Association of America (MLA) rules, which I use, as well. Also, be sure to refer to **Improve Your Writing** for a more in-depth examination of source documentation.

Step 8: Do additional research

Did you discover any gaps in your research as you put together your first draft? Raise some questions that you need additional information to answer? If so, now's the time to head for the library for one last crack at the books.

Step 9: Write the second draft

The goal for this phase is to edit for meaning—improve the flow of your paper, organize your thoughts better, clarify confusing points and strengthen weak arguments.

Focus on all of the problem areas you found. Add new data or information, if need be. Play with sentences, paragraphs, and even entire sections. If you're working with a computer, this is fairly easy to do. You can flip words, cut and add sentences, and rearrange whole pages with a few keystrokes.

If you're working with a typewriter or pencil and paper, you can do the same thing, but with scissors and tape.

As you review your rough draft, ask yourself the following questions:

☞ Do your thoughts move logically from one point to the next?

☞ Is the meaning of every sentence and paragraph crystal clear?

☞ Does every sentence make a point—or support one?

☞ Do you move smoothly from one paragraph to the next?

☞ Do you support your conclusions with solid evidence—research data, examples, statistics?

☞ Do you include a good *mix* of evidence—quotes from experts, scientific data, personal experiences, historical examples?

☞ Do you have a solid introduction and conclusion?

☞ Did you write in your own words and style, without merely stringing together phrases and quotes "borrowed" from other authors?

☞ Have you explained your subject thoroughly? (Don't make the assumption that readers have more knowledge about it than they actually do. Remember: *You're* familiar with the topic now, but you've spent *weeks* on it. Just because something is now "obvious" to you does not mean your readers will know what you are talking about.)

☞ Have you convinced your readers that your thesis is valid?

When you finish editing for content and meaning, print or type a clean copy of your paper, then double-check all of your facts for accuracy:

☞ Did you spell names, terms, and places correctly?

☞ When you quoted dates and statistics, did you get your numbers straight?

☞ Do you have a source note (or preliminary source note) for every fact, expression, or idea that is not your own?

☞ If you quoted material from a source, did you quote that source exactly, word for word, comma for comma, and did you put the material in quotation marks?

Mark any corrections or changes on your new draft. Again, use a colored pen or pencil so you'll easily spot corrections later.

Now take an even closer look at your sentences and paragraphs. Try to make them smoother, tighter, easier to understand.

☞ Is there too much fat? Seize every opportunity to make the same point in fewer words.

☞ Are there places where phrasing or construction is awkward? Try to rearrange the sentence or section so that it has a better flow.

☞ Did you use descriptive, colorful words? Did you tell your reader, "The planes were damaged," or paint a more colorful and creative picture: "The planes were broken-down hulks of rusted metal—bullet-ridden, neglected warbirds that could barely limp down the runway"?

☞ Consult a thesaurus for synonyms that work better than the words you originally chose?

☞ Have you overused particular words? Constantly using the same words makes your writing boring. Check a thesaurus for other possibilities.

☞ How do the words *sound*? When you read your paper aloud, does it flow like a rhythmic piece of music or plod along like a dirge? Vary the length of your sentences and paragraphs to make your writing more exciting.

☞Always remember the point of the paper—to communicate your ideas as clearly and concisely as possible. So don't get lost in the details. Relax. If you have to choose between that "perfect" word and the most organized paper imaginable, opt for the latter.

Again, mark corrections on your draft with a colored pen or pencil. No need to retype your paper yet—unless it's gotten so marked up that it's hard to read.

Step 10: Check your spelling and proofread

All right, here's the part that almost nobody enjoys: It's time to rid your paper of any mistakes in grammar and spelling.

I've told you that your thoughts are the most important element of your paper. It's true. But it's also true that glaring mistakes in grammar and spelling will lead your teacher to believe that you are either careless or downright ignorant—neither of which will bode well for your final grade.

So get out your dictionary and a reference book on English usage and grammar. Scour your paper, sentence by sentence, marking corrections with your colored pen or pencil. Look for:

☞**Misspelled words.** Check every word. If you're using a spell-checking computer program, be careful of sound-alike words. "There" might be spelled correctly, but not if you meant to write "their."

☞**Incorrect punctuation.** Review the rules for placement of commas, quotation marks, periods, etc. Make sure you follow those rules throughout your paper.

☞ **Incorrect sentence structure.** Look for dangling participles, split infinitives, sentences that end in prepositions, and other grammar no-no's.

Step 11: Have someone *else* proofread

Retype your paper, making all those corrections you marked during the last step. Format the paper according to the teacher's instructions. Incorporate your final footnotes and bibliography.

Give your paper a title, one that's as short and sweet as possible, but tells readers what they can expect to learn from your paper.

Find someone who is a good proofreader—a parent, relative, friend—and ask him or her to proofread your paper before you put together the final draft.

Steps 12, 13, and 14: The final draft

Incorporate any changes or errors your proofreader may have caught. Type the final draft. Proof it again—very carefully.

When everything's absolutely perfect, head for the copy shop. Pay the buck or two it costs to make a copy of your paper. After all your hard work, you want to be sure you have a backup copy in case the original is lost or damaged.

Last step? Put your paper in a new manuscript binder or folder. Then, turn it in—on time, of course!

Oral reports

There are some key differences between writing a report and presenting it orally, especially if you don't want to make the mistake of just reading your report in front of the class.

If you've been assigned to give a talk for a class, it will probably fall into one of the following categories:

☞ **Exposition:** a straightforward statement of facts.

☞ **Argument:** trying to change the opinions of at least a portion of the audience.

☞ **Description:** providing a visual picture to your listeners.

☞ **Narration:** storytelling.

The most common forms of oral reports assigned in school will be exposition and argument. You'll find that you will research and organize information for these types of speeches pretty much the way you would a term paper.

As you gather information for your report, making notes on index cards as you did for your term paper, keep this in mind: In order for you to be effective, you must use some different techniques when you *tell* your story rather than *write* it. Here are a few:

☞ **Don't make your topic too broad.** This advice, offered for preparing written reports as well, is even more important when preparing a talk. Try giving an effective speech on "19th Century European Politics," "Shakespeare," or "Updike's Novels" in 15 minutes—frequently the amount of time assigned for oral reports. These topics are more suited to a series of books!

"Rabbit and Babbit: Same Character, Different Towns?", "Disraeli and The British Empire" or "Sex and Sensuality in Shakespeare's Sonnets" are more manageable. Narrowing the scope of your talk will help you research and organize it more effectively.

☞ **Don't overuse statistics.** Although they're very important for lending credibility, too many will weigh down your speech and bore your audience.

☞ **Anecdotes add color and life to your talk.** But use them sparingly, because they can slow down your speech. Get to the punch line before the yawns start.

☞ **Be careful with quotes.** Unlike a term paper, a speech allows you to establish yourself as an authority with less fear of being accused of plagiarism. So you can present a lot more facts without attribution. (But you'd better have the sources just in case you are asked about your facts.)

I've found that trying to shuffle a bunch of papers in front of a class is difficult and that note cards that fit in the palm of your hand are a lot easier to use. But only if the notes on them are very short and to the point, to act as "triggers" rather than verbatim cue cards—hanging on to 300 note cards is as difficult as a sheaf of papers.

Remember: You'll actually be holding these cards in your sweaty palms and speaking from them, so write *notes,* not whole sentences. The shorter the notes—and the more often you practice your report so each note triggers the right information—the more effective your report will be. (And the less you will have to look at them, making eye contact with your class and teacher easier.)

Here are ways to make oral reports more effective:

☞ Pick out one person to talk to—preferably a friend, but any animated and/or interested person will do—and direct your talk to him or her.

☞ *Practice, practice, practice* your presentation. Jangled nerves are often the result of a lack of confidence. The better you know your material, the less nervous you'll be and the better and more spontaneous your presentation.

☞ If you suffer from involuntary "shakes" at the mere thought of standing in front of a roomful of people, make sure you can use a lectern, desk, or something to cling to.

☞ Take a deep breath before you go to the front of the class. And don't worry about pausing, even taking another deep breath or two, if you lose your place or find your confidence slipping away.

☞ If every trick in the world still doesn't steady your nerves, consider taking a public speaking course (Dale Carnegie, *et al),* joining the Toast-masters Club, or seeking out similar extracurricular help.

EPILOGUE

I'm proud of you. You made it all the way through the book. Here's my final advice:

☞ Reread *How to Study*, cover to cover. It's similar to seeing a movie for the second time—you always find something you missed the *first* time.

☞ Practice what I've preached. You had an excuse for flunking before—you didn't know how to study. Now you have absolutely *no* excuse.

☞ Buy, read, and put into practice whichever of the companion volumes you need.

☞ Write me a letter to tell me what helped, how much better you're doing in school, or to let me know what else I can include to add to the value of the books. Send your letters to:

Ron Fry
c/o Career Press
PO Box 687
Franklin Lakes, NJ 07417

BOOK 2

MANAGE
YOUR TIME

MAKE TIME TO STUDY SMARTER

Jim's alarm jolts him awake at 6 a.m.

Because his job keeps him up until midnight most weeknights, he schedules most of his study time for the mornings before classes. And makes sure he never takes a class before 10 a.m.

Unfortunately (for his grades), most mornings he's so tired, he just automatically punches the snooze alarm and sleeps at least another hour.

On a *good* morning, he drags himself out of bed and sits down at his desk to study.

Today seems to be a good morning. He's up by 7, has two cups of coffee, and opens his business ethics text. But Jim, who recognized long ago that he was *not* a morning person, finds his attention wandering. All too soon, he ends up nestling his head on his book and nodding off...until his roommate shakes him awake and informs him he's already late for his first class.

Well, maybe it wasn't going to be such a good morning after all.

Jim's classes end around 1 p.m. He treats himself to lunch in the student union building and, afterward, to an hour of video games. "I deserve a break," he convinces himself. "This day has been totally frustrating so far."

Despite his best efforts, he feels guilty anyway, because he isn't using his free time to study. By 2:30, with only a couple of hours left before he has to go to work, he reluctantly leaves the video arcade. He's falling further behind in his classes every day, so he *knows* he has to use the rest of the afternoon for studying.

Filled with resolve to catch up on all of his school work before he goes to his job, he heads for the library. As he walks, he begins to mentally catalog the various readings, papers, and tests he has to work on. He quickly slows his pace when it suddenly dawns on him that catching up before the end of the *term* would require five or six hours of studying...every day...including weekends.

By the time he gets to the library to study, he's discouraged again. Obviously, anything he can do in the next two hours is a miniscule drop in the bucket compared to what has to be done. Nevertheless, he resolves to do at least a little bit.

As he pulls his books out of his backpack, a scrap of note paper flutters out. It's the piece of paper he wrote his history assignment on two weeks ago...the term paper that's due in two days!

Not only has he not started it yet, his history book is back at his apartment. He decides he'd better run home to get it—the next two hours is the only time he has to work on it before it's due.

On his way home, he runs into a friend. The two of them commiserate about their impossible schedules. By the time Jim finally gets home, he's decided to ask for an extension on his history assignment. It will be the second extension he's asked for, which means he's got *two* overdue assignments, one other term paper, and four finals to prepare for...in the next two weeks.

There's one hour left. "How can I do a paper in 60 minutes?" Jim groans. Deciding he can't, he throws his book bag on his desk and surrenders to the time pressures. There's no way he can get any real studying done in just an *hour*. He crumples on the couch, turns on the TV, and, as the audience gasps at the sight of a 350-lb transvestite sumo wrestler on *Jerry Springer*, asks himself, "Why is *my* life so difficult?"

It's just a matter of time

For Jim, school has become a burden, a time-eating monster that has taken control of his life.

Jim isn't a particularly bad or unusual student. He isn't irresponsible or lazy. He really does want to do well, to get good grades, to prepare himself for a successful career. He's just run out of time.

Let's face it: We all experience problems with time.

We can't control it or slow it down.

We need more of it. And don't know where to find it.

Then we wonder where it went.

But *time* is not really the problem. Time, after all, is the one "currency" that all people are given in equal supply, every day. The problem is that most of us simply let too much of it "slip through our fingers"—because we have *never been taught how to manage our time.* Our parents never sat us down to give us a little "facts of time" talk. And time management skills aren't part of any standard academic curriculum.

Not knowing how to effectively manage our time, we just continue to use the "natural" approach.

Just act naturally

The natural approach to time is to simply take things as they come and do what you feel like doing, without schedule or plan. What the heck—it worked when we were kids. It was easy to live from day to day and never really worry about "where our time went."

You played when you felt like playing—you didn't make *appointments* to play with your friends. There were no *deadlines*—if your model airplane or doll house didn't get done by the end of the week, no problem. You didn't even *own* a calendar—if you had a piano recital coming up, it was your mom's responsibility to remind you to practice, make sure your good clothes were cleaned, and drive you to the recital hall on time.

In fact, sometimes there seemed to be too *much* time—too many *hours* before school was over...too many *days* before summer vacation...too many *weeks* before birthdays...too many *years* before we could learn to drive.

Childhood was a simpler time.

Unfortunately for all of us Peter Pans, there comes a point when the "take-every-day-as-it-comes" approach just doesn't work. For most of us, it hits in high school. (If you're in high school and don't know what I'm talking about, don't worry—you'll find out your first day of college.)

Why? Because that's when we begin to establish goals that are important to *us,* not just to our parents.

We become more involved in extracurricular activities, such as sports, music, or clubs, and must schedule practice times, games, and meetings, while still fulfilling our class obligations and home responsibilities.

In college, we begin thinking about our careers. We take classes that will prepare us for that career, may even try to find a part-time job to give us some exposure to it.

To achieve our goals, whether it's performing in the annual school musical or becoming an architect, we must commit ourselves to the many steps it takes to get there.

We must plan. We must *manage* our time.

Whether you're a high school student just starting to feel frazzled, a college student juggling five classes and a part-time job, or a parent working, attending classes, and raising a family, a simple, easy-to follow time management system is crucial to your success. And despite your natural tendency to proclaim that you just don't have the *time* to spend scheduling, listing, and recording, it's also the best way to give yourself *more* time.

"Harder" isn't the word I'm thinking of

I'm sure many of you reading this are struggling with your increasing responsibilities and commitments. Some of you, like Jim, may be so overwhelmed you've just given up. Those of you who haven't probably figure it's your fault—if you just worked *harder*, spent more time on your papers and assignments, set up camp in the library—then everything would work out.

So you resign yourselves to "all-nighters," cramming for tests and forgetting about time-consuming activities like eating and sleeping. Trying to do everything—even when there's too much to do—without acquiring the skills to *control* your time, is an approach that will surely lead to burn out.

When does it all end?

With classes, homework, a part-time or full-time job, and all the opportunities for fun and recreation, life as a student can be very busy. But believe me, it doesn't suddenly get easier when you graduate.

Most adults will tell you that it only gets *busier.* There will always be a boss who expects you to work later, children who need to be fed, clothed, and taken to the doctor, hobbies and interests to pursue, community service to become involved in, courses to take.

If you're an adult doing all of the latter, I sure don't have to tell you how important time management is, do I?

There may *not* be time for *every*thing

When I asked one busy student if she wished she had more time, she joked, "I'm *glad* there are only 24 hours in a day. Any more and I wouldn't have an excuse for not getting everything done!"

Let me give you the good news: There *is* a way that you can accomplish more in less time, one that's a *lot* more effective than the natural approach. And it doesn't even take more effort. You can plan ahead and make conscious choices about how your time will be spent, and how much time you will spend on each task. You can have more control over your time, rather than always running out of time as you keep trying to do everything.

Now the bad news: The first step to managing your time should be deciding just what is important...and what isn't. Difficult as it may be, sometimes it's necessary for us to recognize that we truly *can't* do it all. To slice from our busy schedules those activities that aren't as meaningful to us so that we can devote more energy to those that are.

You may be a *Star Trek* fan from way back. But is it really the best use of your time to run back to your room to catch the morning rerun...*every* morning?

You may love music so much, you want to be in the orchestra, jazz band, choir, and play with your own garage band on weekends. But is it realistic to commit to all *four?*

Your job at the mall boutique may mean 20 percent off on the clothes you buy. But if you're working there four days a week, taking 15 hours of classes, and working at the food co-op on weekends, when do you expect to study?

If you're raising a family, working part-time, and trying to take a near-full class load yourself, it's probably time to cure yourself of the Super Mom syndrome.

But there *is* enough time to plan

Yet, even after paring down our commitments, most of us are still challenged to get it all done. What with classes, study time, work obligations, extracurricular activities, and social life, it's not easy getting it all in—even without *Star Trek.*

Whether you're in high school, college, or graduate school, a "traditional" student or one who's chosen to return to school after being out in the "real world" for a while, you'll find that the time-management plan outlined in this book will work for you.

My time-management program allows for flexibility. In fact, I encourage you to adapt any of my recommendations to your own unique needs. That means it will work for you whether you are living in a dorm, sharing accommodations with a roommate, or living with a spouse and children. That you *can* learn how to balance school, work, fun, and even family obligations.

The purpose of this book is to help you make *choices* about what is important to you, to help you set *goals* for yourself, to help you *organize* and *schedule* your time, and to develop the *motivation* and *self-discipline* to follow your schedule and reach those goals.

Which will give you the time to learn all the other study skills I write about!

CHAPTER 1

TAKE THE TIME TO PLAN

What if you never developed a plan for your school curriculum, never even chose a major? What if you just "followed your star," wherever it led, taking whatever subjects you felt like, whenever you felt like going to class?

Perhaps you'd take a business class because Michael Eisner made $600 million last year...*and* got to go on Splash Mountain as often as he wanted.

You have a friend who's majoring in psychology, so you'd take a psychology class with her.

Your dad is an engineer and *he* seems to like his job, so you'd throw in a basic science course.

To round out your schedule, you'd take *any* course that that incredibly cute guy is taking, wherever it fits!

If you continue like this for four years, you may have broadened your interests and learned a lot (and/or gotten a boyfriend), but you wouldn't have a degree to show for all your work, and you'd probably find it awfully difficult to find a job when you left school—degreeless, remember?

Planning makes the world go 'round

Consider an even simpler project: Try going grocery shopping without a list. If you're like me and always go food shopping before you've eaten, you'll probably wind up with a cart right out of "junk-food heaven," laden with anything and everything that looks good: soda, chips, sandwich cookies, and ice cream.

You might run out of money at the cash register—how could you figure how much money to bring if you had no idea what you were buying?

Worst of all, when you got home, you may discover that you already had *two* packages of sandwich cookies, a refrigerator *full* of soda, two gallons of ice cream clogging up the freezer, and enough chips to open a delicatessen.

But you didn't get cat food (she's been living on tuna and cereal for two days, you cur) or milk...or anything for that night's dinner.

Whether your goal is to graduate from college or buy groceries for the week, the need for a plan should be clear.

Just as clear, unfortunately, is the fact that far too many people *do* manage their time like the student without a major or the shopper without a list.

I've got a secret

Just like the grocery list and the school curriculum, setting up a plan for managing your time will take effort. But it's an investment of effort that will bring exponential returns.

Wouldn't it be nice to actually have some *extra* time...instead of always "running out of it?"

To feel that you're exerting some control over your schedule, your schoolwork, your *life*...instead of caroming from appointment to appointment, class to class, assignment to assignment, like some crazed billiard ball?

It can happen.

I will not spend a lot of time trying to convince you that this is a "fun" idea—getting excited about calendars and "to-do" lists is a bit of a stretch. You will *not* wake up one morning and suddenly decide that organizing your life is just the most fun thing you can think of.

But I suspect you *will* do it if I can convince you that effective time management will reward you in some very tangible ways.

Presuming all this is true (and I'll wager it is), unless you have some darn good reasons—a solid idea of some of the benefits effective time management *can* bring you—you probably will find it hard to consistently motivate yourself to do it. It has to become a habit, something you do without thinking, but also something you do *no matter what.*

Yes, I have a few of those good reasons ready to trot out, but before I do so, why don't *you* spend several minutes thinking about the potential benefits effective time management might bring you. If you can already spot the potential rewards in your own life, that's even better than waiting for my reasons! Write your ideas in the spaces on the next page.

How time management can help me

_____

_____

_____

_____

_____

_____

_____

_____

_____

_____

_____

_____

_____

_____

_____

_____

_____

_____

_____

_____

_____

_____

_____

Now I'll give you my list.

See if I thought of anything you didn't.

Short-term benefits

A time-management system that fits your needs can help you get more work done in less time. Whether your priority is more free time than you have now or better grades, effective time management can help you reach your objective, because it:

1. **Helps you put first things first.** Have you ever spent an evening doing a busy-work assignment for an *easy* class, only to find that you hadn't spend enough time studying for a crucial test in a more difficult one?

   Listing the tasks that must be done and *prioritizing* them ensures that the most important things will *always* get done—*even when you don't get* everything *done.*

2. **Helps you avoid time traps.** Time traps are the unplanned events that pop up, sometimes (it seems) every day. They're the fires you have to put out before you can turn to tasks like studying.

   You may fall into such time traps because they *seem* urgent...or because they seem *fun.* Or end up spending hours in them...without even realizing you're stuck: You blow an hour of study time at the library because you've left the required study materials at home. Or sit down in front of the TV to relax while you eat dinner and get caught up in a two-hour movie.

   There is no way to avoid *every* time trap. But effective time management can help you avoid most of them. Time management is like a fire-*prevention* approach rather than a fire-*fighting* one: It allows you to go about your work systematically instead of moving from crisis to crisis or whim to whim.

3. **Helps you anticipate opportunities.** In addition to helping you balance study time with other time demands, effective time management can help make the time you *do* spend studying more productive. You will be able to get more done in the same amount of time or (this is even better) do more work in less time. I'm sure you could find *some* way to spend those extra hours each week.

4. **Gives you freedom and control.** Contrary to many students' fears, time management is *liberating,* not restrictive. A certain control over *part* of your day allows you to be flexible with the *rest* of your day.

   In addition, you will be able to plan more freedom into your schedule. For example, you would know well in advance that you have a big test the day after a friend's party. Instead of having to call your friend the night of the party with a big sob story, you could make sure you allocated enough study time beforehand and go to the party without feeling guilty, without even *thinking* about the test.

5. **Helps you avoid time conflicts.** Have you ever lived the following horror story? You get out of class at 5:30, remember you have a big math assignment due, *then* realize you have no time to do it because you have a music rehearsal at 6 p.m.

167

Then you remember that your softball game is scheduled for 7...just before that date you made months ago (which you never did remember!).

Simply having all of your activities, responsibilities, and tasks written down in one place helps ensure that two or three things don't get scheduled at once. If time conflicts do arise, you will notice them well in advance and can rearrange things accordingly.

6. **Helps you avoid feeling guilty.** When you know how much studying has to be done and you have the time scheduled to do it, you can relax—you *know* that the work will get done. If you're going to spend time *thinking* about studying, you might as well just spend the time *studying!*

   Effective time management also helps keep your conscience off your back: When your studying is done, you can *really* enjoy your free time *without* feeling guilty because you're not studying.

7. **Helps you evaluate your progress.** If you know where you should be in class readings or assignments, you will never be surprised when deadlines loom. For example, if you've planned out the whole term and know you have to read an average of 75 pages a week to keep up in your business management class, and you only read *60* pages this week, you don't need a calculator to figure out you are slightly behind. And it's easy enough to schedule a little more time to read next week so you catch up.

   On the other hand, if you only read when it's convenient (such as when your assignment doesn't conflict with your favorite TV shows), you'll never know whether you're behind or ahead. Then one day you suddenly realize you have to be up to Chapter 7...by lunch time.

Good time management helps you know where you are and how you're doing...all along the way.

8. **Helps you see the "big picture."** Effective time management provides you with a bird's-eye view of the semester. Instead of being caught off guard when the busy times come, you will be able to plan ahead—*weeks* ahead—when you have big tests or assignments due for more than one class.

   Why not complete that German paper a few days early so it's not in the way when two other papers are due...or you're trying to get ready for a weekend ski trip? Conflicts can be worked out with fewer problems if you know about them in advance and do something to eliminate them.

9. **Helps you see the "bigger picture."** Planning ahead and plotting your course early allows you to see how classes fit with your overall school career. For example, if you know you have to take chemistry, biology, and pharmacology to be eligible for entrance into the nursing program, and that the courses you will take later will build on those, you will at least be able to see why the classes are required for your major, even if you aren't particularly fond of one or two of them.

   "I have to take statistics because my counselor said it was required" is not as strong a motivator as "It's the next-to-last required class before graduation!"

10. **Helps you learn how to study smarter, not harder.** Students sometimes think time management just means reallocating their time—spending the same time studying, the same time in class, the same time partying, just shifting around these "time segments" so everything is more "organized."

As we'll see later in this book, this is only *partially* true—a key part of effective time management *is* learning how to prioritize tasks. But this simple view ignores one great benefit of taking control of your time: It may well be possible you will be *so* organized, *so* prioritized, *so in control of your time* that you can spend *less* time studying, get *better* grades and have *more* time for other things—extracurricular activities, hobbies, a film, whatever.

Long-term benefits

Besides helping you to manage your time right now and reach your immediate study goals, effective time management will bring long-term benefits.

Have you ever sat in a class and thought to yourself, "I'll *never* use this stuff once I get out of school?"

You won't say that about time-management skills. They will be useful throughout your life.

Learning time management skills now will help you prepare for the future. And the better prepared you are, the more options you will have—learning effective study techniques and earning good grades *now* will increase your range of choices when you graduate. The company you work for or the graduate school you attend could be the one *you* choose, not the one whose choice was dictated by your poor past performance.

Learning how to manage your time now will develop habits and skills you can use outside of school. It may be difficult for you to develop the habits of effective time management, but don't think you're alone—time management presents just as much of a problem to many parents, professors, and non-students. How many people do you know who *never* worry about time?

If you learn effective time-management skills in school, the payoffs will come throughout your life. Whether you wind up running a household or a business, you will have learned skills you will use every day.

Consider the examples of Sam and Taylor, both business executives at a large company. Sam has difficulty managing his time; in fact, he often feels controlled by his job. He's always running to get office supplies to complete a report or gets caught in long, unproductive phone conversations with clients, working on the details of some low-priority task or doing busy work that other people have asked him to do.

The result: A desk always stacked with unfinished (and more important) work. Which means he often has to stay late to finish a report or take work home because he just didn't have time to finish that big presentation or important project when it should have been done—at work.

Taylor, on the other hand, makes a list of weekly priorities every Monday morning and is careful about committing to any projects for which her list clearly shows she doesn't have the time. Instead of spending all her time putting out fires, handling crises, and doing work that she could delegate to someone else, she refers to her priority list often and *always* does the most important things first.

She is realistic and knows that she will never be able to do *everything* she would like. But because she plans, she gets the important projects done...on time. And her boss knows she can count on Taylor to handle extra, emergency assignments.

At the end of the day, Taylor usually feels satisfied that she did a good job. And at the end of the week, rather than worrying about leftover tasks that need to be handled on Saturday or Sunday, she can relax and enjoy her weekend. In fact, she sometimes takes a Friday afternoon off to go to the beach.

Her relaxed weekends, in turn, make her even more effective when she returns to work Monday mornings.

I'm not David Copperfield

Time management is not a magic wand that can be waved to solve problems in school or after graduation. It is not as much a talent as a craft. There is no "time management gene" that you either have or lack, like the ones that produce brown eyes or black hair.

These techniques are tools that can be used to help you reach your short-term and long-range goals successfully.

The important thing to remember is that you *can* be a successful time manager and a successful student *if* you are willing to make the effort to learn and apply the principles in this book.

CHAPTER 2

SPEND TIME TO SAVE TIME

Some people groan aloud when they hear the words "time management." They imagine distressingly organized individuals armed with endless lists, charts, and graphs, chained to a rigid schedule, with no room (or time!) for fun.

If you hate the idea of being tied to a schedule, if you fear that it would drain all spontaneity and fun from your life, I know you'll be pleasantly surprised when you discover that just the *opposite* is true:

Most students are relieved and excited when they learn what a liberating tool time management can be.

Let's explode some of the myths that may be holding *you* back.

Save me from my schedule

Inflexibility is most people's biggest fear—"If I set it all out on a schedule, then I won't be able to be spontaneous and choose what to do with my time later."

Your time-management system can be as flexible as you want. In fact, the best systems act as guides, not some rigid set of "must do's" and "can't do's."

I'm captain of the Time Patrol

Contrary to common belief, time-management skills will not turn you into a study-bound bookworm. How much time do you need to set aside for studying? Ask your career counselor, and he or she will probably echo the timeworn "2:1 ratio"—spend two hours studying *out* of class for every hour you spend *in* class.

Hogwash. That ratio may be way out of line—either not enough time or too much. The amount of study time will vary from individual to individual, depending on your major, your abilities, needs, and goals.

Scheduling time to study doesn't mean that you have to go from three hours of studying a day to eight. In fact, laying out your study time in advance often means you can relax more when you're *not* studying because you won't be worrying about when you're going to get your schoolwork done—the time's been set aside.

How *long* you study is less important than how *effective* you are when you do sit down to study.

The time-management skills in this book are designed to help you get the most out of your study time. The goal is not to spend *more* time studying, but to spend the same or less time, *getting more done in* whatever *time you spend.*

It's too darned involved

Many of you may fear the complexity time management implies. Actually, I recommend simplicity. The more complex your system becomes, the harder it will be to use, and, consequently, the less likely you *will* use it consistently. The more complex the system, the more likely it will collapse.

I, robot

You can design your time-management system to fit your own needs. Some of the skills you will learn in this book will be more helpful to you in reaching your goals than others. You may already be using some of them. Others you will want to start using right now. Still others may not fit your needs at all.

Use the skills that seem most likely to lead you to *your* study goals, meet *your* needs and fit with *your* personality.

For example, two excellent students I know approach study and time management in nearly opposite ways.

Alison plans out almost every detail of her morning and afternoon, scheduling long blocks of time for study, work, and other tasks. On the other hand, she leaves her evenings flexible and, when she goes out, her schedule behind.

Tim prefers to work throughout the day, scheduling all of his activities in smaller blocks of time. He could never spend eight straight hours doing schoolwork, as Alison often does. He also has smaller blocks of free time scattered throughout the day and evening.

Are you like Tim? Like Alison?

Sort of a mix?

Doesn't matter. What *does* is that as long as their systems work for each of them, there is nothing inherently right or wrong, good or bad, about either.

They work.

So much for the myths. Let's look at what is actually required to use time-management skills effectively.

A good notebook and a sharp pencil

In order for time management to work, you have to be able to look at your plan when it's time to use it. It's nearly impossible to make detailed plans very far in advance without having a permanent record. Make it your rule: "If I plan it out, I will write it down." And, preferably, write your plans and schedules for every week and school term in one place so you always know where to find them.

I've provided some schedule formats later in this book for you to photocopy and use. They've been effective for me. (I'll cover them in greater detail in later chapters.) There is a myriad of other schedule planners available in bookstores and office supply stores—you can even create your own on notebook paper or computer.

What's important is that you have *one place to write and keep all your schedule information*, including class times, meetings, study times, project due dates, vacations, doctor appointments, and social events.

Your readiness to adapt and personalize

The time-management system that best suits you will be one that is tailor-made to fit *your* needs and personality. Many of the approaches included in this book are general suggestions that work well for many people, but that doesn't mean each one will be right for you.

Consider the following example: While most parents turn the lights out and keep things quiet when their baby is trying to go to sleep, one baby I know, who spent two months in the hustle and bustle of a newborn intensive-care unit, couldn't sleep unless the lights were *on* and it was *noisy*.

Similarly, although many students will study best in a quiet environment, others may feel uncomfortable in a "stuffy" library and prefer studying in their living room.

Make your study schedule work for *you,* not your night-owl roommate who must plan every activity down to the minute. Alter it, modify it, make it stricter, make it more flexible. Whatever works.

Regular attention and consistent use

We've all had the experience of missing an important appointment or commitment and saying, "I know I had that written down somewhere—I wonder *where!*"

It's easy to *think,* "I'll write it down so I won't forget," but a schedule that is not used regularly isn't a safety net at all. You must *consistently* write down your commitments. You must spend time filling out your schedule every week, every day.

Any efforts you make to manage your time will be futile if you do not have your schedule with you when you need it. For example, you are in art class without your schedule when your teacher tells you when your next project is due. You jot it down in your art notebook and promise yourself you'll add it to your schedule as soon as you get home.

You hurry to your next class, and your geology instructor schedules a study session for the following week. You scribble a reminder in your lab book.

Between classes, a friend stops to invite you to a party Thursday night. You promise you'll be there.

You arrive at work to find out your supervisor has scheduled your hours for the following week. She checks them with you, they seem fine, so you commit to them.

Had you been carrying your schedule with you, you would have been able to write down your art project and schedule the necessary amount of preparation time.

You would have realized that your geology study session was the same night as your friend's party.

And discovered that accepting the work schedule your supervisor presented left you with little time to work on your art project.

Take your schedule with you anywhere and every-where you think you might need it.

When it doubt, take it along!

Keeping your schedule with you will reduce the number of times you have to say, "I'll just try to remember it for now," or "I'll write it down on this little piece of paper and transfer it to my planner later."

Always make a point of writing down tasks, assignments, phone numbers, and other bits of important information in your schedule *immediately*.

A trial run

In order to test its effectiveness, you must give any time-management system a chance to work—give it a trial run. No program can work unless it is used consistently. And consistency won't happen without effort.

It's just like learning to ride a bicycle. It's a pain at first; you may even fall down a few times. But once you're a two-wheel pro, you can travel much faster and farther than you could by foot.

The same goes for the techniques you will learn here—they may take practice and a little getting used to, but once you have maintained a time-management program for a couple of weeks, you will probably find yourself in the habit of doing it. From then on, it will take relatively little effort to maintain.

That's when you'll really notice the payoff—when the task becomes second nature.

CHAPTER 3

SET THE STAGE
FOR SUCCESS

Stacey gets home from work and fixes a sandwich. It's been a long, tiring day. It's after 5 p.m. and she knows she has to start her homework. Sandwich in hand, she clears a spot on the table between the breakfast dishes and gets out her books. She starts to read but finds it difficult to concentrate.

"It's the dishes!" she concludes, holding the dirty dishes responsible for diverting her attention from her studies. She decides to take a break to wash them. Twenty minutes later, Stacey sits down at a clear table.

Five minutes after *that*, however, her mother arrives home from work and begins preparing dinner. Stacey tries to read as her mother cuts vegetables and asks Stacey questions about an upcoming dance.

A half-hour later, after they've finished planning a dress-shopping trip, Stacey can see that her study efforts aren't working. She clears her books off the table so her mother can set it for dinner, and vows to stay up past midnight, if necessary, to get her reading done.

It's obvious that, despite Stacey's motivation to study, she just seemed to be in the *wrong* place at the *wrong* time. That's exactly how many of *you* probably feel when the elements of your study environment are working against you.

What's your best study environment?

There's no one right combination of factors that constitutes a perfect study environment for everyone. However, in order to be effective, you must find the combinations of place and time that work for you.

Of all the suggestions and techniques discussed in this book, careful attention to *where* and *when* you study is probably the simplest and easiest to apply. And the right mix will make a big difference in your productivity.

Unlike Stacey, Kay studies at her desk. She keeps all her materials nearby, avoiding needless trips to other rooms of the house.

She keeps the desk itself clear of books and paper piles so she can spread out her work and study comfortably.

The area is well lit, so she rarely has problems with headaches or eyestrain.

Finally, because she studies in an area removed from the activity of the rest of the house, she is rarely interrupted by others...or distracted by the television, telephone, or dirty dishes.

Who do *you* think gets more done in less time?

Where should you study?

At the library. And realize within the library there may be numerous choices, from the large reading room, to quieter, sometimes deserted specialty rooms, to your own study cubicle. My favorite "home away from home" at Princeton was a little room that seemingly only four or five of us knew about—with four wonderfully comfortable chairs, subdued lighting, phonographs with earplugs, and a selection of some 500 classical records. For someone who needs music to study, it was custom-made for me!

At home. Just remember that this is where distractions are most likely to occur. No one tends to telephone you at the library and little brothers (or your own kids) will not tend to find you easily in the "stacks." It is, of course, usually the most convenient place to make your study headquarters. It may not, however, be the most effective.

At a friend's, neighbor's, or relative's. This may not be an option at all for most of you, even on an occasional basis, but you may want to set up one or two alternative study sites. Despite many experts' opinion that you must study in the same place every night (with which I don't agree), I have a friend who simply craves some variety to help motivate him. He has four different places he likes to study and simply rotates them from night to night. Whatever works for you.

In an empty classroom. Certainly an option at many colleges and perhaps some private high schools, it is an interesting idea mainly because few students have thought of it! While not a likely option at a public high school, it never hurts to ask if you can't make some arrangements. Because many athletic teams practice until 6 p.m. or later, even on the high school level, there may well be a part of the school open—and usable with permission—even if the rest is locked up tight.

At your job. Whether you're a student working part-time or a full-timer going to school part-time, you may well be able to make arrangements to use an empty office, even during regular office hours, or perhaps after everyone has left (depending on how much your boss trusts you). If you're in junior high or high school and a parent, friend, or relative works nearby, you may be able to study from just after school until closing time at their workplace.

A place just for study

Psychologists know that you can often predict human behavior accurately if you know just one thing: the individual's environment at the time. We are conditioned to behave in certain ways based on specific cues from our environments.

Not only are certain environments cues for specific behaviors, the *more* we behave a certain way in a given environment, the *stronger* that tendency becomes. Repetition is the way habits are formed.

Consider the example of a dog. What would the environmental cue of a plastic saucer lead a dog to do?

It all depends on what he has done in the past with that saucer. If it's his food dish, setting it out may make his mouth water. But if his owner usually uses it to play catch with him, he may jump about playfully when he sees it.

How about you? What does your pillow suggest to you? "Sleep" should be your immediate response. So if you study on your bed, propped up by your pillows, you may find yourself falling asleep soon after you open your books. In fact, if you study regularly in your bed, you may eventually not be able to sleep well there!

If possible, designate an area in your room or house that is *just for studying.* You will eventually condition yourself to the extent that just sitting down at your desk will help you gear up for studying.

In order to get to this point, however, you will have to make sure you do not allow your mind to become conditioned to other things while at your study desk or table. If you feel tired or are finding it difficult to concentrate, don't put your head down on your *desk* to rest or daydream. If you need a break, get up and rest in an easy chair or on your bed. Or go take a walk.

If you physically get up and leave your study area when you're not studying, you'll help strengthen the conditioning message: "This desk is only for studying."

Make it pleasant

It helps to make your desk or study area a *positive* place to study. For example, to create a motivating atmosphere, you may want to put up pictures of your dream job to help you remember *why* you're subjecting yourself to these long hours of study and homework.

And don't push yourself to study for unbearable lengths of time. Few things will make you dislike school more than studying until you are sick of the subject matter and your head aches.

Take your own stamina into account. Some people can plop down in a chair, open a book, and read or study for hours. Others find their mind wandering after an hour or two. The former doesn't need a break. The latter, if he or she wants to effectively study after that first hour or two, better schedule short breaks accordingly. Remember: Your study plan should be flexible. Adapt it to *your* needs, strengths, and weaknesses.

Avoid distractions

Consider the location of your desk or study area. Is it in a high-traffic area, where family members or roommates are likely to be walking through, watching TV, or eating? Is it by a window where you can be distracted by passersby or easily daydream because of the wonderful view? The best position for a desk is usually in a quiet, low-traffic area—for example, in a corner or facing a wall. There might not be much of a view, but there won't be so many easy ways to be distracted, either.

Make it convenient

The perfect study environment, an area meeting all of the above criteria, may not be readily accessible to you. A commitment to always study at the library isn't realistic if the library is 10 miles away and you don't have a car.

If you have a two-hour free period between work and class, but it takes you a half-hour to drive home to your study desk, you'd do better to find a quiet coffee shop to read a couple of chapters, even if it isn't as ideal as your own area.

Your study spot should be *accessible* and *convenient.*

Have more than one place

Or maybe I should say your study *spots.*

You may be a student who can (or must) study in a variety of locations, depending on the demands of your schedule. You may want to study in a doctor's office lobby or while you're waiting for an appointment with a professor. Or maybe in the car while you're waiting to pick up your spouse from work or as you carpool to school.

Even if you have one primary study location, occasional changes may be required because of circumstance. Your room and its big oak roll-top desk may be your dream study environment. But if you spend a lot of time on campus—which is a 20-minute drive from home—you'll want to scout out a nice, quiet corner of the library to call your second "study home."

"Do not disturb"

It may help to keep a real or imaginary barrier between you and the outside world while you're studying. Shutting the door to your room helps block out noise and prevents many intrusions. A "Please do not disturb" sign is a great way of telling people you are busy. One student had a pair of Halloween-costume alien antenna he wore whenever he was studying—a friendly reminder to himself and his roommates that he wished to be left alone. In addition to the message you send to other people, the physical act of putting on your "thinking cap" can be a great conditioner—it will put you in the "study mood."

All elements of your study environment

Environment is more than location. Whether you primarily study at school, at home, in the library, or in your car, there are other elements of a study environment that can inhibit or facilitate studying.

Are you in a comfortable chair? It should be pleasant to sit in, though perhaps not as relaxing as a recliner!

What about ventilation and temperature? Does your study spot become stuffy and hot, or so cold you have to wear gloves?

What about keeping the radio or TV on while you're studying? Some people—myself included—work better with a little music in the background, and literally find it *more* difficult to work when it's too quiet. (Though I don't know anyone who works better with the Stones at 90 decibels or while watching *Jeopardy!*)

Before you decide this matter for yourself, you may want to time yourself to see how much you can accomplish without music, then time yourself with music playing. If you feel that music is a positive influence in your study environment, go ahead and play it, but remember that certain types of music are more conducive to studying than others. Familiar tunes, with a steady rhythm, are less distracting than songs with lyrics, a variety of rhythms, and, of course, high decibel levels.

Give your studies the time of day

We've talked about the importance of *place* when you study, and that you should create the *habit* of studying in the same place or places. The same goes for *when* you study as well. As much as possible, create a routine time for when you study. Some students find it easier to set aside specific blocks of time during the day, each day, they plan on studying. In reality, the time of day you will do your work will be determined by a number of factors. Consider the following:

1. **Study when you're at your best.** What is your "peak performance period"—the time of day you do your best work? This varies from person to person—you may be dead to the world till noon but able to study well into the night. Or up and alert at the crack of dawn but distracted and tired if you try to burn the midnight oil.

   Figure out the time of day *you* find it easiest to concentrate and are able to get the most done and, whenever possible, plan to do your most difficult work then.

   Keep in mind that for most people, there are times of the day when it is particularly difficult to concentrate on *anything*—right after a big meal, for example, much of your blood goes to your stomach to work on digesting the food. You may find yourself less alert if you try to study then.

2. **Consider your sleep habits.** Habit is a powerful influence. If you always set your alarm for 7 a.m., you may find that you wake up then even when you forget to set it. If you are used to going to sleep around 11 p.m., you will undoubtedly get quite tired if you try to stay up studying until 2 a.m. And probably accomplish little in the three extra hours.

Although sleep is a physical necessity influenced by biorhythms as well as habitual behavior, we become conditioned to perform certain activities at certain times of the day.

Which is why it is difficult to adjust to a new study time when you start a new schedule and try to study during hours you have previously been sleeping. Try as you might, you'll likely wind up just using your history book for a pillow!

3. **Study when you can.** Although you want to sit down to study when you are mentally most alert, external factors also play a role in deciding when you study. As I mentioned earlier, some students are not able to study consistently in the same study spot, however ideal it is. Same with when you study. You may be most alert during the late afternoon hours, but if you have to work from 1 p.m. to 5 p.m., you're not going to be able to take advantage of that time to study.

Many other factors influence your available study times. Being at your best is a great goal

but not always possible: You must study whenever circumstances allow.

4. **Consider the complexity of the assignment
   when you allocate time.** The tasks themselves may have a great affect on your schedule.
   When I sit down to plan out the chapter of a
   book, for example, I need a relatively long period
   of uninterrupted time—at least an hour, perhaps as many as three—to get my notes in the
   order and think through the entire chapter. If I
   only have half an hour before a meeting or appointment, I wouldn't even attempt to start such
   a project.

Collect your study materials

Have you ever sat down to study, only to realize that
you needed a calculator from another room? On your way
to get it you decide to go through the kitchen to grab a
snack. Your roommate is making dinner, and you ask her
about her new after-school internship. After a few minutes
of chatting, you spot the newspaper on the table and check
the headlines. As you head back to your room, you pause
in the doorway, wondering, "Now what did I come in here
for again?"

Remember time traps? This is one—not having your
materials together, which means you have to spend extra
time gathering them. You risk getting sidetracked and
losing valuable study time.

You can save immense amounts of time simply by
keeping your textbooks, pencils and pens, calculator, and
other necessities within arm's reach.

Some students like to use a three-ring binder for all
their school papers. Lecture notes from each class can be

kept together and marked by a tab. Holes can be punched in handouts and other papers from class and then kept with class notes. In addition, semester or quarter calendars, weekly schedules, phone lists, and other necessities can all be kept in one place. That way you only have to carry around a single binder, not keep track of four, five, six or more different notebooks or folders.

To make sure your binder doesn't get too full or bulky from the semester's work, you can empty the contents occasionally into file folders marked for each class. You may even want to keep a small file holder near your desk to allow quick access to materials from the semester.

This system will keep your class notes and other useful papers organized and easy to find. As you study from day to day, papers often start stacking up on your desk anyway. Create new folders as necessary to hold them.

There are many different ways you can organize your study space and notebooks. You can buy file cabinets, stack plastic baskets on your desk, invest in an inexpensive packet of multicolored folders, etc. The important thing is to always have everything you need handy when you're ready to study, whatever system you devise.

Take it with you

If you study away from your home or room, it is doubly important to have everything you need with you. If you are studying in the library and realize that you forgot your assignment book, you can't just run to the next room and grab it.

Look over your schedule each morning (we'll discuss your Daily Schedule in detail in Chapter 5) and determine what you will need for the day. If you must study lecture notes from your business class that day, make sure you pack your notes that morning—or, because mornings are so hectic, load your briefcase or bookbag the night before.

And don't forget to bring your schedule with you. We've already seen how easily assignments get forgotten if they're not written down immediately!

The more the merrier

If you have materials that you often need *both* at home and at school, it's a good idea to keep a duplicate set of all such essentials at school or in your bookbag or briefcase. Or find a locker in the building in which you spend the most time. It's comforting to know that you will never be without essential supplies...wherever you're studying.

How are you doing?

Let's find out how well you're doing with the principles in this chapter. Sit down at your desk or study area right now and evaluate your own study environment, using the following questions:

1. Do you have one or two special places reserved just for studying? Or do you study wherever seems convenient or available at the time?

2. Is your study area a pleasant place? Would you offer it to a friend as a good place to study? Or do you dread going anywhere near it because it's so depressing?

3. How's the lighting? Is it too dim or too bright? Is the whole desk well-lit or only portions of it?

4. Are all the materials you need handy? Do you have writing instruments? Extra lined paper or scratch paper? A calculator? A garbage can?

Other needed equipment, such as computer supplies or textbooks?

5. What else do you do here? Eat? Sleep? Write letters or read for pleasure? If you try to study at the same place you sit to listen to your music or chat on the phone, you may find yourself doing one when you think you're doing the other!

6. Is your study area in a high-traffic or low-traffic area? How often are you interrupted by people passing through?

7. Can you close the door to the room to avoid disturbances and outside noise?

8. When do you spend the most time here? What time of day do you study? Is it when you are at your best, or do you inevitably study when you're tired and less productive?

9. Are your files, folders, and other class materials near the work area and organized? Do you have some filing system for them? If you wanted to look at your class notes from last month—or last year—would you know where to quickly find them?

Create *your* ideal environment

On page 200 of this chapter, I have included a checklist for you to rate your study environment. If you don't know the answer to one or more of the questions, take the time to experiment.

Many of the items on this chart should be understandable to you now. Remember: *Why* you feel the need for a particular environment is not important. Knowing that you *have a preference* is. Here's what you are trying to assess in each item and how *your* preferences might affect your study regimen:

1. If you prefer "listening" to "seeing," you'll have little problem getting the information you need from class lectures and discussion. In fact, you'll *prefer* them to studying your textbooks. (You may have to concentrate on your reading skills and spend more time with your textbooks to off-set this tendency. Highlighting your texts may help.)

   If you're more of a "visual" person, you'll proba-bly find it easier reading your textbook and may have to work to improve your classroom concen-tration. Taking excellent class notes that you can read later will probably be important for you.

2. This should tie in with your answer to question number 1. The more "oral" you are, the more you should concentrate on listening. The more "visual," the better your notes should be for later review.

   This may make a difference for a number of rea-sons. You may find it difficult to hear or see from the back of the classroom. You may be shy and want to sit up front to make yourself participate. You may find sitting near a window makes you feel less claustrophobic; alternatively, you may daydream too much if near a window and should sit as far "inside" the classroom as possible.

3. Whatever location you find most conducive to studying—given the limitations of your living situation and schedule—should be where you spend the majority of your study time.

4. How to organize your time to most effectively cover the material: This may depend, in part, on the amount of homework you are burdened with and/or the time of year—you may have one schedule during most of the school year but have to adapt during test time, when papers are due, for special projects, etc.

5. To some of you, such preferences may only be a factor on weekends, because your day hours are set—you're in school.

   But if you're in college (or in a high school program that mimics college's "choose your own courses and times" scheduling procedures), you would want to use this factor in determining when to schedule your classes.

   If you study best in the morning, for example, try to schedule as many classes as possible in the afternoons (or, at worst, late in the morning).

   If you study best in the evening, either schedule morning classes and leave your afternoons free for other activities, or schedule them in the afternoons so you can sleep later (and study later the night before).

6. Some of us get cranky if we try to do *anything* when we're hungry. If you study poorly when your stomach is growling, eat something!

7. Most of us grow up automatically studying alone. If we "study with a friend," there's often more horseplay than studying. But don't underestimate the positive effect studying with one or two friends—or even a larger study group—can have on your mastery of schoolwork and on your grades.

I didn't really learn about study groups until college, and then didn't participate much. I wish I had (and wish I had started one in high school)—I realize now I could have saved myself a lot of work and taken advantage of the skills, expertise, and minds of some of my brighter classmates.

8. Just because you perform best under pressure doesn't mean you should always leave projects, papers, and studying for tests until the last minute. It just means if you're well organized, but an unexpected project gets assigned or a surprise test announced, you won't panic.

   If you do *not* study well under pressure, it certainly doesn't mean you occasionally won't be required to. The better organized you are, the easier it will be for you all the time, but especially when the unexpected arises.

9. As we've discussed, some of you (like me) will find it difficult to concentrate with*out* music or some sort of noise. Others could not sit in front of the TV and do *any*thing but breathe and eat.

   Many of you will fall in between—you can read and even take notes to music but need absolute quiet to study for a test or master particularly difficult concepts. If you don't know how you function best, now is the time to find out.

10. Back to organizing. The latter concept—starting and finishing one project before moving on to another—doesn't mean you can't at least sit down and outline an entire night's study plan before tackling each subject, one at a time. Setting up such a study schedule *is* advised. But it

may mean you really *can't* move to another project while the one you're now working on is unfinished. Others of you may have no problem working on one project, switching to another when you get stuck or just need a break, then going back to the first.

11. There's nothing particularly wrong with taking a break whenever you feel the need to keep yourself sharp and maximize your quality study time...as long as the breaks aren't every five minutes and don't last longer than the study periods! In general, though, try to increase your concentration through practice so that you can go at least an hour before getting up, stretching, and having a drink or snack. Too many projects will require at least that long to "get into" or organize, and you may find that breaking too frequently will require too much "review time" when you return to your desk.

Form your own study group

Find a small group of like-minded students—four to six seems to be an optimal number—and share notes, question each other, prepare for tests together. To be effective, obviously, the students you pick to be in your group should share all, or at least most, of your classes.

Search out students who are smarter than you, but not too much smarter. If they are on a level far beyond your own, you'll soon be left in the dust and be more discouraged than ever. On the other hand, if you choose students who are too far beneath your level, you may enjoy being the "brain" of the bunch but miss the point of the group—the challenge of other minds to spur you on.

Study groups can be organized in a variety of ways. Each member could be assigned primary responsibility for a single class, including preparing detailed notes from lectures and discussion groups. If supplementary reading is recommended but not required, that person could be responsible for doing all such reading and preparing detailed summaries.

(The extra work you will thus have to do in one class will be offset by the extra work others will be doing for you.)

Alternatively, everybody can be responsible for his or her own notes, but the group could act as an *ad hoc* discussion group, refining your understanding of key points, working on problems together, questioning each other, practicing for tests, etc.

Even if you find only one or two other students willing to work with you, such cooperation will be invaluable, especially in preparing for major exams.

Here's how to form your own study group and maximize its success:

☞ I suggest four students minimum, probably six maximum. You want to ensure everyone gets a chance to participate while maximizing the collective knowledge and wisdom of the group.

Although group members needn't be best friends, they shouldn't be overtly hostile to one another, either. Seek diversity of experience, demand common dedication.

☞ Try to select students that are at least as smart, committed, and serious as you. That will encourage you to keep up and will challenge you a bit.

☞ There are a number of ways to organize, as we briefly discussed above. My suggestion is to assign each class to one student. That student must truly master that assigned class, doing, in addition to the regular assignments, of course, any or all additional reading (recommended by the professor or not) necessary to achieve that goal, taking outstanding notes, outlining the course (if the group decides that would be helpful), being available for questions about specific topics in the class and preparing various practice quizzes, midterms, and finals, as needed, to help test the other students' mastery.

Needless to say, all of the other students still attend all classes, take their own notes, do their own reading and homework assignments. But the student assigned that class attempts to learn as much as the professor, to actually be the "substitute professor" of that class in the study group. (So if you have five classes, a five-person study group becomes the ideal.)

☞ Make meeting times and assignments formal and rigorous. Consider rigid rules of conduct. For example, miss two meetings, whatever the excuse, and you're out. Better to shake out the frivolous students early. You don't want anyone who is working as little as possible but hoping to take advantage of *your* hard work.

☞ However you organize, clearly decide—early— the exact requirements and assignments of each student. Again, you never want the feeling to emerge that one or two of you are trying to "ride the coattails" of the others.

Studying with small kids

So many more of you are going back to school while raising a family, I want to give you some ideas that will help you cope with the Charge of the Preschool Light Brigade:

Plan activities to keep the kids occupied. And out of your hair. The busier you are in school and/or at work, the more time your kids will want to be with you when you *are* home. If you spend a little time with them, it may be easier for them to play alone, especially if you've planned ahead, creating projects *they* can work on while *you're* working on your homework.

Make the kids part of your study routine. Kids love routine, so why not include them in yours? If 4 p.m. to 6 p.m. is always "Mommy's Study Time," they will soon get used to it, especially if you make spending other time with them a priority and give them something to do during those hours. Explaining the importance of what you're doing—in a way that includes some ultimate benefit for *them*—will also motivate them to be part of your "study team."

Use the television as a baby-sitter. Although many of you will have a problem with this—one that I and my daughter deal with weekly, if not daily—it may be the lesser of two evils. And you can certainly rent (or tape) enough quality shows so you don't have to worry about the little darlings watching seven straight hours of Power Rangers.

Plan your study accordingly. Unless you are right up there in the Perfect Parent Pantheon, all of these things will not keep your kids from interrupting every now and then. You can minimize such intrusions, but it's virtually impossible to eliminate them entirely. So don't try—plan your schedule *assuming* such interruptions will occur. For one, that means taking more frequent breaks to spend five minutes with your kids. They'll be more likely to give you the 15 or 20 minutes at a time *you* need if they get periodic attention themselves. By default, *that* means avoiding projects that can only be done with an hour of massive concentration—you can only work in 15 or 20 minute bursts!

Find help. Spouses can occasionally take the kids out for dinner and a movie (and trust me, the kids will encourage you to study *more* if you do this!), relatives can baby-sit (at their homes) on a rotating basis, playmates can be invited over (allowing you to send your darling to their house the next day), you may be able to trade baby-sitting chores with other parents at school, and professional day care may be available at your child's school or in someone's home for a couple of hours a day. Be creative in finding the help you need and schedule accordingly.

My ideal study environment

How I receive information best:

1. ❑ Orally ❑ Visually

In the classroom, I should:

2. ❑ Concentrate on taking notes ❑ Concentrate on listening
3. ❑ Sit in front ❑ Sit in back ❑ Sit near window or door

Where I study best:

4. ❑ At home ❑ In the library ❑ Somewhere else:

_____

When I study best:

5. ❑ Every night; little on weekends ❑ Mainly on weekends
   ❑ Spread out over seven days
6. ❑ In the morning ❑ Evening ❑ Afternoon
7. ❑ Before dinner ❑ After dinner

How I study best:

8. ❑ Alone ❑ With a friend ❑ In a group
9. ❑ Under time pressure ❑ Before I know I have to
10 ❑ With music ❑ In front of TV ❑ In a quiet room
11. ❑ Organizing an entire night's studying before I start
    ❑ Tackling and completing one subject at a time

I need to take a break:

12. ❑ Every 30 minutes ❑ Every hour ❑ Every 2 hours
    ❑ Every ____ hours

CHAPTER 4

GET THE BIG PICTURE

Now you're ready to plan!

We'll begin by developing a time-management plan for an entire term...before it begins, of course.

This term plan will allow you to keep your sights on the "big picture." To let you see the forest, even when you're in the midst of the trees...and a majority of them are oversized redwoods.

By being able to take in your entire term—every major assignment, every test, every paper, every appointment—you will be less likely to get caught up spending more time on a lower-priority class, just because it requires regularly scheduled reports, while falling behind in a more important one, which only requires reading.

And when you can actually *see* you have a test in accounting the same week your zoology project is due, you can plan ahead and finish the project early. If you decide —for whatever reason—not to do so, at least you won't be caught by surprise when crunch time comes.

It's all routine, Mr. Watson

You can't race off to your ultimate goal until you figure out where *your* starting line is. So the first step to overhaul your current routine is to *identify* that routine, in detail. My suggestion is to chart, in 15-minute increments, how you spend every minute of every day *right now*. Although a day or two might be sufficient for some of you, I recommend you chart your activities for an entire week, including the weekend.

This is especially important if, like many people, you have huge pockets of time that seemingly disappear, but in reality are devoted to things like "resting" after you wake up, putting on makeup or shaving, reading the paper, waiting for transportation, or driving to and from school or work. Could you use an extra hour or two a day, either for studying or for fun? Make better use of such time and you will find all the time you need.

For example, learn how to do multiple tasks at the same time. Listen to a book on tape while you're working around the house; practice vocabulary or math drills while you're driving; have your kids, parents, or roommates quiz you for an upcoming test while you're doing dishes, vacuuming, or dusting; *always* carry your calendar, notebook(s), pens, and a textbook with you—you can get a phenomenal amount of reading or studying done while in line at the bank, the library, the supermarket, or while commuting by bus or train.

Strategy Tip: Identify those items on your daily calendar, whatever their priority, that can be completed in 15 minutes or less. These are the ideal tasks to tackle at the laundromat, while waiting for a book to wind its way to your study cubicle, or while standing in line—anywhere.

One of the inherent advantages of a strictly observed schedule is that it saves time just by "being"—eliminating all that time so many of us waste just sitting down wondering what we should do next! (Not to mention trying to find the materials we need, deciding where we're going to study that night, how long, with whom, etc.) The more time management becomes a *habit*, the more *automatic* such decisions become, and the less time you waste making them.

The other huge advantage, of course, is the discipline such a strict schedule demands. Discipline is a wonderful commodity in that, as far as I've found, the more you're able to discipline *any* single aspect of your life, the easier it is to discipline all others. Just ask any writer who has confronted a blank sheet of paper and stared...for hours..."blocked" by unseen forces. Many will tell you the only way to break free is to continue sitting, day after day, trying again and again, no matter how difficult. You don't think *that* takes discipline?

Collect what you need

As you begin your planning session, make sure you have all of the information and materials you need to make a quality plan. Gather your class syllabuses; work schedule; dates of important family events, vacations or trips, other personal commitments (doctor appointments, birthday parties, etc.); and a calendar of any extracurricular events in which you plan to participate.

Keeping track of your day-to-day activities—classes, appointments, regular daily homework assignments, and daily or weekly quizzes—will be dealt with in the next chapter. For now, I want to talk about those projects—studying for midterm and final exams, term papers, theses, etc.—that require completion over a long period of time. Weeks. Maybe even months.

Creating your Project Board

There are two excellent tools you can use for your long-term planning. The first is a Project Board, which you can put on any blank wall or right above your desk.

It's not necessary for you to construct your own Project Board, though it is certainly the least expensive alternative. There are ready-made charts for professionals available in a variety of formats, including magnetic and erasable. (Yes, you're learning something that you can use throughout your life: Professionals call Project Boards flow charts.) Your local art supply, stationery, or bookstore may have a selection of such items. Otherwise, you can certainly copy the format of the one I've reproduced on pages 208 and 209 of this chapter.

How does the Project Board work? As you can see, it is just a variation on a calendar. I have set it up vertically—the months running down the left-hand side, the projects across the top. You can certainly switch and have the dates across the top and the projects running vertically (in fact, that's the way a lot of the ready-made ones come). It all depends on what space you have on your wall.

Using your Project Board

In the case of each project, there is a key preparatory step before you can use the chart: You have to break down each general assignment into its component parts, the specific tasks involved in any large project. For example, presuming you have been assigned a paper on Dante for your English class, we can identify the steps necessary to complete it as follows:

1. Finalize topic.
2. Initial library research.
3. Prepare general outline.

4. Detailed library research.
5. Prepare detailed outline.
6. Write first draft.
7. Write second draft.
8. Check spelling and proofread.
9. Get someone else to proofread.
10. Type final draft.
11. Proofread again.
12. Turn it in!

Next to each specific task, we have estimated the time we would expect to spend on it.

The second project involves working on a team with other students from your entrepreneurship class to create a hypothetical student business. While the particular elements are different, you'll notice that the concept of breaking the project down into separate and manageable steps and allocating time for each of them doesn't change.

However, because time allocation in later steps depends on what assignments you're given by the group, we have had to temporarily place question marks next to some of them. As the details of this project become clearer and specific assignments are made, your Project Board should be changed to reflect both more details and the specific time required for each step.

You should also include on your Project Board time for studying for all your final exams. Cramming for tests doesn't work very well in the short term and doesn't work at all over the long term, so take my advice and made it a habit to review your class notes on each subject on a *weekly or monthly* basis. Let's presume you agree with me and have decided that every Sunday morning is "review time" and allocated one Sunday a month to review the previous month's work in each subject. We've entered this time on our Board, as well.

As a result of this plan, you'll notice there is little time allocated to "last-minute" cramming or even studying for a specific final the week before it is given—just a couple of hours to go over any details you're still a little unsure of or to spend on areas you think will be on the test. While others are burning the midnight oil in the library the night before each exam, you're getting a good night's sleep and will enter the test refreshed, relaxed, and confident. Seems like a better plan to me.

As a byproduct of this study schedule, by the way, you will find that salient facts and ideas will remain with you long after anybody is testing you on them.

Now that you have your Project Board, what do you do with it? Keep adding any and all other important projects throughout the term and continue to revise it according to actual time spent as opposed to time allocated. Getting into this habit will make you more aware of how much time to allocate to future projects and make sure that the more you do so, the more accurate your estimates will be.

Using a Term-Planning Calendar

The Term-Planning Calendar, an example of which is shown on pages 210 and 211 of this chapter, can be used in concert with or in place of the Project Board.

To use it with the Project Board, start by transferring all the information from the Project Board to your Term-Planning Calendar. Then *add* your weekly class schedule, work schedule, family celebrations, vacations and trips, club meetings, and extracurricular activities. *Everything.* The idea is to make sure your Calendar has *all* your scheduling information, while your Project Board contains just the briefest summary that you can ingest in a glance.

Leave your Project Board on your wall at home; carry your Term-Planning Calendar with you. Whenever new projects, appointments, meetings, etc., are scheduled, add them immediately to your Calendar. Then transfer the steps involving major projects to your Project Board.

To use it in place of the Project Board, just don't make a Project Board. Put all the information—including the steps of all your projects and the approximate time you expect each to take—right on the Calendar.

It's up to you which way to go. Personally, I prefer using *both*, for one simple reason: I like being able to look at the wall and see the entire term *at a glance.* I find it much easier to see how everything fits together *this* way than by trying to "glance" at a dozen different weekly calendars or even three monthly ones.

I also find it difficult to easily see which steps go with which projects without studying the calendar (although I admit color-coding would solve this problem), whereas the very set-up of the Project Board makes such information easy to glean.

High school students may find it easier to use only the Term-Planning Calendar, as they are usually not subjected to quite as many long-term projects as college or graduate students. But once you're in college, especially if you have more than an average number of papers, reports, projects, etc., you'll find the Project Board a very helpful extra tool.

And, yes, I realize it seems a "waste of time" to have to write all these details on both a Project Board and Term-Planning Calendar. But I think you'll find the time you *save* more than makes up for the supposed inconvenience.

Sample Projects Board

MONTH/WEEK		PROJECT: STUDENT CORPORATION
1st MONTH	Week 1	Initial group meeting: Discuss overall assignment and possible products or services—bring list of three each to meeting (1 hour)
	Week 2	Finalize product or service; finalize organization of group and longterm responsibilities of each subgroup. (3)
	Week 3	Subgroup planning and short-term assignments (2)
	Week 4	Work on individual assignment from subgroup (?)
2nd MONTH	Week 1	Work on individual assignment from subgroup (?)
	Week 2	Work on individual assignment from subgroup (?)
	Week 3	Integrate individual assignment with rest of subgroup (?)
	Week 4	Meet with entire group to integrate plans (?)
3rd MONTH	Week 1	Finalize all-group plan; draft initial report (?)
	Week 2	Type and proof final report (?)
	Week 3	
	Week 4	
	DUE DATE	3RD MONTH/end of Week 2

PROJECT: DANTE TERM PAPER	REVIEW/EXAM SCHEDULE
Finalize topic (1 hour)	Review prior month's History notes (3)
Initial library research (2) General outline (1)	Review prior month's English notes (2)
Detailed library research (3) Detailed library research (3)	Review prior month's Science notes (4) Review prior month's Math notes (4)
Detailed library research (3) Detailed outline (1) First draft (4), Additional research (2)	Review 1st MONTH History notes (3) Review 1st MONTH English notes (2) Review 1st MONTH Science notes (4) Review 1st MONTH Math notes (4)
Second draft, spellcheck, proof (10) Independent proof (1) Type final draft and proof (4)	2nd MONTH History notes (3) 2nd MONTH English notes (2) 2nd MONTH Science notes (4) 2nd MONTH Math notes (4)
end of 3RD MONTH	end of 3RD MONTH

Month	Mon	Tue	Wed	Thu	Fri	Sat	Sun
Feb	18	19	20	21	22	23	24
	25	26	27 conference 4-5	28	1	2	3
March	4	5	6	7	8 Afternoon: A.A.P. meeting	9	10
	11 Sociology Presentation	12	13 Math: Ch.1-3	14	15	16	17 Trip Home
	18	19	20 Math: Ch 4	21	22	23	24

Month	Mon	Tue	Wed	Thu	Fri	Sat	Sun
	25	26	27 Math: Ch.5	28	29	30	31
April	1	2	3 No Math Due	4	5	6 Trip to Jim & Dana's	7
	8	9	10 Math: Ch. 6-8	11	12 Sociology paper due!	13	14
	15 Biology Lab Journal Due!!	16 Last day of class	17	18	19	20 Biology Final 3:00	21
	22 Math Final 2:00	23	24	25 ←— CAMPING !!!	26 ☺	27	28

211

CHAPTER 5

ADD THE DETAILED BRUSH STROKES

Your Project Board now lists the major papers, projects, and exams for an entire term. If you've done it the way I do, this Board is now gracing a wall in your room. And you've also filled out a Term Planning Calendar, writing in not just the details on your Project Board, but other key appointments, assignments, and due dates.

It's time to become even more organized. The Project Board and Term Planning Calendar have given you a good start by helping you schedule the entire term. Now it's time to learn about the tools that will help you organize your days and weeks.

For any time-management system to work, it has to be used continually. Before you go on, make an appointment with yourself for the end of the week—Sunday night is perfect—to sit down and plan for the following week. You don't have to spend a *lot* of time—a half hour is probably all it will take—to review your commitments for the week and schedule the necessary study time.

Despite its brevity, this may just be the best time you spend all week, because you will reap the benefits of it throughout the week and beyond!

Step 1: Make your "To-Do" list

First, you must identify everything you need to do this week. Look at your Project Board and/or Planning Calendar to determine what tasks need to be completed this week for all your major school projects. Add any other tasks that must be done—from sending off a birthday present to your sister to attending your monthly volunteer meeting to completing homework that may have just been assigned.

Once you have created your list, you can move on to the next step, putting your tasks in order of importance.

Step 2: Prioritize your tasks

When you sit down to study without a plan, you just dive into the first project that comes to mind. The problem with this approach has been discussed earlier: There is no guarantee that the first thing that comes to mind will be the most important. The point of the weekly Priority Task Sheet is to help you arrange your tasks *in order of importance.* That way, even if you find yourself without enough time for *everything,* you can at least finish the most important assignments.

First, ask yourself this question: "If I only got a few things done this week, what would I want them to be?" Mark these high-priority tasks with an "H." After you have identified the "urgent" items, consider those tasks that are least important, items that could wait until the following week to be done, if necessary. (This may include tasks you consider very important but that don't have to be completed *this week.)* These are low-priority items, at least for this week—mark them with an "L."

All the other items fit somewhere between the critical tasks and the low-priority ones. Review the remaining items. If you're sure none of them are either "H" or "L," mark them with an "M," for middle priority.

Strategy tip: If you push aside the same low-priority item day after day, week after week, at some point you should just stop and decide whether it's something you need to do at all! This is a strategic way to make a task or problem "disappear." In the business world, some managers purposefully avoid confronting a number of problems, waiting to see if they will simply solve themselves through benign neglect. If it works in business, it can work for you in school.

A completed Priority Task Sheet is on page 218 of this chapter. A blank form you can photocopy is on page 242 of chapter 8.

Step 3: Fill in your Daily Schedule

Before you start adding papers, projects, homework, study time, etc., to your calendar, fill in the "givens"—the time you need to sleep, eat, work, attend class. Even if your current routine consists of meals on the run and sleep wherever you find it, build the assumption *right into your schedule* that you are going to get eight hours of sleep and three decent meals a day. You may surprise yourself and find that there is still enough time to do everything you need. (Though all of us probably know someone who sleeps three hours a night, eats nothing but junk food and still finds a way to get straight As, most experts would contend that regular, healthy eating and a decent sleep schedule are key attributes to any successful study system.)

Now you're ready to transfer the items on your Priority Task Sheet to your Daily Schedule forms. (See page 219 of this chapter for a sample completed Daily Schedule, page 243 of chapter 8 for a blank form you can photocopy.)

Put in the "H" items first, followed by the "M" items. Then, fit in as many of the "L" items as you can. By following this procedure, you'll make sure you devote the amount of time needed for your most important priorities. You can schedule your most productive study time for your most important tasks, and plug in your lower priorities as they fit.

Other considerations

Besides the importance of the task and the available time you have to complete it, other factors will determine how you fit your Daily Schedules together. Some factors will be beyond your control—work schedules, appointments with professors, counselors, doctors. But there are plenty of factors you *do* control and should consider as you put together your Daily Schedules each week.

Schedule enough time for each task—time to "warm up" and get the task accomplished, but, particularly when working on long-term projects, not so much time that you "burn out." Every individual is different, but most students study best for blocks of one and a half to three hours, depending on the subject. You might find history fascinating and be able to read for hours. Calculus, on the other hand, may be a subject best handled in "small bites," a half-hour to an hour at a time.

Don't overdo it. Plan your study time in blocks, breaking up work time with short leisure activities. (It's helpful to add these to your schedule as well.) For example, you've set aside three hours on Wednesday afternoon for that research assignment: Schedule a 15-minute walk to the ice cream shop somewhere in the middle of that study block. You'll find that these breaks help you think more clearly and creatively when you get back to studying.

Even if you tend to like longer blocks of study time, be careful about scheduling study "marathons"—a six- or eight-hour stretch rather than a series of two-hour sessions. The longer the period you schedule, the more likely you'll have to fight the demons of procrastination. Convincing yourself that you are really studying your heart out, you'll also find it easier to justify time-wasting distractions, scheduling longer breaks, and, before long, quitting before you should.

Use your Daily Schedule *daily*

Each night (or in the morning before the day begins) look at your schedule for the upcoming day. How much free time is there? Are there "surprise" tasks that are *not* on your schedule but need to be? Are there conflicts you were unaware of at the beginning of the week?

If you plan well at the beginning of the week, this shouldn't happen often. But it invariably does. Just as often, you'll discover a class is canceled or a meeting postponed, which leaves you with a schedule change. By checking your Daily Schedule *daily—either the night before or the first thing in the morning*—you'll be able to respond to these changes.

How do you know whether to enter an assignment on your Daily Schedule or put it on the Project Board first?

If it's a simple task *and* if it will definitely be accomplished within a week—read pages 272-305, study for quiz, meet to discuss cheerleader tryouts with faculty—put it on the appropriate Daily Schedule sheet(s).

If, however, it's a task that is complicated—requiring further breakdown into specific steps—and/or one that will require more than a week to complete, it should be "flow charted" on your Project Board. *Then* the individual steps should be added to your Daily Schedules. (I personally like to plan everything out the night before. It's a fantastic feeling to wake up and start the day completely organized.)

You'll benefit every day

Once you start using your Project Board, Term-Planning Calendar, Priority Task Sheets, and Daily Schedules, you will reap the benefits every day. Throughout the day, you can simply follow your daily schedule.

Anything—even school—seems less overwhelming when you have it broken into "bite-size" pieces and you already know the flavor.

You no longer worry about when you'll get that paper done—you've already planned for it.

You'll accomplish it *all*—one step at a time.

As you get used to managing your time—planning your months, your weeks, and even your days—you'll quickly discover that you seem to have more time than you ever had before.

Priority Rating	Scheduled?	**Priority Tasks This Week** Week of 3/28 through 4/3
		Sociology Paper
H		— Library Search
M		— Outline
L		— Rough Draft
		Math Assignments
H		— Ch. 4
M		— Ch. 5
M		— study for test

Daily Schedule

date: **3/30**

Assignments Due		Schedule	
Bio. Lab work.		5	
Math, Ch. 4		6	
		7	
		8	
		9	Biology ↕
To Do/Errands		10	Sociology ↑
Call Erin – 871-4031		11	↓ ↓ ↓
Books to library		12	Lunch w/ Kim
☐ Bank		1	read: Ch. 5 (soc.) ↕
☐ Groceries		2	
Drop by Jim's		3	Math class
		4	TRAVEL
		5	
Homework		6	Math homework ↕
1) Math Ch. 5 1-9		7	work on paper
2) Sociology paper		8	
(rough draft)		9	
		10	
		11	
		12	

CHAPTER 6

HELP! TIPS, TIPS, AND MORE TIPS

In this book, you've learned a simple, manageable system for getting more done in the amount of time you have available. It is a system geared exactly for people like *you*—students whose school schedules demand a big chunk of time, yet who have a myriad of other commitments, activities, and responsibilities pulling you in other directions.

Your time-management plan should be simple. Why commit to another complicated project that demands your time and mental energies? Yet, no matter how basic and easy your time-management program may be, this doesn't guarantee that you won't be plagued with an occasional time-crunch problem.

As you begin to implement my suggested time-management skills in your life, you are bound to have some glitches. It is impossible to completely avoid these study roadblocks, so let me teach you some problem-solving skills so they don't stop you in your tracks.

Hitting the "wall"

If you run into a "wall" on your path to time-management success, the best solution is to find creative ways to get *around* it, rather than trying to crash your way *through* it.

If you were trying to lose weight, for example, there are a number of different approaches you could take:

1. You could try to alter your *behavior*—eat less, exercise more.
2. Or change your *attitude* toward eating, maybe stop using food as a reward.
3. Or transform your *environment,* keeping the refrigerator stocked with only healthy fruits and veggies...and moving your study area from the kitchen to the bedroom!

Most likely, your weight loss would be the result of a *combination* of changes in all three areas.

Following are several examples of creative and multi-dimensional approaches to solving some typical time-management problems.

Time flies when you're having fun...

...And sometimes even when you're *not.* No matter how hard you try to stick to your schedule, you find that your assignments always take a lot longer than you had planned. You schedule an hour to do your economics homework, and it takes you twice that long. You plan an afternoon at the library for research, and it's closing time before you're ready to leave. It seems like you spend all your time studying—and you're *still* not getting it done.

Solutions: It's time for an attitude check. Are you being too much of a perfectionist? Is it taking you so long to read because you're trying to memorize every word? Make sure your expectations for yourself are realistic. And don't exaggerate the importance of lower-priority assignments.

Consider altering your behavior—with a little help from an alarm clock. If you've planned an hour for your reading assignment, set the clock to go off when you should have completed it. Then, *stop reading.* And go on to the next assignment. If you're not done, reassure yourself that you can go back to it later. You'll probably become conditioned to complete your assignments more quickly, and you won't run the risk of leaving your other, perhaps more important, work unfinished.

"I'm allergic to my desk"

There's nothing wrong with your study area. It's in a quiet corner of the house with few distractions. All your materials are nearby, and the area is well-lit and well-ventilated. But...every time you sit down to study, you find yourself coming up with *any* excuse to leave. Unable to focus on any assignment, your mind would be wandering out the window if there were one in front of you.

Solution: It can happen. You set up the ideal study area, follow your time management system, and stick to your schedule religiously. Your intentions are good. But for some reason, it just doesn't work. Bad vibes, maybe.

What can you do?

Change your environment!

Just as you can condition yourself to study, you can also condition yourself *not* to study in a particular area.

Stick to your schedule, but try another area—another floor in the library, even a place that may not seem to be as conducive to quiet study. Maybe you're one of those people who needs a little music in the background to concentrate.

If changing your environment doesn't help, consider your behavior. Are you trying to study at a time of day when you have too much pent-up energy? Maybe moving your study time earlier or later would help. Try taking a brisk walk or exercising before you begin studying.

Think about other behavior: Have you had several cups of coffee (or cans of soda) prior to your study period? Caffeine overdose—or too much sugar *and* caffeine—could make it very difficult to concentrate.

A conspiracy to keep you from studying

Friends and family call when you're studying because they know that's the best time to reach you at home. Or you're interrupted by phone calls for family members or roommates. Worse yet are the calls from people taking surveys, asking for donations, or trying to sell you.

Solutions: A ringing phone is virtually impossible to ignore. Even if you're determined not to pick it up, it still demands your attention. An answering machine will eliminate your getting roped into lengthy conversations, but your train of thought will still be interrupted.

There are two environment-altering solutions: Unplug the phone while you're studying. Or remove yourself from within hearing distance—go to the library.

A little help from your "friends"

Your roommate, whose study hours differ from yours, always seems to want to spend "quality bonding time" in the middle of your heavy-duty reading assignments.

Solutions: It's not rude to refuse to talk to someone while you're studying. But it often feels like that, and I'd rather feel guilty about not studying than be rude to a friend. A favorite tip from human-relations specialists is to respond in a positive but diverting way—"It sounds like this is important to you. I really want to hear more. Can we talk in an hour when I'm finished with this, so I can concentrate more on your problem?" (Granted, your room-mate would look at you as if you were crazy if you talked like this. Put it in your own words—it's the attitude that's important.)

Another solution might be to put up a "Do Not Disturb" sign, indicating the time you will be available to talk. The visual signal helps remind others that you're busy *before* they unintentionally interrupt you with small talk.

You can't count on anyone

You painstakingly plan your schedule each week, religiously keeping track of each appointment, assignment, and commitment you have. Unfortunately, others don't seem to have the same sense of responsibility as you. Your friends cancel social engagements, you arrive on time for a meeting and no one else in the group shows up, even your teacher postpones the pretest study session.

Solution: Yes, its time for another attitude adjustment. Welcome to the real world!

First of all, there's nothing you can do when someone else cancels or postpones a scheduled appointment. But if you remember, in the very first chapter of this book, I said that fanaticism is not an element of a good time-management program.

Occasional—and sometimes more than occasional—cancellations, postponements, or schedule changes should *not* ruin your schedule.

Try looking at such last-minute changes as *opportunities.* Your doctor canceled your appointment? That means a free hour to get ahead in calculus, read your history assignment, work out at the gym...or just do nothing!

A special note for commuters

If you live at home (as opposed to being housed on campus), there are some special pressures with which you need to be ready to contend:

☞ Travel time. Your commute to school will probably be longer than if you could roll out of bed and walk to class. It will certainly require more wakefulness, even if you just have to stumble to a subway or bus (but especially if you have to drive!). You'll also have travel time problems if you need to use the library after you've returned home, or, for that matter, need to return to the campus for any reason. It's especially important *you* minimize your travel time, planning enough to maximize your use of the campus facilities without scheduling a trip home in between.

☞ While nobody likes walking to class in rain, sleet, or snow—except, perhaps, future postal employees—it is invariably easier to walk a few tree-lined blocks than drive a few miles in inclement weather. Take weather problems into account when scheduling your commute.

☞ The very act of living at home—whether as a child or one "married with children"—brings with it responsibilities to others you could minimize living in a dorm. Be ready to allocate time to these responsibilities and include them in your study schedule. They're as inevitable if you live at home as meat loaf on Tuesdays.

Old habits die hard

As you begin to implement your own system of time management, you may need to rid yourself of some old habits:

1. **Don't make your schedule overly vague.** For example, when Kirsten planned out her day, she simply wrote "study" in the blank spaces on her schedule. Although she had good intentions, she had difficulty actually *studying*. Often she found that the book she needed was still at home, or she had to ask someone about the details of the assignment she needed to finish.

   When you're scheduling your time, be specific about which tasks you plan to do, and when you plan to do them. When Kirsten wrote "read 15 pages in history text" rather than "study" in her calendar, she did not forget her book.

2. **Don't delay your planning.** It's easy to convince yourself that you will plan the details of a particular task when the time comes. You may tell yourself, "I'll just leave my schedule blank and plan the afternoon right after I get out of Biology." But that way it's much too easy to forget your homework when your friends invite you to go to the park or out for a snack.

3. **Write *everything* down.** All of the tools we've discussed and the various other hints should get you into the habit of writing things down. Not having to remember all these items will free up

space in your brain for the things you need to concentrate on or *do* have to remember. As a general rule, write down the so-called little things and you'll avoid data overload and clutter.

4. **Learn to manage distractions.** As a time-management axiom puts it, "Don't respond to the urgent and forget the important." It's easy to become distracted when the phone rings, your baby brother chooses to trash your room, or you realize your favorite TV show is coming on. But don't just drop your books and run off. Take a few seconds to make sure you've reached a logical stopping point. If you haven't, get back to work. If you have, jot down a note to yourself of exactly where you left off and/or anything you want to remember after your break. Then you can enjoy your break without anxiety.

5. **Don't "shotgun" plan.** Even if you haven't been following a systematic time-management approach, you may have had some way of keeping important dates, and events in mind. Some students use what might be called the "shotgun" approach—writing down assignments, dates, and times on whatever is available. They wind up with so many slips of paper in so many places, their planning attempts are virtually worthless.

Record all upcoming events and tasks on your Project Board and/or Term-Planning Calendar. And always have your calendar with you so you can refer to it when you are planning a specific week or day or need to add an appointment or assignment to it.

6. **Don't "overschedule."** As you begin to follow a time-management program, you may find yourself trying to schedule too *much* of your time. Once you get the "effectiveness bug" and become aware of how much you can accomplish, it might be tempting to squeeze more and more into your life.

7. **Be realistic and honest with yourself** when determining those things that require more effort, those that come easier to you. Chances are, you can't complete the outline for your term paper, study three chapters of biology, and do your French literature assignment in the two hours you have between class and work. Schedule enough time to get each assignment done. Whenever possible, schedule pleasurable activities after study time, not before. They will act as incentives, not distractions.

8. **Remember that time is relative.** Car trips take longer if you have to schedule frequent stops for gas, food, necessities, etc.; longer still if you start out during rush hour. Likewise, libraries are more crowded at certain times of the day or year, which will affect how fast you can get books you need, etc. So take the time of day into account.

   And if your schedule involves working with others, you need to take *their* sense of time into account—you may find you have to schedule "waiting time" for a chronically-late friend... always bring a book along.

9. **Be prepared.** As assignments are entered on your calendar, make sure you also enter the items needed—texts; other books you have to

buy, borrow, or get from the library; special materials; etc. There's nothing worse than sitting
down to do that assignment you've put off until
the last minute and realizing that though *you're*
finally ready to get to work, your supplies
*aren't...*and at 10 p.m., you don't have a lot of
options!

10. **Be realistic.** Plan according to *your* schedule,
your goals, and *your* aptitudes, not some
ephemeral "standard." Allocate the time you expect a project to take *you*, not the time it might
take someone else, how long your teacher tells
you it should take, etc. There will be tasks you
accomplish far faster than anyone else, others
that take you much longer.

11. **Be flexible, monitor, and adjust.** No calendar
is an island. Any new assignment will affect
whatever you've already scheduled. If you have
a reasonably light schedule when a new assignment suddenly appears, it can just be plugged
right into your calendar and finished as scheduled. But if you've already planned virtually
every hour for the next two weeks, *any* addition
may force you to change a whole day's plan. Be
flexible and be ready. It'll happen.

    And remember that no plan of action is fool-
proof, so monitor your progress at reasonable
periods and make changes where necessary.
This is *your* study regimen—you conceived it,
you can change it.

12. **Look for more time savings.** If you find
that you are consistently allotting more time
than necessary to a specific chore—giving yourself one hour to review your English notes

every Sunday but always finishing in 45 minutes or less—change your future schedule accordingly. You may use the extra 15 minutes for a task that consistently takes longer than you've anticipated or, if one doesn't exist, quit 15 minutes early.

13. **Accomplish one task before going on to the next one**—don't skip around. If you ever stuffed envelopes for a political candidate, for example, you've probably already learned that it is quicker and easier to sign 100 letters, then stuff them into envelopes, then seal and stamp them, than to sign, stuff, seal, and stamp one letter at a time.

14. **Do your least favorite chores** (study assignments, projects, whatever) first—you'll feel better having gotten them out of the way! And plan how to accomplish them as meticulously as possible. That will get rid of them even faster.

15. **Try anything that works.** You may decide that color coding your calendar—red for assignments that must be accomplished that week, blue for steps in longer-term projects (which give you more flexibility), yellow for personal time and appointments, green for classes, etc.—makes it easier for you to tell at a glance what you need to do and when you need to do it.

Or that you require a day-to-day calendar to carry with you, but a duplicate one on the wall at home.

Once you've gotten used to your class schedule, you may decide to eliminate class times from your calendar and make it less complicated.

16. Adapt these tools to your own use. Try anything you think may work—use it if it does, discard it if it doesn't.

There are thinkers and there are doers.

And there are those who think a lot about doing.

Organizing your life requires you to actually *use* the Project Board, Term Calendar, Priority Task Sheets, and Daily Schedules we've discussed, not just waste more time "planning" instead of studying!

Planning is an ongoing learning process. Dive in and plan for your upcoming school term. Or if you're in the middle of a term now, plan the remainder of it right now. As you use your plan in the upcoming weeks and months, you will come up with new ways to improve your time-management system and tailor it to your own needs.

As you get used to managing your time, planning ahead as well as planning your week and even your days, you'll quickly discover that you seem to have more time than ever before.

I hope you use it wisely and well.

CHAPTER 7

IT'S TIME TO DEAL WITH ADD

Nobody is in favor of illegal drugs. But we also must face and deal with what's happening to the 3 million-plus who are on a *legal* drug—Ritalin, the prescribed drug of choice for kids diagnosed with Attention Deficit Disorder (ADD), hyperactivity, or the combination of the two (ADHD).

I could write a book on ADD, which seems to be the "diagnosis of choice" for school kids these days. Luckily, I don't have to. Thom Hartmann has already written an excellent one—*Attention Deficit Disorder: A Different Perception* (Underwood Books, 1997)—from which I have freely and liberally borrowed (with his permission) for this chapter.

I'm going to have to leave others to debate whether ADD actually exists as a clearly definable illness, whether it's the "catchall" diagnosis of lazy doctors, whether teachers are labeling kids as ADD to avoid taking responsibility for the students' poor learning skills, whether Ritalin is a miracle drug or the one that is medicating creative kids into a conforming stupor.

All of these positions *have* been asserted, and, as hundreds of new kids are medicated every day, the debate about ADD is only likely to continue...and heat up.

That is not my concern in this book.

What I want to deal with here is the reality that many kids, however they are labeled, have severe problems in dealing with school as it usually exists. And to give them the advice they need—especially regarding time-management skills—to contend with the symptoms that have acquired the label "ADD."

Some definitions, please

Just what is ADD? It's probably easiest to describe as a person's difficulty focusing on a simple thing for any significant amount of time. People with ADD are described as easily distracted, impatient, impulsive, and often seeking immediate gratification. They have poor listening skills and have trouble doing "boring" jobs (like sitting quietly in class, or, as adults, balancing a checkbook). "Disorganized" and "messy" are words that also come up a lot.

Hyperactivity, on the other hand, is more clearly defined as restlessness, resulting in excessive activity. Hyperactives are usually described as having "ants in their pants." ADHD, the first category recognized in medicine some 75 years ago, is a combination of hyperactivity and ADD.

According to the American Psychiatric Association, a person has ADHD if he or she meets eight or more of the following paraphrased criteria:

1. Can't remain seated if required to do so.
2. Easily distracted by extraneous stimuli.
3. Unable to focus on a single task or play activity.

4. Frequently begins another activity without completing the first.

5. Fidgets or squirms (or feels restless mentally).

6. Can't (or doesn't want to) wait for his turn during group activities.

7. Will often interrupt with an answer before a question is completed.

8. Has problems with chore or job follow-through.

9. Has trouble playing quietly.

10. Impulsively jumps into physically dangerous activities without weighing the consequences.

11. Easily loses things (pencils, tools, papers) necessary to complete school or work projects.

12. Interrupts others inappropriately.

13. Talks impulsively or excessively.

14. Doesn't seem to listen when spoken to.

Three caveats to keep in mind: The behaviors must have started before age 7, not represent some other form of classifiable mental illness, and occur more frequently than the average person of the same age.

Characteristics of people with ADD

Let's look at the characteristics generally ascribed to people with ADD in more detail.

Easily distracted. Because ADD people are constantly "scoping out" everything around them, focusing on a single item is difficult. Just try having a conversation with an ADD person while the television is on.

Short, but very intense, attention span. Though it can't be defined in terms of minutes or hours, anything an

ADD person finds boring immediately loses their attention. Other projects may hold their rapt and extraordinarily intense attention for hours or days.

Disorganization. ADD children are often chronically disorganized—their rooms are messy, their desks are a shambles, their files incoherent. While people without ADD can be equally messy and disorganized, they can usually find what they are looking for; ADDers *can't.*

Distortions of time-sense. ADDers have an exaggerated sense of urgency when they're working on something and an exaggerated sense of boredom when they have nothing interesting to do.

Difficulty following directions. A new theory on this aspect holds that ADDers have difficulty processing auditory or verbal information. A significant aspect of this difficulty is the very-common reports of parents of ADD kids who say their kids love to watch TV and hate to read.

Daydream. Or fall into depressions or mood swings.

Take risks. ADDers seem to make faster decisions than non-ADDers. This is why Thom Hartmann and Wilson Harrell, former publisher of *Inc.* magazine and author of *For Entrepreneurs Only* (Career Press, 1995), conclude that the vast majority of successful entrepreneurs probably have ADD! They call them "Hunters," as opposed to more staid "Farmer" types.

Easily frustrated and impatient. ADDers do not beat around the bush or suffer fools gladly. They are direct and to-the-point. When things aren't working, "Do something!" is the ADD rallying cry, even if that something is a bad idea.

Why ADD kids have trouble in school

First and foremost, says Thom Hartmann, it is because schools are set up for "Farmers"—sit still, do what you're told, watch and listen to the teacher. This is hell for "Hunters" with ADD. The bigger the class size, the worse it becomes. Kids with ADD, remember, are easily distracted, bored, turned off, always ready to move on.

What should you look for in a school setting to make it more palatable to an ADD son or daughter? What can you do at home to help your child (or yourself)? Hartmann has some solid answers.

☞ Learning needs to be project- and experience-based, providing more opportunities for creativity and shorter and smaller "bites" of information. Many "gifted" programs offer exactly such opportunities. The problem for many kids with ADD is that they've spent years in non-gifted, farmer-type classroom settings and may be labeled underachieving behavior problems, effectively shut out of the programs virtually designed for them! Many parents report that children diagnosed as ADD, who failed miserably in public school, thrived in private school. Hartmann attributes this to the smaller classrooms, more individual attention with specific goal-setting, project-based learning and similar methods common in such schools. These factors are just what make ADD kids thrive!

☞ Create a weekly performance template on which both teacher and parent chart the child's performance, positive and negative. "Creating such a larger-than-the-child system," claims Hartmann, "will help keep ADD children on task and on time."

☞ Encourage special projects for extra credit. Projects give ADDers the chance to learn in the mode that's most appropriate to them. They will also give such kids the chance to make up for the "boring" homework they sometimes simply can't make themselves do.

☞ Stop labeling them "disordered." Kids react to labels, especially negative ones, even more than adults. Saying "you have a deficit and a disorder" may be more destructive than useful.

☞ Think twice about medication, but don't discard it as an option. Hartmann has a very real concern about the long-term side effects of the drugs normally prescribed for ADDers. He also notes that they may well be more at risk to be substance abusers as adults, so starting them on medication at a young age sends a very mixed message. On the other hand, if an ADD child cannot have his or her special needs met in a classroom, not medicating him or her may be a disaster. "The relatively unknown long-term risks of drug therapy," says Hartmann, "may be more than offset by the short-term benefits of improved classroom performance."

Some suggestions for time management

☞ **Use all the time-management forms in this book**, without fail, every single day. Reprioritize, replan, reschedule as needed—and that will probably be more often than those without ADD. And *don't look too far ahead*—concentrate your efforts on short-term goals.

☞ **Organize your time around tasks.** ADDers do well with short bursts of high-quality effort and attention. So *every* task—personal, educational, social, or professional—should be broken into the smallest possible "bite-size" chunks. This will make an ADDer's calendar, to-do list, or priority task sheet appear incredibly long and crowded, but the smaller the tasks, the more he or she will accomplish.

☞ **Break everything into specific goal units.** ADDers are very goal-oriented; as soon as they reach one, it's on to the next. So reestablishing very short-term, "bite-size" goals is essential. Make goals specific, definable, and measurable. And stick to only one priority at a time.

☞ **Create distraction-free zones.** Henry David Thoreau (who evidently suffered from ADD, by the way) was so desperate to escape distraction he moved to isolated Walden Pond. Organize your time and workspace to create your own "Walden Pond," especially when you have to write, take notes, read, or study. ADDers need silence, so consider the library. Another tip: Clean your work area thoroughly at the end of each day.

☞ **Train your attention span.** ADDers will probably never be able to train themselves to ignore distractions totally, but a variety of meditation techniques might help them stay focused longer.

☞ **Utilize short-term rewards.** ADD salespeople don't do well when a sales contest lasts for six months, even if the reward is spectacular, such as a 10-day cruise. But stick a $100 bill on the wall and watch them focus! Those with ADD will not be motivated by rewards that are too ephemeral or too far in the future. They live for the here and now and need to be rewarded immediately.

CHAPTER 8

TIME MANAGEMENT FORMS

In this chapter, I've included blank copies of each of the three key tools introduced in this book: the Term-Planning Calendar, Priority Task Sheet, and Daily Schedule forms. Photocopy as many of these forms as you need, enlarge them to fit in your notebook, and adapt them in any way you see fit to *use* them in *your* time-management program.

Happy planning. And congratulations on committing to a successful time-management program!

Term Planning Calendar

Fill in due dates for assignments and papers, dates of tests, and important non-academic activities and events

Month	Mon	Tue	Wed	Thu	Fri	Sat	Sun

Priority Rating	Scheduled?	**Priority Tasks This Week**
		Week of *through*

Daily Schedule

date:

Assignments Due

	Schedule
	5
	6
	7
	8
	9

To Do/Errands

	10
	11
	12
	1
	2
	3
	4
	5

Homework

	6
	7
	8
	9
	10
	11
	12

BOOK 3

TAKE
NOTES

THERE *IS* A RIGHT WAY TO TAKE NOTES

Have you or one of your friends ever suffered through an inquisition masquerading as a class? One you slithered into every day with the passion of a eunuch?

Let me tell you about my favorite. It was my friend Tony's 8th-grade American history class with Sister Anne Francis (who did *not* appear in *Forbidden Planet* but probably could have made a convincing Monster of the Id). And it was a note-taking nightmare.

Each day, the good sister filled—twice—all eight blackboard panels in the classroom with names, dates, places, wars, rebellions, and treaties—more facts than there are people who have seen Madonna's navel. And the students sat there, silently copying *every word* into their composition books. No heretical abbreviations or blasphemous shorthand for Sister Anne!

They even had to be careful *how* they copied every word. Their penmanship was expected to be just as perfect as Sister Anne's; if it wasn't, their grades suffered. (She checked their notebooks once a week!)

They were assigned no reading and no homework. It wasn't until near the end of the semester that Tony found out why: He discovered a textbook ostensibly assigned to the class on a back shelf—which the good sister was merely copying, word for word, every day, onto the blackboard!

That seems like a useless exercise, doesn't it? When all she had to do was just pass out the text?

Unfortunately, the methods most of you are using to take notes are probably not much more useful.

With one difference—here's the book. (Sorry, sister.)

The pitfalls of poor note-taking skills

Although most of you will have the good fortune *not* to sit in a classroom commanded by an obsessed nun, too many of you will still develop severe cases of carpal tunnel syndrome in crazed efforts to reproduce every single word your teachers utter.

Others will take notes so sparse that, when reviewed weeks—or merely hours later—they'll make so little sense that they might as well have been etched in Sanskrit.

Taking poor notes—which can mean too *few* or too *many*—will undoubtedly mean poor results. As in, "Here's your D and could you please see me after class?"

If you feel compelled to take down your teacher's every pearly word, or recopy your entire text, you certainly won't have much of a social life—where would you ever find the time? Maybe you're so horrified at the prospect of *reliving* those hours of lectures and chapters of text that you simply *never* review your notes. And if you skip note-taking altogether...well, I don't need to tell you what kind of grades you should expect.

Note-taking should be the ultimate exercise in good old American pragmatism. You should take notes only on the material that helps you develop a thorough understanding of your subject...and get good grades, of course. And you should do it in a way that is, first and foremost, useful and understandable to *you*. A method that's easy to use would be a real plus.

Most students have a difficult time developing a good note-taking technique and recognizing the information that always shows up on tests—an understanding of which is essential for good grades.

Failing to learn good note-taking methods, they resort to what *I* think are useless substitutes, such as tape re-corders and photocopying machines.

There is a *right* way to take notes

In this book, I will present the essentials of a note-taking system that works for me and, I'm sure, will work wonders for you. This was not a skill that just came to me, full-blown, like Aphrodite from the ocean, but one that I developed over the years—in high school, college, and on the job as a writer and editor. In the chapters ahead, you will find the distillation of that experience.

And you'll discover that my tried-and-true system is one that is not only easy to learn and *inexpensive,* but one that you can begin using *immediately*—whether taking notes in class, studying a textbook or another reading assignment, gathering information for a term paper, or preparing for an exam.

Here's what you'll learn in ***Take Notes:*** In Chapters 2, 3, and 4, we'll concentrate on what to do *before, during,* and *after* class to ensure award-winning class notes. I'll give you my thoughts on tape recorders, discuss the importance of learning to listen, talk about taking notes in different *kinds* of classes, even teach you some shorthand and mapping techniques.

In Chapters 5, 6, and 7, we'll talk about taking notes from your textbooks, covering everything from highlighting and outlining to time lines and concept trees. Plus a section on working with technical (for example, math and science) texts.

Chapter 8 will help you prepare great notes for oral reports or speeches. Chapter 9 is your chance to practice all of the note-taking skills I'm sure you will have shortly mastered.

What's in it for you?

What are the benefits to you when you learn to take better notes? This book will not only help you become better at writing down essential facts, it will help you improve your *listening* skills. And guide you toward the path of real learning, rather than just learning how to memorize and repeat names, dates, and factoids.

Good note-taking skills will put you in greater control of your time and provide you with a better way to organize your student life. You'll no longer find yourself spending long hours filling notebook after notebook with redundant material, just so you can spend hours rereading it all later. Nor will you ever again need to pull "all-nighters" just before a big test on a subject for which you have inadequate notes.

At test time, you will have the essentials of your class and homework assignments at your fingertips—review will be a breeze.

When you have to research and write a paper, you will have a method that helps you utilize your time in the library and organize the information you gather there more effectively and efficiently. Preparing your reports will be a snap.

But developing your note-taking skills will also benefit you much further down the road. The ability to listen effectively and glean the most salient information from a meeting, speech, or presentation will be a required skill in your future—whether you're a doctor making observations for a patient's file, a business executive taking instructions from your CEO for an important project, or a parent jotting down notes as you meet with your child's teacher.

So, take pen in hand, get some paper and start taking better notes...right now.

CHAPTER 1

GATHER YOUR NOTE-TAKING EQUIPMENT

This chapter is short, because my note-taking system is very simple.

There are no expensive kits to send away for.

No special instruments to buy.

No complicated equipment to learn about.

No convoluted instructions you would need a "techie" to decipher.

Just make sure you have the following materials on hand, and we're ready to go:

1. A ball point pen.
2. A three-ring binder with dividers.
3. Notebook paper.

Okay, it's a *little* more complicated—there's one more essential item you need before you can take effective notes:

4. An active brain.

Taking notes is a *participatory* activity, whether you're sitting in a lecture or reading a homework assignment. You can't expect to take grade-winning notes if the only thing that's working is your *hand.*

In fact, if you could only bring *one* of the four required items to class, you'd be better off leaving pen, paper, and notebook at home.

Ready to go? Do you have everything? Your pen? Paper? Notebook? Brain? Don't worry, I'll show you how to use everything in the following chapters.

Chapter 2

Class notes: Learning to Listen

In one of Bob & Ray's classic radio comedy sketches, Ray plays a talk-show host whose guest is Bob, president of the Slow Talkers of America, which has come to town for its annual convention. The skit goes something like this:

Ray: So, tell me, what brings you to town?
Bob: Well...the...Slow...
Ray: Talkers of America
Bob: Talkers...
Ray: Of America
Bob: Of...
Ray: America
Bob: America...
Ray: Are having their annual convention
Bob: Are...

The impatience of Ray's character is akin to what sometimes happens to *our* minds when we're sitting through a lecture, especially one in which we can find no logical reason to be interested. No matter how fast someone speaks, she cannot deliver information fast enough to keep our minds entirely occupied. The slow pace of orally delivered information is simply not enough to hold our attention.

That's why our thoughts literally go out the window, up to the ceiling, or ahead to Saturday night's date, completely obliterating the lecture from our brain's attention.

This problem is precisely why many businesses are paying big bucks to have their executives take courses on listening. These corporate honchos might be talented, diligent and knowledgeable about their fields, but they are not learning as much as they can from clients and co-workers. Because they never learned how to *listen.*

In fact, many experts in management and education say that listening is one of the most neglected skills in the United States. We assume that if people can *hear,* they can *listen.* But nothing could be further from the truth.

You're probably thinking, "What does all of this have to do with taking notes in class?" The answer: Everything. As I said in the previous chapter, an active brain—one that is prepared to listen and respond—is key to taking effective notes.

I'm convinced that if two students attended a lecture— one copying every word the teacher uttered but not listening to the content; the other listening closely but not taking any notes—the second student would do much better on a surprise quiz at the end of the period.

What makes a good listener *good?*

Have you ever spoken to a good listener? What was it that indicated she was paying attention to you?

☞ She took her eyes off you only occasionally.

☞ She wasn't busy formulating a reply as you were speaking.

☞ She asked frequent questions.

This kind of rapt attention—which you would certainly welcome from anyone sitting through one of *your* stories—is the attitude you should bring to every lecture.

And, believe it or not, note-taking will become a way for you to improve your listening and remember more of the important information your instructors deliver in class.

"Easier said than done," you sigh? Sure it is. The classroom is as warm as a steambath. The guy in front of you is playing tic-tac-toe on his arm. There's a semi-nude game of frisbee going on just outside the window. And the teacher is delivering a droning soliloquy on the Hottentots' use of damask on castle walls.

Sometimes listening actively is a challenge, if not virtually impossible. But there are steps you can take to make it easier.

Sit near the front of the room

Minimize distractions by sitting as close to the instructor as you can.

Why is it the only time people seem to *want* to be in front is when they're attending a play or a concert? I've noticed that adults who attend meetings, high school or college students in lectures, even churchgoers filling up the pews, inevitably head for the *back* of the room first, as if some deadly disease were lurking on those front-row seats. While this practice gives people at meetings the opportunity to exit unnoticed, it does nothing for students—except make it harder to hear or be heard.

The farther you sit from the teacher, the more difficult it is to listen. Sitting toward the back of the room means more heads bobbing around in front of you, more students staring out the window—encouraging you to do the same.

Sitting up front has several benefits. You will make a terrific first impression on the instructor—you might very well be the only student sitting in the front row. He'll see immediately that you have come to class to listen and learn, not just take up space.

You'll be able to hear the instructor's voice, and the instructor will be able to hear *you* when you ask and answer questions.

Finally, being able to see the teacher clearly will help ensure that your eyes don't wander around the room and out the windows, taking your brain with them.

So, if you have the option of picking your desk in class, sit right down front.

Avoid distracting classmates

The gum cracker. The doodler. The practical joker. The whisperer. Even the perfume sprayer. Your classmates may be wonderful friends, entertaining lunch companions, and ultimate weekend party animals, but their quirks, idiosyncrasies, and personal hygiene habits can prove distracting when you sit next to them in class.

Knuckle-cracking, note-passing, whispering, and giggling are just some of the evils that can divert your attention in the middle of your math professor's discourse on quadratic equations. Avoid them (the distractions, not the equations. Sorry.).

Sit up straight

To listen effectively, you must sit correctly, in a way that will let you stay comfortable and relatively still during the entire lecture. If you are uncomfortable—if parts of your body start to ache or fall asleep—your attention will inevitably wander from the instructor's words.

As the old saying goes, "The mind can retain only as much as the bottom can sustain."

Listen for verbal clues

Identifying note-worthy material means finding a way to separate the wheat—that which you *should* write down—from the chaff—that which you should *ignore.* How do you do that? By *listening* for verbal clues and *watching* for the nonverbal ones.

Certainly not all teachers will give you the clues you're seeking. But many will invariably signal important material in the way they present it—pausing (waiting for all the pens to rise), repeating the same point (perhaps even one already made and repeated in your textbook), slowing down their normally supersonic lecture speed, speaking more loudly (or more softly), even by simply stating, "I think the following is important."

There are also a number of words that should *signal* note-worthy material (and, at the same time, give you the clues you need to logically organize your notes): "First of all," "Most importantly," "Therefore," "As a result," "To summarize," "On the other hand," "On the contrary," "The following (number of) reasons (causes, effects, decisions, facts, etc.)."

Such words and phrases give you the clues to not just write down the material that follows but to put it in context—to make a list ("First," "The following reasons"); establish a cause-and-effect relationship ("Therefore," "As a result"); establish opposites or alternatives ("On the other hand," "On the contrary"); signify a conclusion ("Therefore," "To summarize"); or offer an explanation or definition.

Look for nonverbal clues

Studies on human behavior indicate that only a small portion of any message is delivered by the words themselves. A greater portion is transmitted by body language, facial expression, and tone of voice.

I'll spend some time later in this book helping you learn how to identify the most important points of a lecture, but take advantage of the fact that the instructor—through body language, expressions, and tone of voice—will already be doing that identification work for you.

Most instructors will go off on tangents of varying relevance to the subject matter. Some will be important, but, at least during your first few classes with that particular teacher, you won't be able to tell which.

Body language can be your clue.

If the teacher begins looking out the window, or his eyes glaze over, he's sending you a clear signal: "Put your pen down. This isn't going to be on the test. (So don't take notes!)"

On the other hand, if she turns to write something on the blackboard, makes eye contact with several students, and/or gestures dramatically, she's sending a clear signal about the importance of the point she's making.

Of course, there are many exceptions to this rule. For example, my first-year calculus instructor would occasionally launch into long diatribes about his mother or air pollution, with tones more impassioned than any he used working through differential equations.

And there was the trigonometry professor I endured who would get most worked up about the damage being done to the nation's sidewalks by the deadly menace of chewing gum.

Nevertheless, learn how to be a detective—don't overlook the clues.

Ask questions often

Being an active listener means asking *yourself* if you understand everything that has been discussed. If the answer is no, you must ask the instructor questions at an appropriate time or write down the questions you need answered in order to understand the subject fully.

Challenge yourself to draw conclusions from what the instructor is saying. Don't just sit there letting your hand take notes. Let your *mind* do something, too. Think about the subject matter, how it relates to what you've been assigned to read and other facts you've been exposed to.

To tape or not to tape

I am opposed to using a tape recorder in class as a substitute for an active brain for the following reasons:

☞ **It's time-consuming.** To be cynical about it, not only will you have to waste time sitting in class, you'll have to waste more time listening to that class *again*!

☞ **It's virtually useless for review.** Fast-forwarding and rewinding cassettes to find the salient points of a lecture is my definition of torture. During the hectic days before an exam, do you really want to waste time listening to a whole lecture when you could just reread your notes, presuming you had some?

☞ **It offers no back-up.** Only the most diligent students will record *and* take notes. But what happens if your tape recorder malfunctions?

How useful will blank or distorted tapes be to you when it's time to review? If you're going to take notes as a back-up, why not just take good notes and leave the tape recorder home?

☞ **It costs money.** Compare the price of blank paper and a pen to that of recorder, batteries, and tapes. The cost of batteries *alone* should convince you that you're better off going the low-tech route.

☞ **You miss the "live" clues** we discussed earlier. When all you have is a tape of your lecture, you don't see that zealous flash in your teacher's eyes, the passionate arm-flailing, the stern set of the jaw, any and all of which should scream, "Pay attention. I guarantee this will be on your test!"

Having spent all my fury against tape recorders, I concede that there are times they can be useful. Such as when your head is so stuffed up with a cold that "active listening" during a long lecture is virtually impossible.

Or when the material is so obtuse, you know you have to listen to it more than once just to begin to understand it.

Within the first five minutes of the first lecture of my freshman "honors" physics class at Princeton, I was totally lost—and I knew, even then, I would never *not* be lost. I tried tape recording the class, hoping against hope, I suppose, that listening to the monotone drone of formulas and theorems and hypotheses would somehow make more sense in the quiet of my room than it did in a classful of furiously scratching students.

It didn't help. I understood *less* after listening to the tape. But I'll also admit that it *may* have helped someone less scientifically dense than I.

With these possible exceptions noted, I still maintain that a tape recorder will never be an ample substitute for well-developed listening skills.

Note-taking and ADD

Three aspects of ADDers that we discussed previously make it very difficult for them in note-taking situations, especially in a classroom setting: They're easily distracted, have a short attention span and have difficulty processing auditory information. Which means that even if they manage to remain interested, they may be distracted by anything else inside or outside the classroom. If they beat that, they may simply fail to process the lecture everyone else is hearing.

There are four key solutions to these problems. First, despite what I concluded only a couple of paragraphs ago, ADDers *should* tape record lectures. This will enable them to relisten and reprocess information they may have missed the first time around. (Students can also consider asking their professors for their own detailed outlines, notes, or even typed-up lectures that they can duplicate. I have never heard of anyone asking for these, and I can see why professors wouldn't agree, but it's certainly worth a try!)

Second, rather than attempting to take notes using words—even the abbreviations and shorthand I recommend in Chapter 4—ADDers should instead utilize pictures, mapping, diagrams, etc., in lieu of outlines or "word" notes.

Third, they should also learn and practice the process of visualization. Anyone with ADD (or a parent of one) should realize that the mental imaging taught in many memory courses is precisely what will help an ADDer deal with this problem. Practice making visual pictures of things while having conversations; create mental images of lists of things to do; visualize yourself doing things you commit to. And practice paying attention when people talk to you. Listen carefully.

Fourth, joining a study group should be mandatory. A bright ADDer has a lot to add (pardon the pun) to any group, and access to the group's notes may well be life-saving.

CHAPTER 3

CLASS NOTES: SUCCESSFUL STRATEGIES

Note-taking strategies?

What could *possibly* be so complicated about taking notes that one would need *strategies*.

After all, it's just a matter of writing down what the instructor says, isn't it? Okay, maybe not verbatim, just the key stuff, but...

If you want to take notes *effectively,* there is much more to it.

As I've said before, taking down everything the teacher says is *not* an effective strategy. In fact, the most prolific note-takers might be downright *terrible* students.

You can make life easier on yourself if you follow these successful note-taking strategies—and become a *terrific* student in the process.

Know your teacher

First and foremost, you must know and understand the kind of teacher you've got and his or her likes, dislikes, preferences, style, and what he or she expects you to get out of the class. Depending on your analysis of your teacher's habits, goals and tendencies, preparation may vary quite a bit, whatever the class format.

Take something as simple as asking questions during class, which I encourage you to do whenever you didn't understand a key point. Some teachers are very confident fielding questions at any time during a lesson; others prefer questions to be held until the end of the day's lesson; still others discourage questions (or any interaction for that matter) entirely. Learn when and how your teacher likes to field questions and ask them accordingly.

No matter how ready a class is to enter into a freewheeling discussion, some teachers fear losing control and veering away from their very specific lesson plan. Such teachers may well encourage discussion but always try to steer it into a predetermined path (their lesson plan). Other teachers thrive on chaos, in which case you can never be sure what's going to happen.

Approaching a class with the former teacher should lead you to participate as much as possible in the class discussion, but warn you to stay within whatever boundaries he or she has obviously set.

Getting ready for a class taught by the latter kind of teacher requires much more than just reading the text—there will be a lot of emphasis on your understanding key concepts, interpretation, analysis, and your ability to apply those lessons to cases never mentioned in your text at all!

Some teachers' lesson plans or lectures are, at worst, a review of what's in the text and, at best, a review plus some discussion of sticky points or areas they feel may give you problems. Others use the text or other assignments merely as a jumping-off point—their lectures or lesson plans might cover numerous points that aren't in your text at all. Preparing for the latter kind of class will require much more than rote memorization of facts and figures—you'll have to be ready to give examples, explain concepts in context, and more.

Most of your teachers and professors will probably have the same goals: to teach you how to think, learn important facts and principles of the specific subject they teach, and, perhaps, how to apply them in your own way.

In classes like math or science, your ability to apply what you've learned to specific problems is paramount.

Others, like your English teacher, will require you to analyze and interpret various works, but may emphasize the "correct" interpretation, too.

Whatever situation you find yourself in—and you may well have one or more of each of the above "types"—you will need to adapt the skills we will cover in this chapter to each situation.

In general, here's how you should plan to prepare for any class before you walk through the door and take your seat.

Complete all assignments

Regardless of a particular teacher's style or the classroom format he or she is using, virtually every course you take will have a formal text (or two or three or more) assigned to it. Though the way the text explains or covers particular topics may differ substantially from your teacher's approach to the same material, your text is still the basis of the course and a key ingredient in your studying.

You *must* read it, plus any other assigned books, *before* you get to class.

You may sometimes feel you can get away without reading assigned books beforehand, especially in a lecture format where you *know* the chances of being called on are somewhere between slim to none. But fear of being questioned on the material is certainly not the only reason I stress reading the material that's been assigned. You will be lost if the professor decides—for the first time ever!—to spend the entire period asking *the students* questions. I've had it happen. And it was *not* a pleasant experience for the unprepared.

You'll also find it harder to take clear and concise notes because you won't know what's in the text (in which case you'll be frantically taking notes on material you could have underlined in your books the night before) or be able to evaluate the relative importance of the teacher's remarks.

If you're heading for a discussion group, how can you participate without your reading as a basis? I think the lousiest feeling in the world is sitting in a classroom knowing that, sooner or later, you are going to be called on...and that you don't know the material at all.

Remember: Completing your reading assignment includes not just reading the *main* text but any *other* books or articles previously assigned, plus handouts that may have been passed out. It also means completing any non-reading assignments—turning in a lab report, preparing a list of topics, or being ready to present your oral report.

Review your notes

Both from your reading and from the previous class. Your teacher is probably going to start this lecture or discussion from the point he or she left off last time. And you probably won't remember where that point was from week to week...unless you check your notes.

Have questions ready

Go over your questions before class. That way, you'll be able to check off the ones the lecturer or teacher answers along the way and only ask those left unanswered.

Prepare required materials

Including your notebook, text, pens or pencils, and other such basics, plus particular class requirements like a calculator, drawing paper, or other books.

Before we get into how to take notes, it's important to talk about how to set up your notebook(s). There are a variety of ways you can organize your note-taking system:

1. Get one big two- or three-ring binder (probably three or more inches thick) that will be used for all notes from all classes. This will require a hole punch, "tab" dividers, and a healthy supply of prepunched paper.

   You can divide the binder into separate sections for each course/class, in each of which you will keep notes from your lectures and discussion groups, reading lists, assignment deadlines and any course handouts—all material set up in chronological fashion.

   Alternatively, you can further subdivide each section into separate sections for reading notes, class notes, and handouts.

The binder offers several advantages over composition books and spiral notebooks.

☞ It allows for *easy and neat insertion and re-
moval* of notes. If you've written down a page
of notes that you later realize is useless, you
can easily get rid of it.

☞ More importantly, the binder allows you to
supplement and reorganize your notes. You
can—with the aid of an inexpensive hole
puncher—insert handouts and pertinent
quizzes, photostats of articles from periodicals, and completed homework assignments
near appropriate notes. Also, if instructors
expand upon earlier lessons, you can place
your new notes in the right place—they'll
make more sense and be more useful when
you review for exams and term papers.

☞ The binder allows you to *travel light*—you
don't even have to carry it to class; leave it
home. Carry a folder with enough sheets of
blank paper to classes; sort your notes and
file them in your binder every night, an exercise that will take you all of two minutes.

The binder system also has two *dis*advantages:

1. Holes that constantly tear, requiring you to
patiently paste on those reinforcing circles, a
boring and time-wasting task.

2. Woe unto ye who lose your binders, for
within it is everything ye cherish, for surely
ye shall wallow in a sea of incompletes for the
rest of your days.

The former problem can be solved by using either a
spring-operated binding mechanism—which requires no
holes at all, let alone "reinforcements"—or a multipocket

file folder in which weekly or daily notes can be stapled together and filed along with handouts, assignments, etc.

The latter problem can be solved by selectively "culling" your notebook every week so, at worst, you lose a week's worth of material, not an entire semester's.

2. Use one of the above systems but get smaller binders, one for each course/class (with the same options regarding the type of binder and how to protect yourself from losing all your notes—if only from a single class).

3. Use separate notebooks (they're a lot lighter than binders) for notes, both from your reading and class. Use file folders for each class to keep handouts, project notes, and copies, etc. They can be kept in an accordion file or in a multi-pocketed folder.

Whichever system you choose—one of the above or an ingenious one of your own—do *not* use the note-card system discussed in Chapter 4. Although it's my all-time favorite system for preparing research papers, it does *not* work well for class note-taking...I've tried it.

Were you listening before?

A young friend of mine boasted that he finished reading the book, *Green Eggs and Ham*, faster than anyone else in his second-grade class. Pleased that he had discovered one of my (and my daughter's) favorite Dr. Seuss stories, I asked him what he thought of the book. He replied, "I don't know. I was going so fast, I didn't have time to *read* it."

My friend, bright and eager as he is, had missed the point of his reading assignment. And undoubtedly, had his teacher given a *Green Eggs and Ham* test, he would have scored much lower than some of the slower readers in his class.

If you find yourself furiously filling your notebook with your teacher's every pearly word, you might boast the most detailed notes in the class, but I doubt you will truly understand much of what you've so diligently copied.

Why are you taking notes in class?

Are you practicing to enter a speed-writing contest?

Do you want to perfect your dictation-taking skills?

Or are you hoping to actually learn something?

Listen to what your teacher is saying. Think about it. Make sure you understand it. Paraphrase it. *Then,* write your notes.

Learning "selective" listening

Taking concise, clear notes is first and foremost the practice of discrimination—developing your ability to separate the essential from the superfluous, the key concepts, key facts, key ideas from all the rest. In turn, this requires the ability to listen to what your teacher is saying and copying down only what *you* require to understand the concept. For some, that could mean a single sentence. For others, a detailed example will be the key.

Just remember: The quality of your notes usually has little to do with their *length*—three key lines that reveal the core concepts of a whole lecture are far more valuable than paragraphs of less important data.

So why do some people keep trying to take verbatim notes, convinced that the more pages they cover with scribbles the better students they're being? It's probably a sign of insecurity—they haven't read the material and/or don't have a clue about what's being discussed, but at least they'll have complete notes!

Even if you find yourself wandering helplessly in the lecturer's wake, so unsure of what she's saying that you can't begin to separate the important, note-worthy material from the nonessential verbiage, use the techniques discussed in this book to organize and condense your notes anyway.

If you really find yourself so lost that you are just wasting your time, consider adding a review session to your schedule (to read or reread the appropriate texts) and, if the lecture or class is available again at another time, attend again. Yes, it *is*, strictly speaking, a waste of your precious study time, but *not* if it's the only way to learn and understand important material.

Understand the big picture

If you are actively listening, and listening before you write, then your understanding of the "big picture" ought to follow naturally.

Let's say your history teacher is rattling off dates and names of battles from the Franco-Prussian War. Your classmates in the back of the room may go into a panic as they scramble to jot down all the tongue-twisting foreign names that are being spewed out at machine-gun speed.

But *you*, who are sitting up front and listening actively, pause, pen in hand, as your teacher sums up her point: That battle activity increased to a frenzy in the final months before war's end. You jot down a brief note to that effect, knowing that you can check your textbook later for all the names, dates, and details of specific battles.

Your poor friends in the back, although capturing most of the battle names, missed the main point—the big picture— and now will feel compelled to memorize the list of names and dates, even though they can't quite figure out why they copied them down in the first place.

Take notes on what you don't know

You *know* the first line of the Gettysburg address. You *know* the chemical formula for water. You *know* what date Pearl Harbor was bombed. So why waste time and space writing them down?

Frequently, your teachers will present material you already know in order to set the stage for further discussion or to introduce material that is more difficult. Don't be so conditioned to automatically copy down dates, vocabulary, terms, formulas, and names that you mindlessly take notes on information you already know. You'll just be wasting your time—both in class and, later, when you review your overly detailed notes.

Tailor your note-taking to class format

The extent of note-taking required—as well as the importance of those notes to your success in class—will depend to a great extent on the format of each class. There are three different types you'll need to know and adapt to:

1. **The lecture.** Teacher speaks, you listen. Some high-school teachers conduct classes in this relatively impersonal way, but this format is usually adapted for popular college courses, such as Geology 101. In such situations, your teacher might never even know your name. Consequently, your note-taking and listening skills are the only tools you'll be able to use in your quest for top grades.

2. **The seminar.** Again, more common at the college level, seminars are also known as *tutorials* or *discussion groups.* Usually conducted by graduate students, they are often held in conjunction with the larger lectures, giving students a chance to discuss the subject matter in a group of less than 100.

Although this format places a great deal of emphasis on your question-asking-and-answering skills, you should not neglect your note-taking skills. Be all ears while the discussion is flowing, but as soon as possible *after* class, write down the most important points discussed. (Most high school classes are a combination of a lecture— the teacher introducing the particular material in that day's lesson plan—and a discussion group, which may just as often be a question-and-answer session, with the teacher doing the questioning.)

3. **Hands-on classes.** Science and language labs, art classes, and courses in industrial arts will require you to *do* something. But *while* you are doing it, remember to keep a notebook handy.

I had a chemistry teacher who, during labs, quite often launched into extensive theoretical discussions. The less dull-witted among us quickly learned to keep our notebooks close by, capturing facts and figures he never mentioned again—except on the exam!

Observe your instructor's style

All instructors (perhaps I should say all *effective* instructors) develop a plan of attack for each class. They decide what points they will make, how much time they will spend reviewing assignments and previous lessons, what texts they will refer to, what anecdotes they will bring into the lecture to provide comic relief or human interest, how much time they'll allow for questions.

Building a note-taking strategy around each instructor's typical plan of attack for lectures is another key to academic success.

Throughout junior high school and much of high school, I had to struggle to get good grades. I took copious notes, studied them every night, pored over them before every quiz and exam.

I was rewarded for my efforts with straight As, but resented the hours I had to put in while my less ambitious buddies found more intriguing ways to spend their time.

But some of the brighter kids had leisure time, too. When I asked them how they did it, they shrugged their shoulders and said they didn't know.

These students had an innate talent that they couldn't explain, a sixth sense about what to study, what were the most important things a teacher said, what instructors were most likely to ask about on tests.

In fact, when I was in a study group with some of these students, they would say, "Don't worry, she'll never ask about that." And sure enough, she never did.

What's more, these students had forgotten many of the details I was sweating. They hadn't even bothered to write any of them down, let alone try to remember them.

What these students innately knew was that items discussed during any lesson could be grouped into several categories, which varied in importance:

☞ Information not contained in the class texts and other assigned readings.

☞ Explanations of obscure material covered in the texts and readings but with which students might have difficulty.

☞ Demonstrations or examples that provided greater understanding of the subject matter.

☞ Background information that put the course material in context.

As you are listening to an instructor, decide which of these categories best fits the information being presented. This will help you determine how detailed your notes on the material should be. (This will become especially easy as you get to know the instructor.)

An example that comes to mind is that of a physics professor I had who devoted about half of every session to an examination of an important mathematician's or physicist's life and the circumstances surrounding his or her discoveries. At first, I took copious notes on these lectures, only to find that the first two exams were filled, top to bottom, with problems and formulae, not biographical questions.

Needless to say, even *I* figured out that I shouldn't take such comprehensive notes about biographical details.

Read, read, read

Most good instructors will follow a text they've selected for the course. Likewise, unless they've written the textbook themselves (which you will find surprisingly common in college), most teachers will supplement it with additional information. Good teachers will look for shortcomings in textbooks and spend varying amounts of class time filling in these gaps.

As a result, it makes sense to stay one step ahead of your instructors. Read ahead in your textbook so that, as an instructor is speaking, you know what part of the lesson you should write down and what parts of it are *already* written down in your textbook. Conversely, you'll immediately recognize the supplemental material on which you might need to take more detailed notes.

Will you be asked about this supplemental material on your exams?

Of course, if you ask your teacher that question, he'll probably say something like, "You are expected to know everything that's mentioned in this class." That's why it's best to pay attention (and not ask stupid questions you already know the answers to!).

In addition, your experience with the teacher's exams and spot quizzes will give you a great deal of insight into what he or she considers most important.

Instant replay: Review your notes

My friend Tony worked for a time as a reporter on a trade magazine. He would take voluminous notes as sources were talking to him. Days later, as he reread these notes, he'd invariably discover that he really didn't have any full, direct quotes—just snatches of sentences. He couldn't write fast enough to capture the whole thing.

The solution? No, it *wasn't* a tape recorder. It was to read the notes over *immediately* after the conversation. This would allow him to fill in the blanks, putting in the words he couldn't take down at conversational speed.

You should do the same with your class notes. Take the time to look them over briefly at lunch breaks, in study halls, when you go home. Honestly evaluate whether they will be decipherable when it comes time to study for your exams. If not, add to them what you can *while your memory of the class is still fresh.*

Even as you implement these strategies, which will reduce the amount of time you're scribbling notes, you'll still find yourself in situations where you want to capture a lot of information—quickly.

I'll show you how in the next chapter.

CHAPTER 4

MAKING SHORT WORK OF CLASS NOTES

You don't have to be a master of shorthand to stream-line your note-taking. Here are five ways:

1. **Eliminate vowels.** As a sign that was ubiquitous in the New York City subways used to proclaim, "If u cn rd ths, u cn gt a gd jb." (If you can read this, you can get a good job.) And, we might add, "u cn b a btr stdnt."

2. **Use word beginnings** ("rep" for representative, "con" for congressperson) and other easy-to-remember abbreviations.

3. **Stop putting periods** after all abbreviations (they add up!)

4. **Use standard symbols** in place of words. Here is a list that will help you out in most of your classes (you may recognize many of these symbols from math and logic):

≈	Approximately
w/	With
w/o	Without
wh/	Which
→	Resulting in
←	As a result of/consequence of
+	And or also
*	Most importantly
cf	Compare; in comparison; in relation to
ff	Following
<	Less than
>	More than
=	The same as
↑	Increasing
↓	Decreasing
esp	Especially
Δ	Change
⊂	It follows that
∴	Therefore
∵	Because

5. **Create your own symbols** and abbreviations based on your needs and comfort-level.

There are two specific symbols I think you'll want to create—they'll be needed again and again:

Ⓦ That's my symbol for "*What?*" as in "What the heck does that mean?" "What did she say?" or "What happened? I'm completely lost!" It denotes something that's been missed—leave space in your notes to fill in the missing pieces of the puzzle after class.

(M) That's my symbol for "My idea" or "My thought." I want to clearly separate my own thoughts during a lecture from the professor's—include too many of your own ideas (without noting that they *are* yours) and your notes begin to lose some serious value!

Feel free to use your own code for these two important instances; you certainly don't have to use mine.

Although I recommend using all the "common" symbols and abbreviations listed previously *all* the time, in *every* class, in order to maintain consistency, you may want to create specific symbols or abbreviations for each class. In chemistry, for example, "TD" may stand for thermodynamics, "K" for the Kinetic Theory of Gases (but don't mix it up with the "K" for Kelvin). In history, "GW" is the Father of our Country, "ABE" is Mr. Honesty, "FR" could be French Revolution (or "freedom rider"), "IR", the Industrial Revolution.

How do you keep everything straight? No matter what, summarize your abbreviations on each class's notes, perhaps on the front page in a corner. If you're a little more adventurous, create a list on the first page of that class's notebook or a binder section for the abbreviations and symbols you intend to use regularly throughout the semester.

Expanding on your "shorthand"

While you're listening to your instructor, you should be thinking about what you're writing down. Lectures are filled with so many words that will not be at all helpful when you sit down to study for the big exam. Writing all of *those* words down—while missing some of the truly important points of the lecture—is counterproductive: Your notes may look impressively complete, but what are they completely full *of?* All the important stuff, or...?

For instance, if your teacher says, "It's surprising to me that so few people know the role that women pilots played in World War II. We normally hear only about 'Rosie the Riveter' and the role women played at *home*. But the shortage of male pilots at the beginning of the war virtually demanded that women be given a chance, if only, in some areas, to ferry planes, tow targets, or test repaired planes." you could write down something like:

> Wmn's rl/PLs—WW2 < '
> short/men: Ferry Ps/tow tgts/test
> rep Ps

I've written "PL" for pilot and "P" for plane presuming that both words will occur frequently in a lecture on this topic. The more frequently a term occurs, the *more* reason you have to simplify it, preferably to a single letter. But I wrote out "ferry," a word that would not tend to come up too often, as well as "test," figuring the extra "e" in both wouldn't take much time.

Continue to abbreviate *more* as additional terms become readily recognizable—in that way, the speed and effectiveness of your note-taking will increase as the school year grinds on.

I've also noticed that many students are prone to write *big* when they are writing fast and to use only a portion of the width of their paper. I guess they figure that turning over pages quickly means they are taking great notes. All it really means is that they are taking notes that will be difficult to read or use when it's review time.

Force yourself to write small and take advantage of the entire width of your note paper. The less unnecessary movement the better.

In this and the preceding chapter, I've discussed how to prepare and implement a note-taking strategy in class. Now, let's look at a sample lecture so you can practice your newly developed skills.

Here is part of a lecture that was one of my favorites in college. I've numbered the paragraphs here so that they can be easily referred to later.

The Comic Perspective in Comic Novels

1   The comic perspective is one which finds its most successful expression in a presentation of contrasting methods of viewing the world. These could be categorized as that of the cynic and that of the saint. The laughter and the sense of irony that a comic work of literature can instill in its readers is a result of the clash between these methods of seeing the world.

2   If the work of literature is to be considered at all successful, its readers will surely find themselves beset with the task of sorting among the alternatives offered by the idealistic and realistic sensibilities embodied within the characters and/or the narrative voice.

3   The comic novel is one which, at last, must leave its readers experiencing its world in the way a child experiences his: with wonder, honesty, imagination, and confusion.

4   If we conduct an overview of protagonists in great comic novels, we find characters who are very much like children. They are innocent, idealistic, and often naive. Moreover, authors of the great comic novels go to great lengths to deny their characters a detailed past. It is almost as if

the protagonists are born fully grown into the world of the novel.

5   We can learn very few biographical details about Don Quixote. We are told only that he has filled his head with the ideals and dreams of chivalry through his incessant reading of romantic literature. Moving ahead to Dickens, we find in *The Pickwick Papers* a protagonist that the author continually denies a past. It is as if, for Dickens, the intrusion or even the introduction of the past into the present must inevitably bring with it a diminution of integrity and self-sufficiency. In fact, the only instance of Mr. Pickwick attempting to remember his past results in the protagonist falling asleep before he can do so.

6   When we get to the 20th-century comic novels, we notice a continuity of this device. Paul Pennyfeather is delivered into the chaotic world of *Decline and Fall* as if from a womb. Evelyn Waugh devotes three sentences to the history of his protagonist. He is an orphan (someone who by definition cannot know his past) who "lived in Onslow Square with his guardian, who was abysmally bored by his company..."

Although you don't have the luxury of being able to *hear* these words, as, of course, you would in a real lecture, pretend that you were suddenly stripped of the benefits afforded by the printed page—the ability to reread a portion of a lecture that, after all, you wouldn't be able to "rehear."

What would you come up with? How many of the actual words from the lecture would turn up in your notes? Would you be feverishly trying to write down everything the professor said?

While this lecture *sounds* eloquent, it has more sizzle to it than steak. Hence, your notes can be quite brief. Here are what mine looked like (with the paragraph references added):

Cmc Prspctv/Cmc Nvls

1. CP=2 wys 2 C wrld—cynic, saint. Clash=lftr
2. Chrctrs, nrrtr embdy idlsm or rlsm
3. Rdr xprnc=chld's wrld view=cnfused, inncnt
4. Prtgnsts like kids—no past
5. eg Dk/PP, Cv/DQ
6. eg EW/Pnnyf

Lincoln in shorthand

I readily admit that reducing an instructor's eloquent words to this type of shorthand is like summarizing Lincoln's "Gettysburg Address" as:

"Bad war. Guys died. What a shame. Hope it ends soon."

Trying to capture the eloquence and missing half of the teacher's points would make much less sense. And note that very little effort has been put into this "shorthand" approach—a few symbols (=, eg), a couple of obvious substitutions (2 for two, C for see) and the omission of most vowels. Yet it is organized, understandable, and took a minimum of time to write down.

What taking such brief notes will do is allow you to sit back, listen, and watch the instructor. This will help you capture the entire *message* that he or she is communicating, not just the *words*. If you think that the words are very important, try to elaborate on your shorthand while the professor's words are still rattling around in your head—right after the lecture. It's not a bad idea to do this anyway, especially as you start to develop your own note-taking shorthand. It'll allow you to make sure you understand your own abbreviations.

Are you ready to lose the vowels?

Do you think this sort of shorthand will work for you? You probably won't at first. When I first entered college, I found that I couldn't trust my notes. I was trying to write too much down, which meant that I couldn't trust my note-*taking*. As I gained more experience and developed much of the system in this and the previous two chapters, my note-taking became more and more productive.

Just be careful—in your fervor to adopt my shorthand system, don't abbreviate so much that your notes are absolutely unintelligible to you almost as soon as you write them!

Just come up with a note-taking shorthand system that makes sense to *you*. You may certainly choose to abbreviate less, to write a little more. Whatever system you develop, make sure it serves the right purpose: giving you the time to really *listen* to your instructors, rather than writing down only what they say.

Draw your way to good grades

The one problem with this whole note-taking system is that many people find it more difficult to remember words rather than pictures.

Problem solved: ***Mapping*** is another way to take notes that stresses a more visual style—drawing or diagramming your notes rather than just writing them down.

Let me show you how to map the first few pages of this chapter as an example. Start with a clean sheet of paper and, boxed or circled in the center, write the main topic:

Developing shorthand skills

How do you want your picture to read—top to bottom, bottom to top, clockwise in a circle, counterclockwise? I'm going to set mine up top to bottom. After deciding on the first major topic ("How to streamline note-taking") and placing it on your map, add the detail:

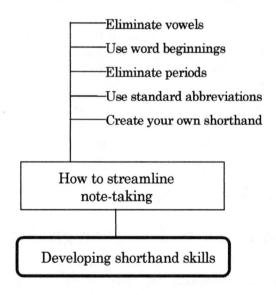

The second major topic ("Expanding your shorthand") and those that follow take their place in the line or circle you've chosen, in the direction you've chosen. I've completed a map containing everything covering up to our discussion of mapping on page 290 of this chapter.

Talk the talk

In many nonlecture classes, you will find that discussion, mostly in the form of questions and answers, is actively encouraged. This dialogue serves to both confirm your knowledge and comprehension of specific subject matter and identify those areas in which you need work.

Whatever the format in which you find yourself, participate in any discussion to the best of your ability. Most teachers consider class participation a key ingredient in the grades they mete out. No matter how many papers and tests you ace, if you never open your mouth in class, you may be surprised (but shouldn't be) to get less than an A.

If you are having trouble following a particular line of thought or argument, ask for a review or for clarification.

Don't ask questions or make points looking to impress your teacher—your real motive will probably be pretty obvious. Remember what you *are* there for—to learn the material and master it.

Based on the professor's preferences and the class setup, ask the questions you feel need answers.

Be careful you don't innocently distract yourself from practicing your now excellent note-taking skills by either starting to analyze something you don't understand, or worse, creating mental arguments because you disagree with something your teacher or a classmate said. Taking the time to mentally frame an elaborate question is equally distracting. All three cause the same problem: *You're not listening!*

Finally, listen closely to the words of your classmates. Knowledge has no boundaries, and you'll often find their comments, attitudes, and opinions as helpful and insightful as your instructor's.

What if you're shy or just get numb whenever you're called on? Ask a question rather than taking part in the discussion—it's easier and, over time, may help you break the ice and jump into the discussion. If you really can't open your mouth without running a fever, consider a remedial course, like Dale Carnegie.

Most importantly, prepare and practice. Fear of standing in front of a class or even of participating from the safety of your seat is, for many of you, really a symptom of lack of confidence.

And *lack of confidence stems from lack of preparation.* The more prepared you are—if you know the material backwards and forwards—the more likely you will be able, even *want,* to raise your hand and "strut your stuff." Practicing with friends, parents, or relatives may also help.

If you are having trouble with oral reports, they are covered separately in Chapter 8. I think you'll find the hints I've included there will eliminate a lot of the fear such talks seem to engender.

What to do *after* class

As soon as possible after your class, review your notes, fill in the "blanks," mark down questions you need to research in your text or ask during the next class, and remember to mark any new assignments on your weekly calendar.

I tend to discourage recopying your notes as a general practice, because I believe it's more important to work on taking good notes the first time around and not wasting the time it takes to recopy. *But* if you tend to write fast and illegibly, it might also be a good time to rewrite your notes so they're readable, taking the opportunity to summarize as you go. The better your notes, the better your chance of capturing and recalling the pertinent material.

It is not easy for most high school students to do so, but in college, where you have a greater say in scheduling your classes, an open period between classes ("one period on, one off") is the perfect opportunity to review that class's notes and prepare for the next one.

Because I stressed so often the importance of reading your texts *before* you stroll into the classroom, let's turn our attention to what you need to do *out*side of class in order to be a star *in* class.

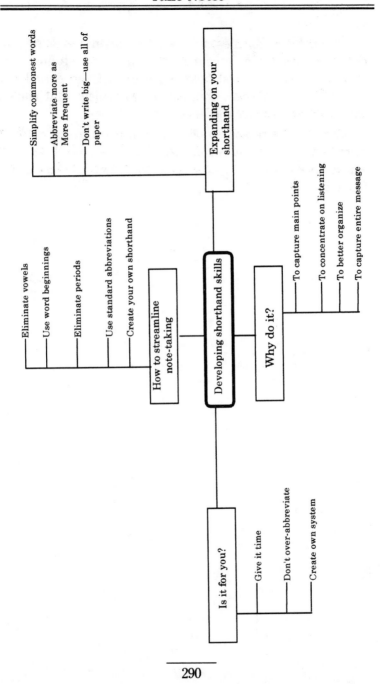

Developing shorthand skills

Expanding on your shorthand
- Simplify commonest words
- Abbreviate more as More frequent
- Don't write big—use all of paper

How to streamline note-taking
- Eliminate vowels
- Use word beginnings
- Eliminate periods
- Use standard abbreviations
- Create your own shorthand

Why do it?
- To capture main points
- To concentrate on listening
- To better organize
- To capture entire message

Is it for you?
- Give it time
- Don't over-abbreviate
- Create own system

CHAPTER 5

TEXTS: READ FIRST, THEN WRITE

I'm sure it's abundantly clear to all of you that not many best-selling authors moonlight writing textbooks. Most of the tomes given to you in classes—even the ones for *literature* classes—are poorly written, badly organized cures for insomnia. Dull is the kindest word to describe all but a few of them.

That said, it's also clear that no matter how dull the prose, your job is to mine the important details from your textbooks to get good grades. Lest you have to wade through that lifeless mass of words more than once, why not take great notes the *first* time through?

You can borrow many of the strategies you implemented for taking notes in class for your attack on your reading assignments. Just as you used your active brain to listen carefully to what your teacher talked about, you can use that same piece of equipment to *read* actively.

☞ Read, then write.

☞ Make sure you understand the big picture.

☞ Take notes on what you don't know.

These same principles we discussed in conjunction with taking notes in class apply to taking notes on your reading materials. But there are some additional strategies you should also consider.

Change the way you read

When we read a book for pleasure, we tend to read, naturally, from beginning to the end. (Though some of us may be guilty of taking a peek at the last chapter of a suspenseful mystery novel.) Yet this linear approach, beginning at point A and moving in a direct manner to point B, is not necessarily the most effective way to read texts for information.

If you find yourself plowing diligently through your texts without having the faintest clue as to what you've read, it's time to change the way you read. The best students don't wade through each chapter of their textbooks from beginning to end. Instead, they read in an almost circular fashion. Here's how:

Look for clues

If we have curled up with the latest Stephen King thriller, we fully expect some clues along the way that will hint at the gory horror to come. And we count on Agatha Christie to subtly sprinkle keys to her mysteries' solutions long before they are resolved in the drawing room.

But most of you probably never tried to solve the mystery of your own textbooks by using the telltale signs and signals almost all of them contain. That's right—*textbooks are riddled with clues* that will reveal to the perceptive student all the note-worthy material that must be captured. Here's where to find them:

Chapter heads and subheads. Bold-faced headings and subheadings announce the detail about the main topic. And in some textbooks, paragraph headings or bold-faced "lead-ins" announce that the author is about to provide finer details. So start each reading assignment by going through the chapter, beginning to end, but *reading only the bold-faced heads and subheads.*

This process of headline reading takes only a few minutes, but it lays the groundwork for a more intelligent and efficient reading of the chapter. You'll have some idea where the author is headed, and this will give you a greater sense of what the most important details are.

End-of-chapter summaries. If you read a mystery from start to finish, the way the author hopes you will, you're likely to get thrown off the scent of the murderer by "red herrings" and other common detective novel devices. However, if you read the last part first, knowing the outcome would help you notice how the author constructed the novel and built an open-and-shut case for his master sleuth. You'd notice a plethora of details about the eventually unmasked murderer that might have gone unnoticed were she just another of the leading suspects. Similarly, knowing what the author is driving at in a textbook will help you look for the important building blocks for his conclusions while you're reading. Although it may not be as much fun to read a mystery novel this way, when it comes to textbook reading and note-taking, it will make you a much more *active* reader, and, consequently, make it much less likely that you will doze off while being beaten senseless by the usual ponderous prose.

Pictures, graphs, charts. Most textbooks, particularly those in the sciences, will have charts, graphs, numerical tables, maps, and other illustrations. All too many students see these as mere filler—padding to glance at, then forget.

If you're giving these charts and graphs short shrift, you're really shortchanging *yourself.* You don't have to redraw the tables in your notes, but it would be helpful to observe how they supplement the text, what points they emphasize, and make note of these. This will help you put them into your own words, which will help you remember them later. And it will ensure that you don't have to continually refer to your textbooks when brushing up for an exam.

Highlighted terms, vocabulary, and other facts. In some textbooks, you'll discover that key terms and information are highlighted within the body text. (And I *don't* mean by a previous student; consider such yellow-swathed passages with caution—their value is directly proportional to that student's final grade, which you don't know.) Whether bold-face, italic, or boxed, this is usually an indication that the material is note-worthy.

Questions. Some textbook publishers use a format in which key points are emphasized by questions, either within the body or at the end of the chapter. If you read these questions *before* reading the chapter, you'll have a better idea of what material you need to pay closer attention to.

These standard organizational tools should make your reading job simpler. The next time you have to read a history, geography, or similar text, try skimming the assigned pages first. Read the heads, the subheads, and the call outs. Read the first sentence of each paragraph. Then go back and start reading the details.

To summarize the skimming process:

1. Read and be sure you understand the title or heading. Try rephrasing it as a question for further clarification of what you will read.

2. Examine all the subheadings, illustrations, and graphics—these will help you identify the significant matter within the text.

3. Read thoroughly the introductory paragraphs, the summary at the end, and any questions at chapter's end.

4. Read the first sentence of every paragraph—this generally includes the main idea.

5. Evaluate what you have gained from this process: Can you answer the questions at the end of the chapter? Could you intelligently participate in a class discussion of the material?

6. Write a brief summary that capsulizes what you have learned from your skimming.

7. Based on this evaluation, decide whether a more thorough reading is required.

Now for the fine print

Now that you have gotten a good overview of the contents by reading the heads and subheads, reviewing the summary, picking up on the highlighted words and information, and considering the review questions that may be included, you're finally ready to read the chapter. If a more thorough reading is then required, turn back to the beginning. *Read one section (chapter, etc.) at a time.*

See if this method doesn't help you get a better handle on any assignment right from the start.

Because you did a preliminary review first, you'll find that your reading will go much faster.

*But...*don't assume that now you can speed through your reading assignment. Don't rush through your textbook, or you'll just have to read it again.

Sure, we've all heard about the boy and girl wonders who can whip through books at 1,000 or even 2,000 words per minute and retain everything they read (or so they claim), but most of us never will read that fast. Which is fine—it's better to read something slowly and *remember* it, than rush it into oblivion.

Many great students—even those in law school or taking umpteen courses on the 19th-century novel—never achieve reading speeds of even close to 1,000 words per minute. Some of them have to read passages they don't understand again and again to get the point.

And there's nothing wrong with that.

This is the most intelligent way to read—with comprehension, not speed—as your primary goal.

Reading technical texts

Math and science texts (or any highly technical ones, such as economics) require slightly different handling. Do everything covered in our discussion of skimming texts, with one addition: Make *sure* you understand the concepts expressed in the various graphs or charts.

But *do not proceed* to the next chapter or even the next section if you have questions about the previous one. You must understand one section before moving on to the next, because the next concept is usually based on the previous one. If there are sample problems, solve those that tie in with the section you have just read to make sure you understand the concepts imparted. If you still fail to grasp a key concept, equation, etc., start again and try again. But *don't* move on—you'll just be wasting your time.

These texts really require a slow, steady approach, even one with a lot of backtracking, or, for that matter, a lot of wrong turns. "Trial and error" *is* an accepted method of scientific research. The key, though, is to make it *informed* trial and error—having a clear idea of where you are heading and *learning* from each error. While trial and error is okay, it is much more important to be able to easily apply the same analysis (solution, reasoning) to a slightly different problem, which requires real understanding. Getting the right answer just because you eliminated every *wrong* one may be a very viable strategy for taking a test but it's a lousy way to assure yourself you've actually learned something.

Understanding is especially essential in any technical subject. Yes, it's easy for some of you to do great on math tests because you have a great memory and/or are lucky and/or have an innate math "sense." Trust me, sooner or later, your luck runs out, your memory overloads, and your calculations become "sense"-less. You *will* reach a point where, without understanding, you will be left confused on the shore, watching your colleagues stroke heroically off to the promised land.

It happened to me in college, where I was (*very* briefly) an electrical engineering major. As long as logarithms and integral calculus were theoretical—just remember the rules, get a little lucky, and count on my built-in math "radar"—I could shine. Not only did I get a perfect 800 on the math section of the SAT, I got an 800 on the *Calculus Achievement Test* (now the SAT-II). A budding mathematical genius, *ne c'est pas?*

Sure. Until I had to actually show I *understood* the concepts underlying all the rules and calculations, to use that understanding as the basis for practical reasoning and applying the concepts. Remember the TV show *Lost in Space?* Me during freshman year physics *and* physical chemistry.

Good-bye, "math sense." Hello, English major.

CHAPTER 6

TEXTS: NOW GET OUT YOUR PEN

Mr. Lonney's assignment sounded simple enough: Read the photocopy of *The Atlantic* magazine article about Hemingway's years in Key West for a quiz on Friday. A fairly typical assignment that three students in the class chose to tackle in three completely different ways:

Sally read the article with her legs over the side of a sofa during a *Star Trek* rerun. In this way, she missed most of the salient points in the article, though not what the trouble with tribbles really was (for the 13th time). During commercials, however, she really hunkered down and paid close attention to what she was reading. This made Sally quite proud of herself—she usually didn't bother to read assignments at all, particularly ones as boring as this one.

Kevin spent an hour at his desk on Thursday night reading the article—twice—and highlighting what he felt were the most important parts. He was confident that he had a good grasp of the material and completely understood the most important points of the article.

Barb spent about three hours going back and forth between the article and a legal pad, writing down long, complete sentences that, all told, summarized the salient points and a good many details of the article pretty well. She planned to read over the notes during the study hall she had before Mr. Lonney's class.

Who got the best grade?

Barb put in the most time. And she did get an A. Kevin earned a B+. Sally was pretty happy with the C- she didn't have to work too hard for.

Who had the right approach?

Barb, right?

Wrong. The answer is that old favorite of the multiple-choice test: none of the above.

A is not for effort

Even though the ends in some way justified Barb's means, the amount of effort she puts into most of her assignments also ensures that she doesn't have much of a personal life. She regularly works until 11 p.m. during the week, and puts in quite a few hours cracking the books on weekends.

Admirable?

Or overkill?

Well, then, you're thinking, why doesn't Kevin have the right idea? After all, he put in only an hour and got a grade pretty darn close to Barb's.

Actually, if Kevin had spent the *same* amount of time—but used it more wisely—he could have turned that B+ into an A...with*out* working *harder.*

Work smarter, not harder

The right approach to Mr. Lonney's assignment lies somewhere between Kevin's and Barb's. (Sorry, Sally.) Careful reading and good notes are essential to earning good grades consistently. But taking good notes on written materials does not have to take a lot of time. With a good note-taking system, Barb could have gotten to bed an hour earlier (or caught that *Star Trek* rerun herself).

Effective note-taking skills should:

☞ *Help you recognize* the most important points of a text.

☞ *Make it easier* for you to understand those important points.

☞ *Enhance your memory* of the text.

☞ Provide a *highly efficient* way to study for your exams.

Let's learn how to take better notes on this sort of material and practice doing it.

Go for the gold, ignore the pyrite

Step one in effective note-taking from texts is to write down the *principle* points the author is trying to make. These main ideas should be placed either in the left-hand margin of your note paper, or as headings. *Do not write complete sentences.*

Then, write down the most important details or examples the author uses to support each of these arguments. These details should be noted under their appropriate main idea. I suggest indenting them and writing each idea on a new line, one under the other. Again, *do not use complete sentences.* Include only enough details so that your notes are not "Greek to you" when you review them.

A note-taking exercise

Let's practice these steps using the following article.

The Effects of Mabel Dodge Luhan on the Cultural and Social Life of Taos, New Mexico

Mabel Dodge Luhan had an extraordinary effect on the life of the little mountain town of Taos, New Mexico. From the time she arrived in 1917 until her death in 1962, Mabel was the social and cultural life of the town. She not only brought her own personality to the artists' colony, but numerous artists and writers to visit Taos as well. Some of them remained in the area for the rest of their lives.

The gatherings of these famous people—D.H. Lawrence, Georgia O'Keeffe, Greta Garbo, Leopold Stokowski and others—in Mabel's house served as a kind of "salon" where important members of the American and European artistic communities met, discussed each other's work, and spread the word about Taos and Mabel when they returned to New York, California, or Europe. Their enthusiasm helped bring even more famous people to visit Taos.

The social scene in Taos centered on Mabel. Because she was a personal friend of most of the people who visited her, as well as being wealthy, domineering, and extremely active, she reigned as the head of the social order in the town during her entire lifetime. The other prominent members of the community—the artists, the wealthy ranchers, the merchants—all formed a pecking order beneath her.

Mabel's support of the artistic community earlier in this century helped spread the fame of these artists—and increased the sale of their works. The prominence of Taos as an artists' colony, thanks in part to Mabel, encouraged even more artists to move to Taos, which, in turn, increased the number of visitors who came to town to buy art or simply to look at it—while spending money at the restaurants, hotels, bars, and gift shops. This trend has continued—Taos today is a major art center in the U.S. with dozens of art galleries and tourist-related shops.

The historic, as well as artistic, aspects of Taos were promoted by Mabel. Her artist friends painted people, places, and events connected to the local Spanish and Native American cultures. These paintings, and the media attention given to the historic aspects of the town, helped spread the fame of Taos.

Today, Mabel's house and her grave, in the historic Kit Carson Cemetery, are two of many attractions that tourists visit when they come to town.

It is difficult to imagine what Taos would be like today had Mabel Dodge Luhan not taken up residence there in 1917. For 45 years, her promotion of the little town gave it worldwide fame. Artists, historians, writers, and tourists began to visit Taos. Each year, the number of visitors—and social and cultural events, art galleries, and historic tours—increases, thanks to the influence of Mabel Dodge Luhan.

As you read any article, you'll notice, of course, that certain words appear repeatedly. Rather than write them down again and again during your note-taking, develop an easy-to-use shorthand for the article and write a key to it across the top of the page.

For instance, in this article, the author uses several terms that can be easily abbreviated: M (for Mabel Dodge Luhan—you didn't write MDL, did you?); T (Taos); a&w (artists and writers); a (art); NA (Native American).

Here's what my notes might look like:

1. intro   —ovrvw M on T

             —brt a&w, stayd

2. social —top dog
—salon
—a&w brt a&w
—a scene

3. cult. —hist. Sp/NA
—hse/gr

4. conc. —wht lke w/o M?
—M's effect
—yrly vsts incr./M

Which, if you can't understand it, translates as:

1. Introduction
   A. Overview of Mabel Dodge Luhan's influence on Taos.
   B. She brought artists and writers to visit, some of whom then moved there.

2. Social effects
   A. Mabel was the head of "society" in Taos.
   B. She created a "salon" atmosphere in her home.
   C. Her friends, the famous artists and writers, brought other artists and writers to Taos—and to Mabel.

3. Cultural effects
   A. Historic aspects, especially the promotion of the Spanish and Native American cultures.
   B. Her own house and grave today are part of the historic/cultural scene.

4. Conclusion
   A. Taos wouldn't be the same without her.
   B. Thanks to her, it's a bustling town today filled with artistic residents and visitors.

C. The cultural and social scene—which she developed—continues to increase in numbers and importance.

Getting it all down

Now, read the next article and take notes on it using the method outlined above. Then, compare what you've written with the sample notes I've included following it.

Whither South Africa?

The bickering that has gone on among both white and black South African dissidents, primarily over whether to boycott that country's first free elections, is reminiscent of the playground squabbles we went through as children. Bosom buddies one moment, down-in-the-dirt antagonists the next, back in class again minutes later.

Is such bickering merely a method of negotiation, a way for each of the sides, but primarily the African National Congress and the Zulu nationalists, to convince the other that unless their demands are met, they may well scuttle the entire process? Again, is it not like the child who, denied the field at first base, takes his ball and goes home, allowing pride to overcome his desire to play ball, no matter what position he is given?

Perhaps, but the real passions that lie behind such brinkmanship cannot be denied. And neither can the very real sense that for many of the "players," there is far more emotion at work than political maneuvering or logic.

Most of the citizenry is tired of the daily deadlines, the factionalism, the ever-changing alliances, enemies turning into friends overnight, friends waking up enemies. Breakthroughs are announced in newspapers' morning editions only to be proved false by the evening.

This disarray has in many cases overshadowed the active campaigning by Nelson Mandela's African National Congress and President F. W. de Klerk's National Party, the two major factions in the election. Their campaign has been further eroded by the party that has, so far at least, opted out of the elections altogether—the Zulu nationalists' Inkatha Freedom Party. It is unthinkable that they and their mercurial leader, Mangosuthu G. Buthelezi, will hold themselves out of the election process entirely. They simply have too much to lose—patronage, credibility, and the ability to incorporate their own platform in the newly formed government—to boycott the elections entirely.

But Buthelezi and his party have defied logic and done the unthinkable before. While many observers believe his holdout to be a shrewd strategic move, one that will enable him to extract every possible concession before he enters the electoral fray, others remember his withdrawal from negotiations last year that many feel would have enabled him to displace de Klerk as the titular opposition leader and expand his influence beyond the predominantly Zulu province of Natal. Instead, he became even more insular and isolated, scared off many former supporters and lost the votes of many who were ready to make him the alternative to Mandela and the ANC.

Applying the system

How closely do your notes resemble something like this?

Bick in SA

I.   Boyct? Neg ploy by ANC/Z?
II.   Real pass→emtn/pol mnvring
III.   Cits no lke chngs, factionsm, dly deads
IV.   Bick ovrshdws cam.—2 maj facts (ANC/NM, Natl P/DK).

V.   Z-I-MB-OUT? 2 mch lse?
VI. MB strat? CF prev withd neg. Cd hv displcd DK.
     But isol, scrd sups, lst vts ANC.

Another exercise: What's the question?

Of course, reading in this way will make your notes that much more succinct and valuable, as will another device for making yourself a more active reader: asking yourself questions about the material. For example:

☞ What are the most important points in the section I've just read?

☞ What information from this section is my instructor likely to ask about in the next exam?

☞ What important theories/ideas from my other reading are covered, explained, or expanded here?

As you read the text, try thinking of note-taking as just writing down the answers to questions about the material.

For instance, let's take a look at this brief passage, adapted from the article, "Days of Trauma and Fear," which appeared in the April 4, 1994 edition of *Time*:

Mexico is not a seamless unity but a mosaic of dissimilar people afforded unequal progress. Only the top half has joined the 20th century; the rest is mired in unyielding poverty. Until recently, inflation was at 50% and, despite a number of federal initiatives, the gap between rich and poor continues to widen: The poorest Mexicans' share of the national income declined from 5% eight years ago to 4.3% today.

Others are taking advantage of Mexico's growing clout in global markets and getting rich in the bargain. Mexico's gross domestic product has grown from $2,525 per capita just four years ago to $4,324 last year. But as we've already seen, these encouraging statistics mask a situation that makes Mexico one of the most unequal countries in the world.

The recent assassination of leading presidential candidate Luis Donaldo Colosio, the ruling party's handpicked successor to President Carlos Salinas de Gortari, crippled the confidence of the country striving to climb the slippery ladder to "First World" nation status. The murder was only the latest blow in a year that has featured violent rebellion in the southern state of Chiapas led by the Zapatista National Liberation Army, economic uncertainty and political disruption at a time when many citizens thought they had finally achieved a semblance of stability, peace and prosperity.

The Mexican stock market reacted violently, even for a market for which the word volatile would normally be an understatement—plunging 100 points soon after opening, though it closed the day down less than 1 percent.

The author is throwing around a handful of statistics and a few mouthfuls of Hispanic names in describing the current state of the economy in Mexico.

Should we remember the statistics about per capita income, poor Mexicans' share of income, the stock market loss? Should these statistics appear in our notes?

If we read linearly, starting at the beginning and plodding along to the last word, we probably would be tempted to write down these numbers and what they mean in our notes. But taking the article as a whole, it can readily be summarized without really worrying about the numbers: "Mexico's been having problems, is a very unequal society, the assassination has probably made it all worse."

Therefore, the statistics are not especially important, but the enormity of the problem to which they give credence *is.* The names bring up the same problem (and solution) dealt with in the South African article: Whenever possible, simplify and just note, somewhere, your abbreviations. Just as I substituted ANC for African National Congress, NM for Nelson Mandela, DK for de Klerk, and so on, so you should abbreviate Luis Donaldo Colosio, Carlos Salinas de Gortari, Chiapas, and the Zapatista National Liberation Army. These are the terms most likely to be repeated again and again in any article on the current political or economic situation in Mexico.

A note on primary sources

Primary sources (what *Freud* said, rather than what some textbook author *says* he said) present some unique note-taking challenges.

Although textbooks give you digested information, primary sources require you to do more work to get to the heart of the matter. In the sciences (social and physical), literary criticism, history, and philosophy, original thinkers will present assertions and findings. They might suggest new theories or other explanations of events or phenomena. And in doing any of the above, they will very likely support or seek to disprove established beliefs and theories.

Your notes on primary source documents should summarize the author's assertions. Under each of the summaries, you should make notes on the arguments and evidence the author presents in support of these conclusions.

The process here can be similar to that outlined previously. You can first skim the document to see what the author is presenting that's truly *new* (or, at least, was new when he wrote it), and then go back to see how he proves these claims.

For instance, if you are assigned *Thus Spake Zarathustra* by Nietzsche in your Philosophy 101 course, the headings in your notes might be:

1. The dominant force in history is the "will to power."
2. A "transvaluation of values" is necessary to produce a system of morality that produces greatness rather than goodness.
3. Blending Dionysian instinct with Apollonian reason and ethics will result in the "Ubermensch" (Superman).
4. Democracy promotes conformity and suppresses excellence.
5. God is dead.

You could easily gather these by skimming the text—because of Nietzsche's tendency to use aphorisms—or by reading a good introduction to it. Then, as you read the text more thoroughly, you'd want to note how the philosopher supports these assertions.

In this chapter, I pointed out some of the components to look for when taking notes from reading assignments, and touched on one of the most important tools to help you get down the material in an organized manner. In the next chapter, I'll give your an even more powerful tool—outlining.

CHAPTER 7

OUTLINES AND OTHER TOOLS

I have a confession to make: To this very day, I resent having to write an outline for a book, article, or research project. I'd much rather (and do) just sit down and start writing.

Even though I know that doing an outline is a great way to organize my thoughts so that I can write more quickly, it just seems to take more time that I could spend actually *writing*.

Well, I would have hated myself in school if I knew then what I know now: You should do outlines while you are *reading*, as well.

Outlines will help you review a text more quickly and remember it more clearly.

And outlining texts will make you a *better* writer.

Many students underline in their textbooks or use magic markers to "highlight" them. This is a sure sign of masochism, as it guarantees only one thing: They will have to read a great deal of the deadly book again when they review for their exams.

Others write notes in the margin. This is a little bit better as a strategy for getting better grades, but marginalia usually make the most sense only in context, so this messy method also forces the student to reread a great deal of text.

What's *the* most effective way to read and remember your textbooks? *(Sigh.)* Yes, the outline.

Reverse engineering

Outlining a textbook, article, or other secondary source is a little like what the Japanese call "reverse engineering"— a way of developing a schematic for something so that you can see exactly how it's been put together. Seeing how published authors build their arguments and marshal their research will help you when it comes time to write your own papers.

Seeing that logic of construction will also help you a great deal in remembering the book—by putting the author's points down in *your* words, you will be building a way to retrieve the key points of the book more easily from your memory.

What's more, outlining will force you to distinguish the most important points from those of secondary importance, helping you build a true understanding of the topic.

The bare bones of outlining

Standard outlines use Roman numerals (I, II, III, etc.), capital letters, Arabic numerals (1, 2, 3, 4...), and lowercase letters and indentations to show relationship and importance of topics in the text. You certainly don't have to use the Roman-numeral system, but your outline should be organized in the following manner:

Title

Author

I. First important topic in the text

  A. First subtopic

    1. First subtopic of A

      a. First subtopic of 1

      b. Second subtopic of 1

    2. Second subtopic of A

II. The second important topic in the text

Get the idea? In a book, the Roman numerals usually would refer to chapters; the capital letters to subheadings; and the Arabic numbers and lower-case letters to blocks of paragraphs. In an article or single chapter, the Roman numbers would correspond to subheadings, capital letters to blocks of paragraphs, Arabic numerals to paragraphs, small letters to key sentences.

What's he getting at?

We understand things in outline form. Ask an intelligent person to recount something and he'll state the main points and only enough details to make his words interesting and understandable.

The discipline of creating outlines will help you zero in on the most important points an author is making and capture them, process them, and, thereby, retain them.

Sometimes an author will have the major point of a paragraph in the first sentence. But just as often, the main idea of a paragraph or section will follow some of these telltale words: *therefore, because, thus, since, as a result.*

When we see these words, we should identify the material they introduce as the major points in our outline. The material immediately preceding and following almost always will be in support of these major points. The outline is an extraordinary tool for organizing your thoughts, and your time.

Let's practice what we're preaching

Turn to Chapter 9, which is an excerpt from my own *101 Great Answers to the Toughest Interview Questions* (Career Press, 1994) and then outline it. Let's see how well you've been paying attention!

Create a time line

I always found it frustrating to read textbooks in social studies. I'd go through chapters on France, England, the Far East, and have a fairly good understanding of those areas, but have no idea where certain events stood in a global context.

To help overcome that difficulty, consider drawing a time line that you can update periodically. The time line will help you visualize the chronology and remember the relationship of key world events.

For instance, a time line for the earliest years in the history of the United States might look like this (I would suggest a horizontal time line, but the layout of this book makes reproducing it that way difficult. So here's a vertical version):

1776	The American Revolution
1783	The Articles of Confederation
1786	Shay's Rebellion
1789	Ratification of the Constitution
1791	The Federal Reserve Bank
1795	The XYZ Affair
1798	The Alien and Sedition Laws

Comparing this to other time lines in your notebook would put these events in the context of the end of the Napoleonic Era and the French Revolution.

Draw a concept tree

Another terrific device for limiting the amount of verbiage in your notes and making them more memorable is the concept tree. Like a time line, the concept tree is a visual representation of the relationship among several key facts. For instance, one might depict the categories and examples of musical instruments this way:

Musical Instruments

Brass	Percussion	String	Wind
Bugle	Bongo	Banjo	Bagpipes
Cornet	Cymbal	Bass	Bassoon
French horn	Drum	Cello	Clarinet
Saxophone	Piano	Guitar	Flute
Trombone	Tambourine	Harp	Harmonica
Trumpet	Triangle	Viola	Oboe
Tuba	Xylophone	Violin	Recorder

Now we can give credence to the old saying, "A picture is worth a thousand words," because time lines and concept trees will be much more helpful than mere words in remembering material, particularly conceptual material. And developing them will ensure that your interest in the text will not flag too much.

Add a vocabulary list

Many questions on exams require students to define the terminology in a discipline. Your physics professor will want to know what vectors are, your calculus teacher will want to know about differential equations, your history professor will want you to be well-versed on The Cold War, and your English literature professor will require you to know about the Romantic Poets.

As you read your textbook, be sure to write down all new terms that seem important and their definitions. I used to draw a box around terms and definitions in my notes, because I knew these were among the most likely items to be asked about and the box would always draw my attention to them when I was reviewing.

Most textbooks will provide definitions of key terms. Even if they don't, the meanings of most terms can be inferred from the text.

This is an important point: Even if your textbook does not define a key term, make sure you write the term down in your notes *with* a definition. It will be much harder months later to remember what the term means.

In addition, even if the author does provide a definition, your notes should reflect *your* understanding of the term. Take the time to rephrase and write it in your own words. This will help you remember it.

I would also recommend writing down examples for terms that you might have trouble remembering. If you're reading an English textbook and you come across the term *oxymoron*, which is defined by the author as "a figure of speech combining seemingly contradictory expressions," wouldn't it be better if your notes on figures of speech read something like this:

oxymoron:	jumbo shrimp, cruel kindness
onomatopoeia:	PLOP, PLOP, FIZZ, FIZZ
metaphor:	food for thought
simile:	this is *like* that

Wait, you're not done yet

After you've finished making notes on a chapter, go through them and identify the most important points, which are the ones that might turn up on tests, either with an asterisk or by highlighting them. You'll probably end up marking about 40 to 50 percent of your entries. When you're reviewing for a test, you should *read* all of the notes, but your asterisks will indicate which points you considered the most important while the chapter was very fresh in your mind.

To summarize, when it comes to taking notes from your texts or other reading material, you should:

☞ Take a cursory look through the chapter before you begin reading. Look for subheads, highlighted terms, and summaries at the end of the chapter to give you a sense of the content.

☞ Read each section thoroughly. Although your review of the chapter "clues" will help your understanding of the material, you should read for comprehension rather than speed.

☞ Make notes immediately after you've finished reading, using mapping, the outline, time line, concept tree, and vocabulary list methods of organization as necessary.

☞ Mark with an asterisk or highlight the key points as you review your notes.

CHAPTER 8

TAKING GREAT NOTES FOR ORAL REPORTS

The English poet John Donne wrote, "Death be not proud," and no wonder: In many public opinion polls in which respondents were asked to rate their biggest fears, public speaking—and *not* the good old grim reaper—won...hands down.

This leads one to wonder why there haven't been more horror films made about standing up in front of an audience than about ax murderers. And makes anyone who has done a considerable amount of public speaking wonder why more people simply don't do the sensible thing to overcome their fear of "lecternship"—prepare and practice.

Researching, taking and properly using notes, and rehearsing, should ensure that you will have nothing but a mild case of the butterflies before you have to get up in front of your classmates, professors, or any other audience, friendly or otherwise.

Good notes are your lifeline when you stand up to say what's on your mind. They should act as cues to remind you where your talk should go next, and they should make you feel secure that you can get through the ordeal.

However, the *wrong* kind of notes can be a crutch that guarantees not success, but audience boredom. You've probably seen any number of people get up in front of an audience and just read some papers they have in front of them.

Is there any *better* cure for insomnia?

Organize your talk for maximum effect

I've done so much public speaking throughout my career that I've actually grown to enjoy it—in fact, I look forward to talking to a room full of strangers. I don't think that would be the case at all were it not for a piece of valuable advice I acquired quite a few years ago:

There is only one best way to organize a speech:
Tell them what you are going to say; say it;
then, tell them what you said.

An outline for a speech is going to be different than one for a term paper, because of the way effective presentations must be organized. Unlike readers, your listeners will not have a piece of paper in front of them to ponder and review. Your classmates and teacher will be relying on ear and memory to make sense of your talk, so you will have to be somewhat repetitious, though, hopefully, in a barely noticeable way.

When organizing your facts for your talk, you can use the same method—the index cards—as you used in preparing your term paper. But as you put together your outline, follow my advice: Tell them what you're going to say, say it, then tell them what you said. It's that simple.

Create your outline

Now that you have the information and colorful quotes you need to make a convincing speech, start organizing it. Go through your cards and decide the best way to arrange them so that they build toward a convincing argument. Then, using the order you've established, go through the cards and develop an outline.

Let's say you were assigned to take one side of the argument, "Should drugs be legalized?" Your outline might look like this:

The Opening

I.   Drugs should be legalized

II. This will help solve, not deepen, the drug crisis in this country

III. Keeping drugs illegal assures that criminals get rich and government funds get wasted

The Middle

I.   The reasons to legalize drugs

   A. Artificially inflated prices

      1. Costs are inflated 2,500 percent

   B. Public funds are being wasted

      1. Law enforcement is not working

      2. Funds for rehabilitation are paltry

      3. Education funds are inadequate

II. Control would be easier

   A. It has worked in other countries

   B. Licensing would increase revenues

   C. Harsh penalties would curb sales to minors

319

    D. Drug addicts would be known and
       available for counseling
  III. Prohibition doesn't work
    A. Statistics to support statement
    B. Parallels with Roaring Twenties

The Closing

  I.   The costly, ineffective War on Drugs
  II.   Legalization sounds radical, but it would
       work
  III. The alternative is far more dangerous

As you can see, the speech will restate the same points three times as a way of emphasizing them and assuring that they will be remembered.

Learning to fly without a net

Now read through it several times. Read it to yourself to make sure you haven't left out any important facts or arguments. Then read it aloud to see how it flows, fixing as necessary.

Now, it's time to go without a net. Stand in front of a mirror and try giving the speech, start to finish, looking at nothing but your own beautiful face. But have your notes close by.

How did you do? What parts of the speech did you remember with no trouble? Where did you stumble? If you're like 99 percent of the human race, you probably had to wrench your eyes from the mirror now and then to look at your notes.

Of course, you're not ready for an audience yet. Nor should you expect to be at this point. You'll want to practice many more times before you face your listeners. The purpose of this exercise is to help you identify what areas you really know—and which are going to require a little prompting.

Your next step is to distill your talk even further on additional note cards. For those areas with which you're most familiar, the ones you remember without looking at your notes, jot down a simple phrase, even a symbol, that prompts you to continue with your talk. For those details you're a little unsure of, write as much detail as you need. As you continue to practice speaking, you should further distill the information on your note cards, until what you have is the barest framework possible.

My advice for preparing your final note cards is much like the advice that veteran travelers offer on packing for a long trip: Put only the bare necessities in your suitcase. Then, take half of them out.

Mistakes novices make, and you shouldn't

This all makes giving an oral report sound scary, doesn't it? It certainly did to me at one time. I took a course on public speaking at the American Management Association, one of the leading providers of continuing adult education. Because I made my living with printed words, I wanted to have lots of them in front of me so I wouldn't feel naked. I'd hide behind my legal pad!

But the instructor, to whom I've been grateful countless times since, would allow us to bring only three index cards for a three-minute talk. And each card could have no more than 10 words written on it.

Certainly many students in the class stumbled, but they probably hadn't rehearsed. On the other hand, I guarantee you that, as a relative novice at public speaking, you will make one (and maybe all) of these "Big Three" mistakes if you bring your entire text with you:

☞ You will read from it, failing to make eye contact with your audience. This will help to ensure that you lose *their* interest and *your* credibility. How familiar can you be with a subject if you have to *read* your entire speech?

☞ If you stop reading for a second to ad lib or look at your listeners, you will lose your place. It's much harder to find that key word that will jog your memory on a full page of text than on an index card.

☞ You won't be familiar enough with your speech, because, after all, you will have it there with you, so why bother rehearsing or memorizing anything?

As I've become more polished as a public speaker, I've noticed that having only the cards has encouraged me to ad lib more. And, by and large, these are the most well received parts of the speech. Talking relatively freely, with the help of only the sparest notes, is one way to make sure the "real you" comes through.

And that's who the audience is there to hear, right?

Please take note

I've begun to think of my notes for speeches as the purest form of the craft we've described in this book. You are distilling ideas down to a phrase, a word, a number, perhaps just a symbol (hey, it sort of worked for "the Artist") that will help you remember under pressure.

Often, the very *process* of taking notes is enough, in itself, to ensure that a fact, an impression, or a formula, will last in your memory for a long time. Note-taking is stripping data down to its essence.

Although I've made many suggestions about the best way to take notes, remember that it is a very individualistic and pragmatic art. Each of you should figure out what works best for you, then refine your technique using the suggestions made in these chapters. It will be worth the effort.

In the next chapter, I've reproduced an excerpt from one of my other books—*101 Great Answers to the Toughest Interview Questions, 2nd Edition*—on which to practice your newly mastered note-taking and outlining skills. And I've shown my own outline of the chapter, too. Just don't peek at my notes before you take your own!

CHAPTER 9

LET'S PRACTICE
WHAT WE'VE
PREACHED

Starting on the next page, I've reprinted an excerpt (most of Chapter 2) from my book, *101 Great Answers to the Toughest Interview Questions, 2nd Edition*.

Practice outlining it (see Chapter 7) and taking notes on it. You'll soon see how well you learned the lessons of this book—or identify the chapters you need to go back and reread!

On pages 336 and 337, I've given you two blank pages to fill in your outline. On pages 338 and 339, I've reproduced my own. Don't peek until you finish yours! See how close you get to this "model" (though it's certainly not the only "solution"). And note that I've written out much more of it than I normally would (as opposed to applying my own shorthand), purely for the sake of readability.

If you find you have a lot of trouble with this exercise, forget what I said about linear reading—go back and read *Take Notes* again, from start to finish!

What you're up against

The days of filling out the standard application and chatting your way through one or two interviews are gone. These days, interviewers and hiring managers are reluctant to leave anything to chance. Many have begun to experiment with the latest techniques for data-gathering and analysis. For employers, interviewing has gone from an art to a full-fledged science.

Does this make you feel like a specimen under a microscope? Get used to it. Times are tougher for companies, so it's natural to assume that interviews will be tougher for their prospective employees.

In the many years I've subscribed to human resources journals, I've noticed an increasing number of new interviewing methods developed to help interviewers measure, as accurately as possible, how well prospective candidates would perform on the job. The "database interview," the "situational interview," and the "stress (confrontational) interview" are only a few of the special treatments you might encounter on your way to landing the ideal job.

The good news is that companies hoping to survive in our new service economy will depend on the human element—you—as their most valuable business asset. But because there are more "humans" competing for fewer jobs, employers will be focused on hiring only the very best applicants.

Interviewing has always been a challenge. But these days it is serious business. Consider:

The incredible shrinking company. Rampant downsizing has left fewer jobs. At the same time, the "cost of hire"—the amount of money it takes to land a suitable candidate for a job—has escalated dramatically in recent years.

From business suit to lawsuit. Lawsuits against employers for wrongful discharge and other employment-related causes have also increased exponentially over the past decade. Hiring mistakes can be costly, making it more important than ever for companies to be sure the people they do hire will be right for the job.

The great cattle call. Although the labor force is indeed shrinking as a result of the much ballyhooed "baby bust," you're liable to face a new kind of competition as a job applicant. These days, you can expect to bump into fellow candidates at every level of experience on the way to or from your first interview—or your fourth.

Where does that leave you?

More employers seem to be looking for a special kind of employee—someone with experience, confidence and the initiative to learn what he or she needs to know. Someone who requires very little supervision. Someone with a hands-on attitude—from beginning to end.

Because it's difficult to tell all that from an application and handshake, here's what's happening:

Passing the test(s). You'll probably have to go through more interviews than your predecessors for the same job—no matter what your level of expertise. Knowledge and experience still give you an inside edge. But these days, you'll need stamina, too. Your honesty, your intelligence, your mental health—even the toxicity of your blood—may be measured before you can be considered fully assessed.

Braving more interviews. You may also have to tiptoe through a mine field of different types of interview situations—and keep your head—to survive as a new hire.

Don't go out and subscribe to a human resources journal. Just do all you can to remain confident and flexible—and ready with your answers. No matter what kind of interview you find yourself in, this approach should carry you through with flying colors.

Let's take a brief no-consequences tour of the interview circuit.

Level 1: The screening interview

If you are pursuing a job at a mid-size or large company (any organization of more than 250 employees), your first interview is likely to begin in the human resources department.

What can you expect? Let's say you're applying for your dream job as a middle manager at ABC Widget Co. Arriving on time for your first interview, you're greeted by Heather.

Heather is a lower-level person in the human resources department. She's been given a bare-bones introduction to the duties and responsibilities you must have to operate successfully in the position you're after. If she's not completely up to speed, it's probably not her fault. The person who will manage this new position (the hiring manager) may not have had time to fill out a detailed position description, or to tell Heather exactly what he or she is looking for.

Regardless of how much she's got to go on, Heather's job is pretty simple: weed out the number of candidates whose resumes jibe with the short version of the job description, so that the hiring manager will have fewer candidates to interview.

After you've gotten through the preliminaries, Heather is likely to follow a script. She will ask questions to see if you have the qualifications for the position: the appropriate degree, the right amount of experience, a willingness to relocate, and so on.

Heather will be trying to determine whether you've been completely truthful on your resume. Did you work where and when you claim? Have the titles and responsibilities you're bragging about? Make the salaries you've stated?

The screening interview may also drift into a few qualitative areas. Does she think you're sufficiently enthusiastic? Do you sound intelligent? Exhibit any obvious emotional disturbances? Are you articulate? Energetic? Are you the type of person who would fit well within the department, and the company?

Getting past the gate

If you pass the screening hurdle, Heather may resort to an arsenal of professional interviewing techniques. Remember, Heather is trained and practiced in the science of interviewing.

Although it's still up to the hiring manager to decide whether you'll still be checking the classified ads next week, Heather has the power, at this point, to keep you from meeting the hiring manager! She is, in effect, the gatekeeper.

But once you get past the gate, be careful of what's on the other side.

1. The stress interview

Anyone who's been through one of these never forgets it. The stress interview is designed to cut through the veneer of pleasantries to the heart of the matter. To see what a candidate is really made of.

I was subjected to a stress interview before I'd ever heard of the technique—not the best way to prepare, believe me.

Several years ago, I applied for an editorial position at a major publishing company. I made it past the first hurdle, a screening interview conducted in the corporate office. Next, I was invited to come back to meet the director of personnel, Carrie. After greeting me pleasantly, Carrie led me back to her rather palatial office. We chatted for a few minutes as I settled in. Then everything changed. Suddenly, I was undergoing an interrogation—worthy of the secret police in a country on Amnesty International's Top Ten.

Assuming that I had been given good reviews by the first screening interviewer, I was shocked when Carrie began firing. First she questioned my credentials. Why, she wondered sarcastically, had I majored in liberal arts rather than something "practical." She demanded to know what in the world made me think that I could edit a magazine (even though I had been doing it quite well for years).

Each successive question skittered in a dizzying new direction. If the first question was about my work experience, the next launched into my fitness routine, and the next, my favorite movie.

Carrie's questions did exactly what I later discovered they were intended to do—they made me feel confused, fearful, and hostile. I behaved badly, I admit. I answered most of her questions in monosyllables, avoiding her eyes.

Needless to say, I was not offered the job.

But I did learn some valuable lessons from Carrie that day:

☞ **Never let them see you sweat.** In other words, no matter how stressful the situation, stay calm. Never take your eyes from the interviewer. When he or she finishes asking a question, take a few seconds to compose yourself and then, and only then, answer.

☞ **Recognize the situation for what it is.** It is nothing more than an artificial scenario designed to see how you react under pressure. The interviewer probably has nothing against you personally.

☞ **Don't become despondent.** It's easy to think that the interviewer has taken a strong dislike to you and that your chances for completing the interview process are nil. That's not the case. The stress interview is designed to see if you will become depressed, hostile, or flustered when the going gets tough.

☞ **Watch your tone of voice.** It's easy to become sarcastic during a stress interview, especially if you don't realize what the interviewer is up to.

2. The situational interview

"What would happen if everyone else called in sick and...?"

There's nothing quite like the terror of the hypothetical question. Especially when it is a product of the interviewer's rich imagination. We'll talk more about these devils in Chapter 9. But for now, know that the hypothetical question should start a red light flashing in your consciousness. It is your signal that you are about to undergo an increasingly popular type of interview—the situational interview.

The premise is sound. Present the candidate with situations that might, hypothetically, occur on the job in order to gauge the degree to which he or she demonstrates the traits that will lead to success.

But what's good for the interviewer is often deadly for the interviewee. You will have to devote a great deal of thought to each of these questions. If you find yourself caught in this snare, stay calm and use the homework you have already done on your personal inventory to untangle yourself.

3. The behavioral interview

The hypothetical is just too "iffy" for some interviewers. This breed is more comfortable staying in the realm of the known, so they will dig deep into your past experience hoping to learn more about how you have already behaved in a variety of on-the-job situations. Then, they'll attempt to use this information to extrapolate your future reactions on this job.

How did you handle yourself in some really tight spots? What kinds of on-the-job disasters have you survived? Did you do the right thing? What were the repercussions of your decisions?

Be careful of what you say. Every situation you faced was unique in its own way, so be sure to let the interviewer in on specific limitations you had to deal with. Did you lack adequate staff? Support from management? If you made the mistake of plunging in too quickly, say so and admit that you've learned to think things through. Explain what you'd do differently the next time around.

That said, my advice would be to steer away from the specifics of a particular situation and emphasize the personal strengths and expertise you'd feel comfortable bringing to any challenge you're likely to face.

4. The team interview

Today's organizational hierarchies are becoming flatter. That means that people at every level of a company are more likely to become involved in a variety of projects and tasks—including interviewing you for the job you're after.

How does this happen? That depends on the company. The team interview can range from a pleasant conversation to a torturous interrogation. Typically you will meet a group, or "team," of interviewers around a table in a conference room. They may be members of your prospective department or a cross section of employees from throughout the company who you can expect to work with at some time or other in your new position.

The hiring manager or someone from human resources may chair an orderly session of question-and-answer—or turn the group loose to shoot questions at you like a firing squad. When it's all over, you'll have to survive the assessment of every member of the group.

Some hiring managers consult with the group after the interview for a "reading" on your performance. Others determine their decision using group consensus. The good news is that you don't have to worry that the subjective opinion of just one person will determine your shot at the job. Say one member of the group thinks you "lacked confidence" or came across as "arrogant." Others in the group may disagree. The interviewer who leveled the criticism will have to defend his or her opinion to the satisfaction of the group—or be shot down.

A group of people is also more likely (but not guaranteed) to ask you a broader range of questions that may uncover and underline your skills and expertise. Just take your time—and treat every member of the team with the same respect and deference you would the hiring manager.

Level 2: The hiring interview

You've made it this far. But don't relax yet. Your first interview with the person who will manage your prospective position is not likely to be a walk in the park. You may be stepping out of range of the experience and interviewing talent of the human resources professional—into unknown territory.

And you could wander there for a while.

Why? Experienced interviewers are trained to stay in charge of the interview, not let it meander down some dead-end, nonproductive track. There is a predictability to the way they conduct interviews, even when they wield different techniques.

A little knowledge is a dangerous thing

On the other hand, the hiring manager is sure to lack some or all of the screening interviewer's knowledge, experience, and skill—making him or her an unpredictable animal.

The vast majority of corporate managers don't know what it takes to hire the right candidate. Few of them have had formal training in conducting interviews of any kind. To make things worse, most managers feel slightly less comfortable conducting the interview than the nervous candidate sitting across their desks from them!

For example, a manager might decide you are not the right person for the job, without ever realizing that the questions he or she asked were so ambiguous, or so off the mark, that even the perfect candidate could not have returned the "right" answer. No one monitors the performance of the interviewer. And the candidate cannot be a mind reader. So more often than is necessary, otherwise perfectly qualified candidates are apt to walk out the door for good simply because the manager failed at the interview!

Foiling the inept interviewer

But that doesn't have to happen to you. You can—and should—be prepared to put your best foot forward, no matter what the manager who is interviewing for the job does or says. That begins with having the answers to 101 questions at the ready. But it doesn't stop there. Because the interviewer may not ask any of these questions.

What do you do then? In the chapters that follow, you'll see how you can give even the most dense of managers the feeling that you are the best person for the job.

Simply put, you're a step ahead of the game if you realize at the outset that managers who are interviewing to hire are after more than just facts about your skills and background. They are waiting for something more elusive to hit them, something they themselves may not be able to articulate. They want to feel that somehow you "fit" the organization or department.

Talk about a tough hurdle! But knowing what you're up against is half the battle. Rather than sit back passively and hope for the best, you can help the unskilled interviewer focus on how your unique skills can directly benefit—"fit"—the department or organization using a number of specific examples.

One word of caution. Don't come on so strong that you seem to be waging a campaign. You will come off as overzealous and self-serving. You lose. Just keep quietly and confidently underlining the facts (your expertise) and enthusiastically showing (discovering together) how well these "puzzle pieces" seem to fit the job at hand.

That certain something

One afternoon, Alexander, my boss and the publishing director for the magazine I was running, asked me to stop by his office to meet a promising young candidate a friend had referred. "I know you don't have any positions open right now, Ron," he told me. "But could you take the time just to say hello?"

I was up to my ears with work, but I took a few moments to find out a little bit about Lynn. I asked her a few preliminary questions: Where was she working? What were her strengths? What was she looking for? I had planned to be out of there in five minutes.

But, somehow, we were still talking a half-hour later. By that time, I knew she was a terrific writer and editor. And I understood why she was thinking about making a move.

I still couldn't offer her a job. But she had impressed me so much in that informal meeting that when the managing editor spot opened up on my magazine a few months later, I didn't think twice. I called Lynn. After a more thorough and formal interview, she got the job.

What made Lynn such a winner? She displayed just those traits that I keep stressing, the traits employers are always looking for, no matter what the job description: confidence, enthusiasm, experience, and dependability.

Your outline of this chapter

_____

_____

_____

_____

_____

_____

_____

_____

_____

_____

_____

_____

_____

_____

_____

_____

_____

_____

_____

_____

_____

_____

_____

_____

_____

_____

_____

_____

_____

_____

_____

_____

_____

_____

_____

_____

_____

_____

_____

_____

_____

_____

_____

_____

_____

_____

_____

_____

_____

_____

_____

_____

_____

_____

My outline of this chapter

State of Interviewing Today

Key:　I= interview　　IR= interviewer
　　　　E= employer　　C= candidate

I. Overview
  A. Irs reluctant 2 lve anything 2 chance
  B. I gone » are 2 science.
  C. Many new I methods developed & used
  D. I more downsizing than ever
    1. Downsizing left fewer jobs, cost/hire up
    2. Lawsuits up
    3. More competition
    4. Es looking 4 "perfect" Cs
      a. So + Is, + tests
      b. Different kinds of Is

II. Screening I
  A. W/ human resources
  B. Job: weed out Cs
  C. Will follow script
  D. Then 2 prof. I techniques
    1. Stress I
      a. Purpose: confuse/intimidate
      b. How handle?
        (1) Stay calm
        (2) Not personal
        (3) Don't get depressed/angry

    2. Situational I

        a. Hypothetical questions

        b. Require thought, stay calm, use personal inventory

    3. Behavioral

        a. Dig into experience

        b. Explain details, tell what to do different

        c. Emphasize personal strengths/expertise

    4. Team I

        a. Group interview, orderly or like firing squad

        b. Usually mean group input, even gp. decision

        c. Usually ask broader range of questions

III. Hiring I.

    A. Hiring mgr unpredictable IR

        1. Not prof Irs

        2. May B uncomfortable 2

    B. Dealing w/ inept IR

        1. Have answers ready

        2. Irs lking 4 "chemistry"

        3. Don't B 2 aggressive

IV. What Es lking 4

    A. Enthusiasm

    B. Confidence

    C. Experience

    D. Dependability

BOOK 4

"ACE"
ANY TEST

CHAPTER 1

SO, WHAT ARE YOU AFRAID OF?

"All we have to fear is fear itself."
—Franklin Delano Roosevelt

FDR was *almost* right. The only thing you *may* have to fear is fear itself. But, frankly, you *don't* have to. You just have to conquer it or beat it into submission so that you can get on with your life—and your biology exam.

But it doesn't hurt to have a little anxiety. You don't want to become so complacent that you lose that edge you need to be truly "up and running" for the test.

Let's spend a few minutes talking about why tests scare people, and then I'll help you learn how to spend your time studying instead of wasting it on anxiety attacks.

Bees do it, even famous people do it

I still remember a documentary on a famous singer I saw on TV years ago. The camera had been following her around while she went to rehearsal, got her make-up on and talked with her manager.

The scene I remember most was the shot of her as she waited backstage to be announced, looking nervous, horrified, petrified, regretful that she'd ever entered show business, and extremely vulnerable. (Presuming she remembered she was being filmed, this was the *controlled* panic.)

But, when the announcer called her name and the roar of applause began, she walked with a determined gait to the stage, smiled, took the microphone and never looked back. Her famous voice filled the auditorium, and the audience went wild. If she had those little panics and still passed the test, why shouldn't you?

Speech? Sure, right after I kill myself!

Truly successful entertainers or public speakers will usually admit they get those little knots in their stomachs just before they have to perform. They would be the first ones to tell you that not only is it okay to go through a nervous moment or two, it's actually a benefit, giving them the adrenaline rush they need to do a good job.

Frankly, I usually don't get nervous anymore before a speech or TV appearance—I've just done too many of them—but I will never forget the sweating, slobbering basket case I became when I had to actually stand up and do a book report in 7th grade! Even after thousands of public appearances, there are still times when the old nerve ends tingle a bit while backstage. Know what? I always give a *better* speech.

Let's put that back into the context of your exam-taking: You may have taken a test in the past where you thought you knew everything, did little if any studying—and got a bad grade. Don't go too far the other way.

But don't get too tensed up either. Keep a little anxiety in your life. Just keep it under control and in perspective.

Why is there terror present in the first place? Because we don't want to fail. We realize that, within the next 30 or 60 minutes, a percentage of our grade will be determined by what we write or *don't* write down on a piece of paper, or which box we color in with our No. 2 pencil.

So, what are you afraid of?

Now, why do some people fail? What does it mean when someone proclaims they don't "test well"? For many, it really means they don't study well (or, at the very least, study *enough*). For others, it could mean they are easily distracted, unprepared for the type of test they are confronting or simply unprepared mentally to take *any* test (which may well include mentally sabotaging yourself into a poor score or grade, even though you know the material...backwards and forwards).

Take heart—very few people look forward to a test; more of you are afraid of tests than you'd think. But that doesn't mean you *have* to fear them.

We all recognize the competitive nature of tests. Some of us rise to the occasion when facing such a challenge. Others are thrown off balance by the pressure. Both reactions probably have little to do with one's level of knowledge, relative intelligence, or amount of preparation. The smartest students in your class may be the ones most afraid of tests.

Sometimes, it's *not* fear of failure—it's fear of *success*. You think to yourself, "If I do well on this exam, my parents will expect me to do well on the next exam—and the teacher will think I'm going to do well every day!"

Fear of success gets boring nearly as quickly as would-be martyrs and know-it-all busybodies. Look at it this way: You'll have to deal with some sort of pressure every day of your life. So you might as well opt for the *good* kind—"Way to go, genius, keep up the good work!"—rather than the other—"I just don't understand why Tim does so poorly in school. He just doesn't apply himself."

Nobody likes Saralee anyway

Another reason for failure? Some people can't deal with competition. All they can think about is what Saralee is doing. Look at her! She's sitting there, writing down one answer after another—and you know they're all correct!

Who cares about Saralee? I sure wouldn't. Only one person in that room should be concerned with Saralee and Saralee's performance. That's right. Just as only one person should be concerned with *your* performance. Make it all a game: Compete with yourself. See if you can't beat your previous test scores. Now, that's positive competition!

My daughter, Lindsay, clarified this point when she ran the 100-yard dash for her 1st-grade track team. Despite the fact she was the second fastest of nearly 30 girls, she cried at the end of the race because she wasn't *first*. Is there a little too much pressure here? Can I hear a "Keep it in perspective"? Amen.

You don't have to join the club

Some people thrive on their own misery and are jealous if you don't thrive on it, too. They want to include you in all of their hand-wringing situations, regardless of whether you really know or care about what's happening. These are people to avoid when you're preparing for an exam—the Anxiety Professionals.

"Oh, I'll never learn all this stuff!" they cry. You might not win points with Miss Manners if you say, "If you'd shut up and study, you might!" You *can* have the pleasure of *thinking* it—on your way to a quiet place to study alone.

Watch out for those "friends" who call you the night before the exam with, "I just found out we have to know Chapter 12!" Don't fall into their trap. Instead of dialing 911, calmly remind them that the printed sheet the professor passed out two weeks ago clearly says, "Test on Chapters 6 through 11." Then hang up, get on with your life, and let them wring their hands all the way to the bottom of the grading sheet. (Of course, if *you* don't bother to check what's going to be on the test, a call like this *will* panic you...and waste your time.)

Focus on the exam

If you have trouble concentrating on your preparations for the exam, try this: Think of your life as a series of shoe boxes (the Imelda Marcos Theory). The boxes are all open and lined up in a nice, long, neat row. In each shoe box is a small part of your life—school, work, romantic interest, hobbies, *ad Florsheim*. Although you have to move little pieces from one box to another from time to time, you can—and should—keep this stuff as separate as possible.

Of course, you *can* make it easier to do this by *not* going out of your way—certainly before an especially big or important test—to add *more* stress to an already stressful life. Two days before the SAT is *not* the time to dump a boyfriend, move, change jobs, take out a big loan, or create any other waves in your normally placid river of life.

You're already an expert

For years you've taken pop quizzes, oral exams, standardized tests, tests on chapters, units, whole books, and whole semesters. For the most part, you've been successful.

If you haven't been as successful as you'd like, keep reading. For the remainder of this book, we'll review what you can do to change all that. All this experience, coupled with the real-life "tests" I've already mentioned, demonstrates that you're pretty good—even excellent. Stop for a moment and pat yourself on the back. You are a successful test-taker, in spite of a little fright here and there.

One in a million

Just admitting that you're not at ground zero can help you realize that preparing for an exam is not in itself a whole new task of life—it's merely part of a continuum.

Think of this fraction: 1 over 1 million. Your life is the big number. Your next test is the little number. All the "ones" in your life add up to the 1 million; they are important, but all by themselves, they can't compare to the Giant, Economy-Sized Number of Life. Write "1/1,000,000" at the top of your next test to remind yourself of that. That alone should kill off a bunch of stomach butterflies.

"Extra" tests give extra help

If you want to practice the many recommendations you're going to get in this book, including what I'm sharing with you in this important first chapter, take a few "extra" tests just to give yourself some practice. It will also help you overcome unacceptable levels of test anxiety.

Get permission from your teachers to retake some old tests to practice the test-taking techniques and exorcise the High Anxiety Demon. Take a couple of standardized tests that your counseling office might have, too, because the color-in-the-box answer sheets and questions in printed form have their own set of rules (which, as you can guess, we'll talk about later in this book).

A little perspective, please

The more pressure you put on yourself—the larger you allow a test (and, of course, your hoped-for good scores) to loom in your own mind—the less you are helping yourself. Of course, the bigger the test really *is*, the more likely you are to keep reminding yourself of its importance.

No matter how important a test really may be to your career—and your scores on some *can* have a major effect on where you go to college, whether you go on to graduate school, whether you get the job you want—it is just as important to *de-emphasize* that test's importance in your mind. This should have no effect on your preparation—you should still study as if your life depended on a superior score. It might!

A friend of mine signed up to take the Law School Admission Test (LSAT), not just once, but twice. The first time, he did "Okay, not great." By the time the second date rolled around, he had come to his senses and decided not to become a lawyer. But because he had already paid for the thing, he took the LSAT again anyway. Are you already ahead of me? That's right—a 15-percent improvement with *no* studying. Does that tell you something about trying to downplay all this self-inflicted pressure?

Keeping the whole experience in perspective might also help: Twenty years from now, nobody will remember, or care, what you scored on *any* test—no matter how life-threatening or life-determining you feel that test is now.

Don't underestimate positive thinking: Thoughts *can* become self-fulfilling prophecies. If you tell yourself often enough, "Be careful, you'll fall over that step," you probably will. If you tell yourself often enough, "I'm going to fail this test," you just might. Likewise, keep convincing yourself that you are as prepared as anyone and are going to "ace" the sucker, and you're already ahead of the game.

How to lower your AQ (Anxiety Quotient)

To come to terms with the "importance" of a test, read the list below. Knowing the answers to as many of these questions as possible will help reduce your anxiety:

1. What material will the exam cover?
2. How many total points are possible?
3. What percentage of my semester grade is based on this exam?
4. How much time will I have to take the exam?
5. Where will the exam be held?
6. What kinds of questions will be on the exam (matching, multiple-choice, essay, true/false...)?
7. How many points will be assigned to each question? Will certain types of questions count more than others? How many of each type of question will be on the exam?
8. Will it be an open-book exam?
9. What can I take in with me? Calculator? Candy bar? Direct line to the test gods?
10. Will I be penalized for wrong answers?

Take a hike, buddy

Finally, to shake off pretest anxiety, take a walk. Or a vigorous swim. In the days before an exam, no matter how "big" it is, don't study too hard or too much or you'll walk into the exam with a fried brain.

Please don't think that advice loses its power at the classroom door. Scheduling breaks during tests has the same effect. During a one-hour test, you may not have time to go out for a stroll. But during a two- or three-hour final, there's no reason you should not schedule one, two, or even more breaks on a periodic basis—whenever you feel you need them most. Such time-outs can consist of a bathroom stop, a quick walk up and down the hall or just a minute of relaxation in your seat before you continue the test.

No matter what the time limits or pressures, don't feel you cannot afford such a brief respite. You may need it *most* when you're convinced you can *least* afford it, just as those who most need time-management techniques "just don't have the time" to learn them.

Relax, darn it!

If your mind is a jumble of facts and figures, names and dates, you may find it difficult to zero in on the specific details you need to recall, even if you know all the material backwards and forwards. The adrenaline rushing through your system may make "instant retrieval" seem impossible.

The simplest relaxation technique is deep breathing. Just lean back in your chair, relax your muscles, and take three very deep breaths (count to 10 while you hold each one). For many of you, that's the only relaxation technique you'll ever need.

There are a variety of meditation techniques that may also work for you. Each is based upon a similar principle—focusing your mind on one thing to the exclusion of everything else. While you're concentrating on the object of your meditation (even if the object is nothing, a nonsense word, or a spot on the wall,) your mind can't be thinking about anything else, which allows it to slow down a bit.

CHAPTER 2

CREATING THE TIME TO STUDY

"Work expands so as to fill the time available for its completion."
—Cyril Parkinson, Parkinson's Law

"I recommend that you learn to take care of the minutes, for the hours will take care of themselves."
—Lord Chesterfield

Let's start by making a major adjustment in our thinking: Time is our *friend*, not our enemy. Time allows us space in each day or week or month to do a lot of fun things and to reach certain milestones in order to advance our careers, get diplomas or degrees, establish and develop relationships, go on vacations, and all that good stuff.

It also allows us to prepare for tests. (Let's not get carried away and forget the focus of this book.) This chapter includes some simple time charts that will help you work on *when, where,* and *how* you manage the various demands on your time.

Look at it this way: Between now and next Wednesday, whether you are preparing to play in the state basketball tournament, writing a paper about the Mississippi Delta, or holding down three jobs (or, heaven help you, all of the above), you have exactly the same amount of time as the rest of us. It's what you *do* with that time that makes the difference.

How are you going to get from here to there? Are you just going to go crashing along, like an elephant trampling down banana trees, or are you going to get there by following a plan? Good. That's the right answer. See? You just passed *another* test. Congratulations.

The vital statistics

How often have you made a "to-do" list and then either forgotten it, lost it, or ignored it? To-do lists have incredible merits, but they're not much good if you don't use them.

Let's run through the composition and execution of a to-do list for a shopping expedition as an example. Here's what I do when I am making up a list of errands:

First, after writing down where I have to go, I turn the paper over and make individual lists of items for each stopping place. I may have Smith's Drugstore on the "where to go" front side of the list, but on the back I have listed shaving cream, bubble gum, newspaper, hair spray, and prescription.

Am I (A) obsessive-compulsive or (B) merely organized? If this were a real test, the right answer would be (B).

By separating the *where* from the *what*, I am able to focus on getting from the post office to the drugstore to the hardware store without trying to separate the toothpaste from the tool kit. On the other hand, when I am heading down Aisle 3B, I can concentrate on what items I need from this particular stop.

I do one more thing on my shopping list: If I need to take anything with me (return a videotape, drop off my cleaning, take an article to be photocopied, etc.), I place a "T" (meaning "take") with a circle around it beside the place for which I need the "T" item. That way, I don't get to Smith's only to discover that I forgot to bring the prescription form. (If convenient, put all the "T" items, along with the list, beside the door so you won't have to search for them when it's time to leave.)

Now, why am I sharing all this detailed information on my shopping-list habits when we're supposed to be talking about getting ready for your zoology exam? Because the methods and the rationale are similar to your management of time. Here's what my list does for me:

☞ I don't forget anything.

☞ I save time.

☞ I get things done easily.

☞ I "save" my brain for what's important.

Attention, Study-Smart shoppers!

Think of the time between now and your next exam as your shopping trip. You want to use this time most effectively so that: 1) You don't forget anything; 2) you work efficiently (save time); 3) you arrange your studying so it's done as easily as possible; and 4) you concentrate on the important details, not on *all* the details (big difference!).

How much time do you have? Unless I missed something in the paper this morning, we all have 24 hours a day. But you and I know that's not what we're talking about here. We have to subtract sleeping, eating, commuting, and obligations like work and classes...whoa! Any time left?

Sure there is. But first you need to get a handle on what you *must* do, what you *should* do, and what you *want* to do. Let's refer to them as our H, M, and L priorities.

The H ("high") priorities are those things we *must* do between now and the next test.

The M ("medium") priorities are those things we *should* do, but we could postpone without being jailed or written out of the will.

The L ("low") priorities are those things we want to do but are *expendable*. At least until you have finished taking this next exam.

Time-saving tip: Remember my advice from **Manage Your Time**, if you push aside the same low-priority item day after day, week after week, at some point you should decide if it's something you need to do at all! This is a strategic way to make a task or problem "disappear."

Yes, Virginia, it's all right to sleep

An "H" is sleeping, eating, and attending class, especially the class in question. You simply can't ignore these.

An "M" is getting your family car's oil changed or taking your cat to the vet for a checkup. Important, but unless the car's dipstick shows that it has no oil or the cat is so sick it's trying to dial the vet itself, these tasks can be delayed for a handful of days.

An "L" is going to the Hitchcock Film Festival or partying with friends up at the cabin in the mountains.

In **Manage Your Time**, I give you three different forms to use. I'm including them in this book as well. The first one, the Term Planning Calendar, helps you sort out and manage the big picture. The second, Priority Tasks This Week, breaks the semester down into seven-day periods. The third, Daily Schedule, will reduce it to a focused day-by-day format.

Let's talk about the Term-Planning Calendar on page 367 of this chapter. Simply put, this is a series of monthly calendars with all the important events listed on them. Sounds pretty simple. Actually, it is. Even if you've only got six weeks left in the semester, go ahead and fill out one of these.

Don't just list school-related items ("Biology semester exam, 9 a.m." on May 3); put down the "H" items from the rest of your life, too ("Trip to Chicago" on March 22).

One very good reason for listing all the social/personal/non-academic items is for you to determine which of those are going to remain in the "H" category. For example, if you discover that you have planned a trip to Chicago for the weekend before your French midterm the following Monday, you'd better cry *"Sacre bleu!"* and decide the Chicago trip is an "L" and must be moved to another time.

Get the picture?

One of the most important reasons for writing down exactly what is coming up is to get that big picture. Once you've filled in all the due dates of term papers, unit tests, midterms, finals, project reports, etc., take a good look at the results.

Are there a bunch of deadlines in the same week or even on the same day? During finals and midterms, of course, this really can't be helped and there's no way to take the tests at another time.

Perhaps you can do something about some of the other deadlines. If you have a French test covering three units on the same day that you have to turn in a paper on the "Influence of the Beatles on British Foreign Policy" and a status report on your gerbil project for sociology, take the plunge and decide that you will get the paper and the project status report done early so that you can devote the time just prior to that day to studying for your French test.

You can't make decisions like that, however, if you don't have the ability to sit back and get an overall view. I like to sit back—literally—and look at the Term Planning Calendar so I can easily see where several deadlines are on the same day or week.

Looking at everything that is coming up will help you decide what is really an "H" and what is not. It need not cut into your social life, but it does mean that you may need to rearrange some things or say no to some invitations that come smack in the middle of your gathering data on gerbils.

But you can frolic on the nights and weekends that are far enough away from your "H" priorities. When personal "H" events come up (you really can't miss your sister's wedding no matter how much the gerbils need you), your Term Planning Calendar gives you enough warning so that you can make sure your school work doesn't suffer.

"I should have planned better"

Once you have a grasp of your obligations for a term at a time, bring the tasks down to the week at hand by filling out the Priority Tasks This Week form (see the sample on page 368 of this chapter). When planning study time for a test during the week, find the answers to these two questions: 1) How much time do I *need* to devote to studying for this exam? and 2) How much time do I *have* to study for this exam?

It's fairly easy to determine the answer to the second question. After all, there are a finite number of hours between now and the exam, and your personal and other school "H" priorities will use up 80 or 90 percent of them.

But the first question calls for a fairly definitive answer, too, or else you will never be able to plan.

Consider these other questions when figuring out the time needed:

☞ How much time do I usually spend studying for this type of exam? What have been the results? (If you usually spend three hours and you consistently get Ds, perhaps you need to reassess the time you're spending or, more accurately, *mis*spending.)

☞ What grade do I have going for me now? (If it's a solid B and you're convinced you can't get an A, you may decide to devote less time to studying for the exam than if you have a C+ and an extra-good grade on the exam would give you a solid B. Just make sure you aren't overconfident and end up with an exam grade that will ruin your B forever.)

☞ What special studying do I have to do? (It's one thing to review notes and practice with a study group—more on that later in the book—but if you need to sit in a language lab and listen to hours of tapes or run the slower group of gerbils through the alphabet once more, plan accordingly.)

☞ Organize the materials you need to study, pace yourself, and check to see how much material you have covered in the first hour of review. How does this compare to what you have left to study? Not every hour will be of equal merit (some hours will be more productive than others, while some material will take you longer to review), but you should be able to gauge pretty well from this first hour and from your previous experience.

Be careful how you "divvy up" your valuable study time. Schedule enough time for the task, but not so much time that you burn out. Every individual is different, but most students study best for blocks of about one and a half to three hours, depending on the subject. You might find history fascinating and be able to read for hours. Calculus, on the other hand, may be a subject that you can best handle in small bites, a half-hour to an hour at a time.

Don't overdo it. Plan your study time in blocks, breaking up work time with short leisure activities. It's helpful to add these to your schedule as well. You'll find that these breaks help you think more clearly and creatively when you get back to studying.

Even if you tend to like longer blocks of study time, be careful about scheduling study "marathons"—six- or eight-hour stretches rather than a series of two-hour sessions. The longer the period you schedule, the more likely you'll have to fight the demons of procrastination. Convincing yourself that you are really studying your heart out, you'll also find it easier to justify time-wasting distractions, scheduling longer breaks and, before long, quitting before you should.

Don't be dazed

Now we get to the Daily Schedule (see the sample on page 369 of this chapter), the piece of paper that will keep you sane as you move through the day.

Your Term Planning Calendar will most likely be on the wall beside your study area in your dorm, apartment, or house. Your Priority Tasks This Week should be carried with you so that you can add any items that suddenly come up in class ("Oh," your teacher says, "did I forget to tell you that we have a quiz on Friday on the first two chapters?") or in conversation ("Go skiing with you this weekend? With you *and* your gorgeous twin? Let me check my calendar!").

Carry your Daily Schedule so that you can be sure not to forget *anything*. The Daily Schedule, by the way, is divided into four categories:

1. **Assignments due.** What has to be turned in on this day. Check before you leave for class. (This is like the "T" notation on my shopping list.)

2. **To do/errands.** Don't depend on your memory. It's not that you can't remember; it's that you shouldn't *have* to remember. This column will help you plan ahead (for example, actually buying a birthday present before the birthday) and save you last-minute panic when you should be studying for the upcoming exam.

   As with any to-do list, make sure each item is really an item and not a combination of several steps (or stops). "Phone home" is one item; "arrange details for spring dance" is not.

3. **Homework.** When the teacher gives out homework assignments, here's where you can write them down so they're all together, complete with due dates, page numbers, and any other information from the teacher.

4. **Schedule.** The actual list of events for the day from early morning to late at night. This is especially important when you have something extraordinary happening. For example, suppose that your teacher tells you to meet her in a different room for your 9:30 biology class. Again, if you depend on your memory alone, you will most likely be the only one who isn't getting to dissect a frog over in McGillicuddy Hall.

In fact, you should highlight any unusual happenings with a brightly colored pen just to remind yourself. Take a moment to glance over the day's schedule *twice*. Look at it the night before, to psych yourself up for the coming day and make sure you didn't forget to do any special assignments. Then, glance at it again while you're having a quiet moment during your nutritious breakfast on the very day.

Using these time-saving tools effectively

Organizing your life requires you to actually *use* these tools. Once you have discovered habits and patterns of study that work for you, continue to use and hone them.

When you're scheduling your time, be specific about which tasks you plan to do and when you plan to do them.

Don't delay your planning. It's easy to convince yourself that you will plan the details of a particular task when the time comes. You may tell yourself, "I'll just leave my schedule blank and plan the afternoon right after I get out of biology." But that way it's much too easy to forget your homework when your friends invite you to go to the park or out for a snack.

Plan according to *your* schedule, *your* goals, and *your* aptitudes, not some ephemeral "standard." Allocate the time you expect a project to take *you*, not the time it might take someone else, how long your teacher says it should take, etc. Try to be realistic and honest with yourself when determining those things that require more effort or those that come easier to you.

Whenever possible, schedule pleasurable activities *after* study time, not before. They will then act as incentives, not distractions.

Be flexible and ready. Changes happen and you'll have to adjust your schedule to accommodate them.

Monitor your progress at reasonable periods and make changes where necessary. Remember, this is *your* study regimen—you conceived it, you can change it.

If you find that you are consistently allotting more time than necessary to a specific chore—giving yourself an hour to review your English notes every Sunday but always finishing in 45 minutes or less—change your future schedule accordingly. You may use the extra 15 minutes for a task that consistently takes *longer* than you've anticipated for, or if such doesn't exist, quit 15 minutes early. Isn't scheduling great?

As assignments are entered on your calendar, make sure you also enter items needed—texts, other books you have to buy, borrow or get from the library, and special materials such as drawing pads, magic markers, graph paper, etc.

You may decide that color coding your calendar—red for assignments that must be accomplished that week, blue for steps in longer-term assignments, yellow for personal time and appointments, green for classes, etc.—makes it easier for you to tell at a glance what you need to do and when you need to do it.

Adapt these tools for your own use. Try anything you think may work—use it if it does, discard it if it doesn't.

Do your least favorite chores (study assignments, projects, whatever) first—you'll feel better having gotten them out of the way! Plan how to accomplish them as meticulously as possible. That will get rid of them even faster.

Accomplish one task before going on to the next one—don't skip around. If you ever stuffed envelopes for a political candidate, for example, you've probably learned that it is quicker and easier to sign 100 letters, then stuff them into envelopes, then seal and stamp them, than to sign, stuff, seal, and stamp one letter at a time.

If you see that you are moving along faster than you anticipated on one task or project sequence, there is absolutely nothing wrong with continuing onto the next part of that assignment or the next project step.

If you are behind, don't panic. Just take the time to reorganize your schedule and find the time you need to make up. You may be able to free up time from another task, put one part of a long-term project off for a day or two, etc.

The tools we've discussed and the various other hints should get you into the habit of writing things down. Not having to remember all these items will free up space in your brain for the things you need to concentrate on or *do* have to remember.

Learn to manage distractions. As a time-management axiom puts it, "Don't respond to the urgent and forget the important." Some things you do can be picked up or dropped at any time. Beware of these time-consuming and complicated tasks that, once begun, demand to be completed. Interrupting at any point might mean starting all over again. What a waste of time *that* would be!

If you're writing and have a brainstorm—just as the phone rings (and you *know* it's from that person you've been waiting to hear from all week)—take a minute to at least jot down your ideas before you answer the phone.

Nothing can be as counterproductive as losing your concentration, especially at critical times. Learn to ward off those enemies that would alter your course and you will find your journey much smoother.

One way to guard against these mental intrusions is to know your own study clock and plan your study time accordingly. Each of us is predisposed to function most efficiently at specific times of day (or night). Find out what sort of study clock you're on and schedule your work during this period.

Beware of uninvited guests and *all* phone calls: Unless you are ready for a break, they'll only get you off schedule.

More subtle enemies include the sudden desire to sharpen every pencil in the house, an unheard-of urge to clean your room, an offer to do your sister's homework. Anything, in other words, to avoid your own work. If you find yourself doing anything *but* your work, either take a break then and there or pull yourself together and get down to work. Self-discipline, too, is a learned habit that gets easier with practice.

Saying no (to others or yourself) will help you insulate yourself from these unnecessary (and postponable) interruptions. Remember, you are seeking to achieve not just time—but *quality* time. Put your "do not disturb" sign up and stick to your guns, no matter what the temptation.

Going into "test training"

Now that you have discovered the value of keeping track of upcoming events, including exams—and the possibility that you can actually plan ahead and keep your life from getting too crazy even during finals week—we can talk a little about the days prior to the exams themselves.

If you have an upcoming exam early in the morning and you are afraid you won't be in shape for it, do a bit of subterfuge on your body and brain.

Get up early for several days before the exam, have a good breakfast, and do homework or review your notes. This will help jump-start your brain and get it used to the idea of having to solve equations or think seriously about the Punjab at an earlier-than-usual hour.

On the other end of the day, take care to get to bed early enough. Forego the late-night parties and the midnight movie on TV and actually devote enough time to getting some serious ZZZZZs.

Cramming doesn't work

In case I didn't mention it yet, *cramming does not work.* We've all done it at one time or another, with one excuse or another—waited until the last minute and then tried to fit a week's, month's, or entire semester's worth of work into a single night or weekend. Did it work? Doubt it.

After a night of no sleep and too much coffee, most of us are lucky if we remember where the test *is* the next day. A few hours later, trying to stay awake long enough to make it back to bed, we not only haven't learned anything, we haven't done well on the test we crammed for!

How to cram anyway

Nevertheless, despite your resolve, best intentions, and firm conviction that cramming is a losing proposition, you may well find yourself—though hopefully not too often—in the position of needing to do *some*thing the night before a test you haven't studied for at all. If so, there are some rules to follow that will make your night of cramming at least marginally successful.

Be realistic about what you can do. You absolutely *cannot* master a semester's worth of work in one night. The *more* you try to cram in, the *less* effective you will be.

Be selective and study in depth. The more you've missed, the more selective you must be in organizing your cram session. You *can't* study it all. In this case, it's better to know a lot about a little rather than a little about a lot.

Massage your memory. Use every memory technique you know (and those in *Improve Your Memory*) to maximize what you can retain in your short-term memory.

Know when to give up. When you can't remember your name, give up and get some sleep. Better to arrive at the exam with some sleep under your belt, feeling as relaxed as possible.

Consider an early morning versus a late-night cram. Especially if you're a morning person, but even if you're not, I've found it more effective to go to bed and get up early rather than go to bed late and get up exhausted.

Spend the first few minutes writing down whatever you remember now but are afraid you'll forget, especially when your mind is trying to hold on to so many facts and figures it seems ready to explode.

Get a copy of my latest book—*Last Minute Study Tips.* It will help you prepare for a test that's weeks, days, hours, or just minutes away...and do better on it.

As time goes by

Be honest with yourself. Don't block out two hours to study for your calculus exam *today* when you suspect your best friend will entice you to go with him to get a pizza and talk about anything *but* calculus. If you have budgeted six hours to prepare for the entire exam, you've just cheated yourself out of a third of the time.

It's okay to write down "pizza with Binky" for those two hours. Just be realistic and honest and budget your study time when you will truly be studying.

Term Planning Calendar

Fill In due dates for assignments and papers, dates of tests, and Important non-academic activities and events

Month	Mon	Tue	Wed	Thu	Fri	Sat	Sun

Priority Rating	Scheduled?	**Priority Tasks This Week** *Week of* *through*

Daily Schedule   *date:*

Assignments Due   Schedule

Assignments Due	Schedule
	5
	6
	7
	8
	9

To Do/Errands

To Do/Errands	
	10
	11
	12
	1
	2
	3
	4
	5

Homework

Homework	
	6
	7
	8
	9
	10
	11
	12

CHAPTER 3

WHEN SHOULD YOU *REALLY* START STUDYING?

Once upon a time, there was a hard-working student named Mel. He read his books, took good notes, rarely missed a day of school, and always did his homework. Sitting next to him was a guy named Steve. This guy *sort of* took notes, *kind of* read his book, and *usually* did his homework. Well, okay, not usually, but *kind of* usually—if he came to class at all.

The day of the big test came. Hard-working Mel got a D and slouchy, lazy Steve got an A.

If you believe this bears any resemblance to reality, please read and reread every one of the books in my **How to Study Program**. All nine of them. You need all the help you can get.

The first day of the test of your life

Well, maybe I shouldn't really say "test of your life." Even the SAT isn't *that* important or scary!

What I really want to emphasize in this chapter was hinted at in the "once upon a time" story above: You don't start preparing for a test a couple of days before. You begin when you walk into the classroom on the first day—or even *before* that.

Too many students think the exam is out there all by itself—floating out in space like a balloon that got loose from a bawling kid at a carnival. Nope.

Everything you do in that course—attending every class, applying listening skills, taking good notes, doing your homework, and reading all the assignments—helps you in "studying" for the exam.

For whom the alarm clock tolls

Yes, my friend, it may be cruel and it may be cold, but getting out of bed and going to class is the first step toward passing the final that's four months away.

"Oooh, missing that biology class just this one time can't huuuuurrrrrrt!" you moan as you roll over and bury your head under the pillow.

Obviously, if this is you, you've got to start by getting to bed a little bit earlier, planning ahead a little bit more, and deciding that going to class is something you must do automatically.

Now that you're here...

All right. I got you out of bed and inside the classroom. You're awake, polite, respectful, and listening. Now what?

Actually, that question should have been asked last night or several nights ago. You can't just waltz into class and be up to speed. When you arrive, you're expected by your teacher to have:

1. Read the assignment.
2. Brought your notes/textbooks with you.
3. Brought your homework assignment.
4. Opened your notebook to the right page, opened the textbook to the current chapter, and taken out your homework to hand it in.

Before that bell rings for class to begin, have your work ready to go so you don't waste time trying to find everything. Of course, if you've done a last-minute check back home or in the dorm, you'll know for sure that you've got the right books, notebooks, homework assignments, etc. Teachers get really tired of hearing, "I left it at home/in the car/in the dorm/with my girlfriend."

Pop goes the quiz

Not all tests, as you know by now, are announced. Your teacher may decide, out of malice, boredom, or his or her lesson-plan book, to give you a pop quiz.

Now, how can you score well if you, first of all, aren't in class and, second of all, haven't read the new material and periodically reviewed the old? And suppose it's an open-book test and you don't have a book to open?

Let's face it. Biology, U.S. history, Economics or Whatever 101 may not be your favorite subject, but that doesn't mean you have to have an attitude about it. "Proving" you can't or won't do well in a class proves nothing.

The next steps

Let's move on to what you should do during class, after class, and before class.

First, during class, you need to listen and observe. Not a difficult task, even when the teacher isn't going to win any elocution or acting awards. Identifying noteworthy material means finding a way to separate the wheat—that which you *should* write down—from the chaff—that which you should *ignore.*

How do you do that? By *listening* for verbal clues and *watching* for nonverbal ones.

Many teachers will invariably signal important material in the way they present it—pausing (waiting for all the pens to rise), repeating the same point (perhaps even one already made and repeated in your textbook), slowing down their normally supersonic lecture speed, speaking more loudly (or more softly), and even by simply stating, "I think the following is important."

There are also a number of words that should *signal* noteworthy material (and, at the same time, give you the clues you need to organize your notes logically): "first of all," "most importantly," "therefore," "as a result," "to summarize," "on the other hand," "on the contrary," "the following (number of) reasons (causes, effects, decisions, facts, etc.)."

Words and phrases such as these give you the clues to not just write down the lecture material that follows but to put it in context—to make a list ("first," "the following reasons"); establish a cause-and-effect relationship ("therefore," "as a result"); establish opposites or alternatives ("on the other hand," "on the contrary," "alternatively"); signify a conclusion ("therefore," "to summarize"); or offer an explanation or definition.

Don't just listen, watch!

If the teacher begins looking out the window, or his eyes glaze over, he's sending you a clear signal: "This isn't going to be on the test. (So don't take notes!)"

On the other hand, if she turns to write something on the blackboard, makes eye contact with several students, and/or gestures dramatically, she's sending a clear signal about the importance of the point she's making.

Of course, there are many exceptions to this rule. My first-year calculus instructor would occasionally launch into long diatribes about his mother or air pollution, in tones more impassioned than any he ever used working through differential equations.

There was also the trigonometry professor I endured who got all worked up about the damage being done to the nation's sidewalks by the deadly menace of chewing gum.

Nevertheless, learn to be a detective—don't overlook the clues.

Teachers like to see students take notes. It shows them that you are interested in the topic at hand and that you think enough of what is being said to write it down. (If you've ever stood at the front of the room, you can usually tell who's taking notes and who's writing a letter to that friend in Iowa.)

You are your own best note-taker

I'm sure you have observed in your classes that some people are constantly taking notes, while others end up with two lines on one page. Most of us fall in between.

The person who never stops taking notes is either writing a letter to that friend in Iowa or has absolutely no idea what *is* or is *not* important.

The results are dozens of pages of notes (by the end of the semester) that may or may not be helpful. This person is so busy writing down stuff that he isn't prepared or even aware that he can ask and answer questions to help him understand the material better. To use that old adage, he can't see the forest for the trees. He is probably the same person who takes a marking pen and underlines or highlights every other word in the book.

Compare him to the guy who thinks note-taking isn't cool, so he only writes down today's date and the homework assignment. He may write something when the teacher says, "Now, write this down and remember it," but he probably just scribbles some nonsense words. After all, he's cool.

Watch him sweat when it's time to study for the exam. He's stuck with a faulty memory and a textbook that may not contain half the material that will be on the test.

Notes: Tools of the trade

For a time, I found it very useful to type my notes after I'd written them in class. First of all, my handwriting won't win any prizes. I noticed early on that very few people asked to borrow my notes. "Is this word 'Madagascar' or 'Muncie'?" they'd ask a little too loudly.

Second, typing the notes gave me an opportunity to have a quick review of the class, spell out most of my abbreviations, and—most importantly—discover if I missed anything. This gave me time to check my textbook or ask a classmate for the missing information. You don't want to discover this at midnight the night before the test.

A neater version of my notes was also extremely helpful when it came time to study for the test. I could read what was there, I had highlighted the most important elements and the whole batch of notes just made more sense.

Why did I say I did this "for a time"? Because I stopped doing it my second year of college and have not done it since. I concluded that the "cons"—primarily the time I was wasting—just outweighed the "pros" discussed above.

Instead, I concentrated on developing my own shorthand system that minimized the need to rewrite anything and maximized my ability to capture "noteworthy" materials the first (and only) time around. (If you missed my explanation of this system, go back to **Take Notes** and study it now.)

Reading is fundamental

Reading improves reading. If you hate reading or consider yourself a slow reader, keep at it anyway. Read anything and everything. Read at nights and on weekends. Read cereal boxes (even though the ingredients can often be as scary as a Stephen King novel) and newspapers and magazines and short stories and...well, you get the idea.

Let's look at how you can use your reading skills—and improve them—to get higher grades. Here are some suggestions that help people read more efficiently:

1. When a chapter in a textbook has questions at the end, read the questions first. Why? They will give you an idea of what the chapter is all about and they will be "clues" as to what you should look for in the text.

2. Some of the *words* in each chapter will help you concentrate on the important points and ignore the unimportant. Knowing when to speed up, slow down, ignore, or really concentrate will help you read both faster *and* more effectively.

   When you come across words like "likewise," "in addition," "moreover," "furthermore," and the like, you should know nothing new is being introduced. If you already know what's going on, speed up or skip what's coming entirely.

When you see words like "on the other hand," "nevertheless," "however," "rather," "but," and their ilk, slow down—you're getting information that adds a new perspective or contradicts what you've just read.

Lastly, watch for payoff words such as, "in conclusion," "to summarize," "consequently," "thus"— especially if you only have time to hit the high points of a chapter.

3. Underline or highlight main points in the text. Don't, like our friend I mentioned earlier, mark too much or your efforts will be meaningless. At the same time, pay special attention to words and phrases the author has highlighted by placing them in italics or in boldface.

4. Don't skip over the maps, charts, graphs, photos, or drawings. Much of this information may not be in the text. If you skip it, you're skipping vital information.

5. What's the big picture here? We can get bogged down in the footnotes and unfamiliar words and lose touch with the purpose of the chapter. Keep these simple steps in mind:

  ☞ If there is a heading, rephrase it as a question. This will support your purpose for reading.

  ☞ Examine all subheadings, illustrations, and graphics, as these will help you identify the significant matter within the text.

  ☞ Read the introductory paragraphs, summary, and any questions at the end of the chapter.

  ☞ Read the first sentence of every paragraph— this is generally where the main idea is found.

☞ Evaluate what you've gained from the process: Can you answer the questions at the chapter's end? Could you intelligently participate in a class discussion of the material?

☞ Write a brief summary of what you have learned from your skimming.

6. Shortly before class, look over the chapter again. Review what you and the author have decided are the most important points and mark topics you want the teacher to explain. (It's much better to have valid questions rather than trying to look smart by having a quota of questions each time. Teachers know the difference.)

15 questions to help you

Beyond grasping the meaning of words and phrases, critical reading requires that you ask questions. Here are 15 questions that will help you effectively analyze and interpret most of what you read.

1. Is a clear message communicated throughout?
2. Are the relationships between the points direct and clear?
3. Is there a relationship between your experience and the author's?
4. Are the details factual?
5. Are the examples and evidence relevant?
6. Is there consistency of thought?
7. What is the author's bias or slant?
8. What is the author's motive?
9. What does the author want you to believe?
10. Does this jibe with your beliefs or experiences?

11. Is the author rational or subjective?
12. Is there a confusion between feelings and facts?
13. Are the main points logically ordered?
14. Are the arguments and conclusions consistent?
15. Are the explanations clear?

Obviously, this list of questions is not all-inclusive, but it will give you a jump start when critical reading is required. Remember, the essential ingredient to any effective analysis and interpretation is the questions you ask.

After class

The best time to study for your next class is right after the last one. Say you have Government 101 at 9:30 a.m. on Tuesdays and Thursdays. As soon as you can after your Tuesday class, review the day's notes, type them if possible, and complete the reading and homework for Thursday.

Why? Because the class is fresh in your mind. Your notes are crying out to be reviewed and corrected or added to, and you have a level of understanding that may not be there Wednesday night at 9 p.m.

Then, spend a little time on the same class and the same materials as close as possible to the next class. Let's say you can do that at 8:30 a.m. on Thursday. The *big* study time is ASAP after Tuesday's class; the little *quick-let's-review* time comes shortly *before* Thursday's class.

Now, let's refine these study habits for the next test.

CHAPTER 4

STUDY SMARTER, NOT HARDER

Charles de Secondat, Baron de Montesquieu, said, "You have to study a great deal to know a little." I'm going to be so bold as to amend what the baron said: "You have to study a reasonable amount to know a great deal." Why change his centuries-old words? Because we know a lot about study techniques that he didn't and we can concentrate on studying *smarter*, not harder.

Let's look at how we can study a reasonable amount and do well on the exams that are intended to find out if we know what we think we do.

The pharaohs wouldn't approve

Let me tell you about my Inverted Pyramid Theory. The top is very wide, the bottom very narrow. This is symbolic of the way you should study for a test. Begin with all possible materials (all notes, book chapters, workbooks, audio tapes, etc.) and briefly review everything to determine what you need to spend time with and what you can put aside.

I also call this separating the wheat from the chaff. The wheat is the edible good stuff that's taken from the field and turned into Chocolate Sugar Munchies. The chaff stays behind. The chaff was important at one time but no longer is needed. The same is true of some of the material you've gathered for this next test. Now try this:

1. Gather all the material you have been using for the course: books, workbooks, handouts, notes, homework, previous tests, and papers.

2. Compare the contents with the material you will be tested on and ask yourself: What exactly do I need to review for this test?

3. Select the material for review. Reducing the pile of books and papers will be a psychological aid— suddenly, it'll seem as if you have enough time and energy to study for the test.

4. Photocopy and complete the Pre-Test Organizer on pages 437 and 438 of chapter 9. Consider carefully the "Material to be covered" section. Be specific. The more detailed you are, the better job you'll do in reviewing all the areas that you should know. This exercise will help you *quantify* what you need to do. Instead of wandering aimlessly through your materials, you will have told yourself just where this information is.

5. As you review the material and conclude that you know it for the test, put a bold check mark on the "Okay" line. You are, to use my example, inverting the pyramid, or shrinking the amount of material you need to study.

   Now you have time not only to spend on the stuff that's giving you grief, but to seek out other sources (fellow students, the teacher, the library, etc.) and get to the heart of the matter.

6. By the time the test is given, you should have reduced the "pyramid" to nothing. Go into the test and do well!

The way of all flash

You probably remember flashcards from elementary school. On one side was a picture, on the other, a word. Or one side held a definition ("Someone who studies bugs"), and the other, the word being defined ("entomologist").

Using flashcards is a great way to test yourself. It also works for two people studying together or for a group. It works well for studying vocabulary, short answers, definitions, matching ("Boise" and "potato"), even true and false.

Learn from your mistakes

If you have access to old exams written by the same teacher, especially if they cover the same material you're going to be tested on, use them also for review.

Chances are, the very same questions will *not* appear again. But the way the test is prepared, the kinds of questions, the emphasis on one kind of question over another (100 true/false, 50 multiple-choice, and one—count 'em— one essay), will give you clues to what your own test will be about.

At the same time, see if you can find anyone who had this teacher for this class last year or last semester. Can they give you any advice, tips, hints, or warnings?

Once you've discovered the type of test facing you, you'll want to figure out what's going to be *on* it (and hence, what you need to study). Remember, it's rarely, if ever, "everything."

In general, take the time to eliminate from consideration, with the possible exception of a cursory review, material you are convinced is simply not important enough to be included on an upcoming test. This will automatically give you more time to concentrate on those areas you are sure *will* be included.

Then create a "To Study" sheet for each test. On it, list specific books to review; notes to recheck; specific topics, principles, ideas, and concepts to go over; etc. Then just check off each item as you study it. This method will minimize procrastination, logically organize your studying and give you ongoing "jolts" of accomplishment as you complete each item.

All teachers are not equal (or fair or...)

In an ideal world, all teachers would be filled with knowledge they eagerly and expertly shared with their students. Their lectures would be exciting and brief. Their tests would be fair and accurate measurements of what the students should have learned.

Before you tell me a story about flying pigs, let me say that, in spite of the criticism schools and teachers have been getting for years, there are a lot of teachers out there like that. If you don't think you've had one yet, your turn is coming up.

In the meantime, though, let's consider Weird Al (or Weird Alice.) His personality may come out, unfortunately, when he writes and grades his tests. If you're lucky, you'll be forewarned by his former students so that you can be prepared as much as possible.

Watch for these danger signs. Even if he never seems to know when the next test will be, try to get that answer out of him. Believe me, you want to ask. It's better to discover today that it's a week from Thursday rather than finding out the Wednesday before.

If he says he doesn't know what the test will cover, keep asking him. Also ask what types of questions will be on the test (true/false, multiple choice, essays, etc.) and what percentage of the test will be devoted to each. By your questions, you are helping him shape the test in his mind, and giving him the information he needs to give back to you.

Once you've taken the test, check your corrected test paper carefully. If a right answer was marked wrong, let him know. If the question is too ambiguous and you think your answer could be right as well as the one *he* says is right, let him know.

And now, h-e-e-e-e-r-r-e-e-e's the SAT

Well, you did it. You registered to take the SAT or ACT and the Day of Reckoning is approaching.

I'll share some specifics on taking *any* test in the next few chapters, but for right now, just remember that any hours-long national standardized test requires a lot of the same skills and the same planning as any unit quiz, chapter test, midterm, or final.

Because these standardized tests are intended to test your general knowledge of many areas, rather than grill you on the details from Chapter 14 of your chemistry book, you can and you *cannot* study for them. You cannot study specific material. On the other hand, you have been studying for them all your life.

This test will seek to find out what you know about a lot of different subjects. Some of the answers will come from knowledge you gained years before. Others will come from your ability to work out the problems right there, using techniques and knowledge you gained this semester.

To prepare for any standardized test—the SAT, ACT, GRE, GMAT, etc.—I have one big suggestion: Determine, based on your past test-taking experiences and your comfort levels, what your weak areas are. Do you continually and completely mess up essay questions? Do analogies spin you out of control? Do you freeze at the sight of an isosceles triangle?

Seek out teachers, librarians, and school counselors who can guide you to samples of these kinds of questions. Ask your teachers and fellow students for advice on handling the areas you feel you are weak in, take the sample tests, then work on evaluating how you did. Keep testing yourself and keep evaluating how you are doing.

Get advice from other students who say things like, "Analogies? Piece of cake!" Find out if they really can do them easily and get tips from them (and from what I say in the following chapters).

Also, a solid review of basic math and English will be valuable. If geometry is not your strong suit, find a book that contains lists of the fundamentals and spend time reviewing information that you will be expected to exercise on the SAT. Do the same with the other subject areas to be tested. If your library doesn't have such materials, get advice from teachers or from the counseling office.

Put me in, coach!

Should you take one of those SAT preparation courses? Is it worth the money, the time, the effort, the bother?

The answer is a definite maybe. It depends on a handful of factors: First of all, ask others for recommendations. Listen closely to why they liked or disliked a particular course (their reasons may not match your reasons—tread carefully here). Ask particularly about each course's effectiveness and results.

Decide if you have the time and money to take a course. If you do, which kind do you want? There are coaching classes taught by people, but there are also book/cassette tape combos and computer programs. Ask your school counseling office for recommendations. The office may even have copies of some of the programs. If you don't have the money, ask about financial aid and other ways to reduce tuition.

Evaluate the professionalism of whatever course you're considering. How good are the materials? Do they look complete and professionally prepared, or do they consist of a sheaf of badly photocopied forms and a ratty binder? Can you attend a meeting free to get a feel for the procedures? Will they furnish you with the resumes of your instructors? Will those instructors be accessible outside of class?

Finally, are there any money-back guarantees? The best companies—in this or any field—stand behind their product, even if that means giving full refunds to dissatisfied customers.

There's method in their madness—I think

The standardized-test coaching programs should deal with two areas. I'll call them Method and Content.

Method is the study of *how* to take a test, specifically how to take the SAT, ACT, GRE, whatever. That portion of the course will cover much of the same material that you're reading in this book, especially the material we're going to look at in the next two chapters.

Content deals with practicing the sort of stuff that will be on the specific test you are taking: vocabulary words, math problems, essay questions, analogies, and so on.

The two areas overlap, of course. When you work math problems, there are methods you utilize to get the answer, just as there is content.

Practicing for the SAT by answering questions that are similar in content to what you will later be tested on is a valuable exercise, but it's only half the equation. The other half is the feedback you get from your coach (or teacher, counselor, or fellow students) on what you did, how you did it, and why you did what you did. It won't do you any good to keep messing up on analogies, for example, if you can't stop and figure out how to do them right.

CHAPTER 5

ESSAY TESTS: WRITE ON!

Essay questions. Some students love them. Some hate them. Personally, I think *all* "objective" tests are harder than essay tests. Why? An objective test of any kind gives the teacher much more latitude, even the option of focusing *only* on the most obscure details (which, granted, only the truly sadistic would do). As a result, it's much more difficult to eliminate areas or topics when studying for such a test. It's also rare to be given a choice—answer 25 out of 50—whereas you may often be given, for example, five essay questions and have to choose only three. This greatly increases the odds that even sporadic studying will have given you some rudimentary understanding of one or two of the questions, whereas you may be lost on a 100-question true-false test.

Why else did I like essay tests? Less could go wrong on an essay test—there were only three or four questions to read, not 100 potential *mis*reads. I could think of a few questions, not hundreds. I could take the time to organize (a strength) and write (another strength). It was also easier to budget time among three or four essay questions than among 150 multiple-choice.

Whether you love or hate essays, there are some important pointers to ensure that you at least score better on them.

Of course you know this, but...

Really advanced schools with big budgets provide typewriters or computers for their students so they can write essays in the classroom. But we can't all have 90210 as our ZIP code. The rest of you will have to work with a pen.

First of all, make sure it's a good, comfortable pen. If you hate ballpoints and swear by felt-tipped pens, then go for it. Actually, go for *them*. Only someone who wants a really bad grade shows up with one pen. Naturally, it will run out, begin to leak, break, or all of the above if you have only one. If you have two (or, for the truly superstitious, three or more) then, of course, the first pen will be working like that annoying drum-beating rabbit when your grandchildren are taking the SAT on Mars.

Think before you ink

Approach essay questions the same way you would a paper. Although you can't check your textbook or go to the library to do research, the facts, ideas, comparisons, etc., you need are in your own cerebral library—your mind.

Don't ever, *ever* begin writing the answer to an essay question without a little "homework" first. I don't care if you're the school's prize-winning journalist.

First, dissect the question. Are you sure you know what it's really asking? What are the verbs? Don't "describe" when it calls for you to "compare and contrast." Don't "explain" when it tells you to "argue." Underline the verbs. (See pages 394 through 396 for a list of the most-used such verbs in essay tests and what each is instructing you to do.) And please *don't*, intentionally or otherwise, misread the question in such a way that you answer the question you'd *like* rather than the one you've actually been given.

Then, sit back a minute and think about what you are going to say. Or less than a minute, depending on how much time you have, but *don't* just start writing.

Here's a step-by-step way to answer essay questions:

Step one: On a blank sheet of paper, write down all the facts, ideas, concepts, etc., you feel should be included in your answer.

Step two: Organize them in the order in which they should appear. You don't have to rewrite your notes into a detailed outline—why not just number each note according to where you want to place it?

Step three: Compose your first paragraph, working on it just as long and as hard as I suggested you do on your papers. It should summarize and introduce the key points you will make in your essay. *This is where superior essay answers are made or unmade.*

Step four: Write your essay, with your penmanship as legible as possible. Most teachers I've known do *not* go out of their way to decipher chickenscratch masquerading as an essay and do *not* award high grades to it either.

Step five: Reread your essay and, if necessary, add points left out, correct spelling, grammar, etc. Also watch for a careless omission that could cause serious damage—leaving out a "not," for example.

If there is a particular fact you know is important and should be included but you just don't remember it, take a guess. Otherwise, just leave it out and do the best you can.

If the rest of your essay is well-thought-out and organized and clearly communicates all the other points that should be included, I doubt most teachers will mark you down too severely for such an omission.

Remember: Few teachers will be impressed by length. A well-organized, well-constructed, specific answer will always get you a better grade than "shotgunning"—writing down everything you know in the faint hope that you will actually hit something. Don't waste your time (and your teacher's).

Start out right, with a brief, to-the-point first paragraph that doesn't meander or "pad." ("What were the similarities between Dante's Beatrice and Joyce's Molly Bloom? To truly answer this question, we must first embark upon a study of Italian and Irish literature, politics, and culture at the time..." Have we wasted enough of our precious time trying to cover up our lack of knowledge here?) End your essay with a clearly-written and organized paragraph that offers more than just a summation of what you've already written.

Worry less about the specific words and more about the information. Organize your answer to a fault and write to be understood, not to impress. Better to use shorter sentences, paragraphs, and words—and be clear and concise—than to let the teacher fall into a clausal nightmare from which he may never emerge (and neither will your A!).

If you don't have the faintest clue what the question means, ask. If you still don't have any idea of the answer—and I mean *zilch*—leave it blank. Writing down everything you think you know about the supposed subject in the hopes that one or two things will actually have something to do with the question is, in my mind, a waste of everyone's time. Better to allocate the time you would waste to other parts of the test and do a better job on those.

The best-organized beats the best-written

Although I think numbering your notes is as good an organizational tool as jotting down a complete outline, there is certainly nothing wrong with fashioning a quick outline. Not one with Roman numerals—this outline will consist of a simple list of abbreviated words, scribbled on a piece of scrap paper or in the margin of your test booklet.

The purpose of this outline is the same as that of those fancy ones: to make sure you include everything you need and want to say—in order.

It's important to write well. But excellent writing, even pages and pages of it, will not get you an excellent grade unless you write quality answers—hard-hitting, incisive, and direct.

Think of the introduction and the conclusion as the bread of a sandwich, with the information in between as the hamburger, lettuce, tomato, and pickle. Everything is necessary for it all to hang together, but the main attraction is going to be what's between the slices.

Give me some space, man

Plan ahead. Write your essay on every other line and on one side of the paper or page only. This will give you room to add or correct anything without having to write it so small that it is illegible and, therefore, doesn't earn you any credit.

It also helps keep the whole paper neater and, psychologically, that should help you get a slightly better grade. Most teachers won't admit it, but they will give a few more points to tests that are neat, clean, and done with a good pen. Think about it. How many slobs do you know who are A students?

Proof it!

Budget your time so that you can go back over your essay, slowly, and correct any mistakes or make any additions. Check your spelling, punctuation, grammar, and syntax. (If you don't know what syntax is, find out. You'll need to know for the SAT.) It would be a shame for you to write a beautiful, thorough essay and lose points because of careless errors.

When you're done, you're *almost* done

Resist the temptation to leave the room or turn in your paper before you absolutely must. Imagine the pain of sitting in the cafeteria, while everyone else is back in the classroom, continuing to work on the test, and suddenly remembering what else you could have said to make your essay really sparkle. But it will be too late!

Take the time at the end of the test to review not only your essay answers, but your other answers as well. Make sure all words and numbers are readable. Make sure you have matched the right questions with the right answers. Even make sure you didn't miss a whole section by turning over a page too quickly or not noticing that a page was missing. Make sure you can't, simply *can't*, add anything more to any of the essay answers. Make sure. Make sure. Make sure.

If you're out of time, are you out of luck?

You may find yourself with two minutes left and one full essay to go. What do you do? As quickly as possible, write down every piece of information you think should be included in your answer, and number each point in the order in which you would have written it. If you then have time to reorganize your notes into a better-organized outline, do so. Many teachers will give you at least partial credit (some very near *full* credit) if your outline contains all the information the answer was supposed to. It will at least show you knew a lot about the subject and were capable of outlining a reasonable response.

One of the reasons you may have left yourself with insufficient time to answer one or more questions is you knew too darned much about the previous question(s), and you wanted to make sure the teacher *knew* you knew, so you wrote...and wrote...and wrote...until you ran out of time.

Be careful—some teachers throw in a relatively general question that, if you wanted to, you could write about until next Wednesday. In that case, they aren't testing your knowledge of the whole subject as much as your ability to *edit* yourself, to organize and summarize the *important* points.

Just remember that no matter how fantastic your answer to any one essay, it is going to get 1/5 the overall score (presuming five questions)—that is, 20 points, never more, even if you turn in a publishable book manuscript. Meanwhile, 80 points are unclaimed.

If you've mastered the tips and techniques in this chapter, you will, from now on, "be like Ron": You'll positively drool when you see a test that's nothing but essays!

Common instructional verbs

Compare   Examine two or more objects, ideas, people, etc., and note similarities and differences.

Contrast   Compare to highlight differences. Similar to *differentiate, distinguish*.

Criticize	Judge and discuss merits and faults. Similar to *critique*.
Define	Explain the nature or essential qualities.
Describe	Convey the appearance, nature, attributes, etc.
Discuss	Consider or examine by argument, comment, etc.; debate; explore solutions.
Enumerate	List various events, things, descriptions, ideas, etc.
Evaluate	Appraise the worth of an idea, comment, etc., and justify your conclusion.
Explain	Make the meaning of something clear, plain, intelligible, and/or understandable.
Illustrate	Use specific examples or analogies to explain.
Interpret	Give the meaning of something by paraphrase, by translation, or by an explanation based on personal opinion.
Justify	Defend a statement or conclusion. Similar to *support*.
Narrate	Recount the occurrence of something, usually by giving details of events in the order in which they occurred. Similar to *describe*, but only applicable to something that happens in time.
Outline	Do a general sketch, account, or report, indicating only the main features of a book, subject, or project.
Prove	Establish the truth or genuineness by evidence or argument. Similar to *show*, *explain why*, *demonstrate*. (In math, verify validity by mathematical demonstration.)

Relate   Give an account of events and/or circumstances, usually to establish associations, connections, or relationships.

Review   Survey a topic, occurrence, or idea, generally but critically. Similar to *describe, discuss, illustrate, outline, summarize, trace.* Some test-makers may use these words virtually interchangeably, although one can find subtle differences in each.

State   Present the facts concisely. May be used interchangeably with *name, list, indicate, identify, enumerate, cite.*

Summarize State in concise form, omitting examples and details.

Trace   Follow the course or history of an occurrence, idea, etc.

CHAPTER 6

OBJECTIVE TESTS: DISCRIMINATE AND ELIMINATE

Some people prefer objective tests to essays. After all, in multiple-choice questions, the answer is staring you in the face (and secretly sticking out its tongue at you, if you don't recognize it). You just have to be able to figure out which one it is.

In this chapter, we're going to look at different types of objective questions and some of the methods to use to answer each type, based primarily on "the process of elimination."

If you learn nothing else from this chapter, learn this: The process of elimination has saved many a person from failure. It may just save you.

Place prong A into dovetail Y using tube 4

A very key point of preparation for *any* kind of test: Read and understand the directions. Otherwise, you could seemingly do everything *right*, but not follow your teacher's explicit directions, in which case everything's *wrong*.

If you're supposed to check off *every* correct answer to each question in a multiple choice test—and you're assuming only *one* answer to each question is correct—you're going to miss a lot of answers!

If you're to pick one essay question out of three, or two out of five, that's a lot different than trying to answer every one. You won't be able to do it. Even if you do, the teacher will probably only grade the first two. Because you needed to allocate enough time to do the other three, it's highly doubtful your first two answers will be so detailed and so perfect that they will be able to stand alone.

Are the questions or sections weighted? Some tests may have two, three, or more sections, some of which count for very little—10 or 20 percent of your final score—while one, usually a major essay, may be more heavily weighted—50 percent or more of your grade. Let this influence the amount of energy you devote to each section.

Beware of time. If questions or sections are weighted, you'll want to allow extra time for those that count for 90 percent of the score and whip through the 10-percent section as the teacher is collecting booklets.

I know students who, before they write a single answer, look through the entire test and break it down into time segments—allocating 20 minutes for section one, 40 for section two, etc. Even on multiple-choice tests, they count the total number of questions, divide by the time allotted, and set "goals" on what time they should reach question 10, question 25, etc.

I never did it, but I think it's a great idea—if it turns out to be a workable organizational tool for you and not just one more layer of pressure.

If there are pertinent facts or formulas you're afraid you'll forget, I think it's a good idea to write them down somewhere in your test booklet before you do anything else. It won't take much time, and it could save some serious memory jogs later.

When a guess isn't just a guess

Will you be penalized for guessing? The teacher may inform you that you will earn two points for every correct answer, but *lose* one point for every incorrect one. This will certainly affect whether you guess or skip the question—or, at the very least, how many potential answers you feel you need to eliminate before the odds of guessing are in your favor.

There is usually nothing wrong with guessing, unless, of course, you know wrong answers will be penalized. Even then, the question is how *much* to guess.

If there's no penalty for wrong answers, you should *never* leave an answer blank. But you should also do everything you can to increase your odds of getting it right. If every multiple-choice question gives you four possible answers, you have a 25-percent chance of being right (and, of course, a 75-percent chance of being wrong) each time you have to guess.

But if you can eliminate a single answer—one you are reasonably certain cannot be right—your chances of being correct increase to 33 percent.

And, of course, if you can get down to a choice between two answers, it's just like flipping a coin: 50-50. In the long run, you will guess as many right as wrong.

Even if there is a penalty for guessing, I would probably pick one answer if I had managed to increase my chances of getting the right one to 50-50.

Presuming that you've managed to eliminate one or more answers but are still unsure of the correct answer and have no particular way to eliminate further, here are some real insider tips to make your "guess" more educated:

☞ If two answers sound alike, choose neither.

☞ If the answers that are left to a mathematical question cover a broad range, choose the number in the middle.

☞ If two quantities are very close, choose one of them.

☞ If two numbers differ only by a decimal point (and the others aren't close), choose one of them. (Example: 2.3, 40, 1.5, 6, 15; I'd go with 1.5 or 15. If I could at least figure out from the question where the decimal point should go, even better!)

☞ If two answers to a math problem *look* alike— either formulas or shapes—choose one of them.

Remember: This is not the way to ace a test—these are just some tried-and-true ways to increase your guessing power when *you have absolutely nothing else to go on and nothing left to do.*

Eliminate the obvious and sort-of obvious

Suppose the question was as follows: "The first U.S. President to appoint a woman to the Cabinet was: (A) Franklin D. Roosevelt, (B) Herbert Hoover, (C) Abraham Lincoln, or (D) Jimmy Carter."

"Heck if I know," you may be saying to yourself. But you know more than you think! Most likely, you can get the answer down to two choices pretty quickly. Why is that? Think for a moment about women's rights and the role of women in American society. Okay, that's long enough.

You're absolutely correct to eliminate, right away, Abraham Lincoln. It wasn't that he was a bad guy; you just have to remember that women didn't even have the right to vote at that time, and laws and customs kept women from doing most of what they are doing today. The likelihood of a woman being in the President's Cabinet in the 1860s is very, very, very slim.

Let's go to the other extreme. You may be fuzzy on who was in Jimmy Carter's Cabinet, but even if you are too young to remember Carter, you're guessing that he was recent enough not to be the first president to appoint women in that role. Score another point for the process of elimination.

Now comes the hard part. If you have any knowledge of history, and I hope you do, you know that the two remaining choices were, at least, presidents during the 20th century...in other words, after women were granted the right to vote.

You may not be able to get past this choice. But even if you can't, and you blindly select one or the other, your chance of selecting the correct answer is one out of two. Even if your teacher deducts points, I would go ahead and put down (A) or (B).

Those of you who know a little more about history are going to remember that Roosevelt was loved or hated for his dramatic changes in government, while Hoover was the poster boy for The Status Quo Society. If that difference in their styles and actions comes to mind, then you'd be 100-percent correct to choose FDR.

Check it out, check it out!

Use this process of elimination for all types of objective questions. Depending on whether you can eliminate any of the answers and whether you feel you can "afford" to lose the points will help you decide how to answer the question.

If there is time during a test for you to come back to questions and look at them one more time, go ahead and put a line through the answers you know can't be correct. That will simply save you time. You will ignore the answers that are struck out and concentrate on the ones that remain. A small point, but it can save you several seconds per question.

What about going back, rechecking your work, and changing a guess? How valid was that first guess? It was probably pretty darn good (presuming you had some basis for guessing in the first place). So good that you should *only* change it *if:*

☞ It really was just a wild guess and, upon further thought, you conclude your guess answer really should be eliminated (in which case your next guess is, at least, not quite so wild).

☞ You remembered something that changed the odds of your guess completely (or the answer to a later question helped you figure out the answer to this one!).

☞ You miscalculated on a math problem.

☞ You misread the question (didn't notice a "not," "always," or another important qualifier).

Get visual

Throughout a test, don't miss an opportunity to draw a picture for yourself if it will help you understand the question and figure out the right answer. If the question deals with any sort of cause-and-effect that has several steps in it, literally draw or write down those steps very quickly, using abbreviated words or symbols. This may help you see missing pieces, help you understand relationships between parts, and, thus, help you select the right answer.

16 tips for "acing" multiple-choice tests

1. Be careful you don't read too much into questions. Don't try to second-guess the test preparer, get too elaborate, and ruin the answer.
2. Underline the key words.
3. If two choices are very similar, the answer is probably neither one of them.
4. If two choices are opposite, one of them is probably correct.
5. Don't go against your first impulse unless you are *sure* you were wrong. (Sometimes you're so smart you scare yourself.)
6. Check for negatives and other words that are there to throw you off. ("Which of the following is *not....*")
7. The answer is usually wrong if it contains "all," "always," "never," or "none." I repeat, usually.
8. The answer has a great chance of being right if it has "sometimes," "probably," or "some."
9. When you don't know the right answer, look for the wrong ones.
10. Don't eliminate an answer unless you actually know what every word means.
11. Read every answer (unless you are wildly guessing at the last minute and there's no penalty). A sneaky test maker will place a decoy answer that's *almost* right (or *seems* logically right) first, tempting you to pick it before you've even considered the other choices.
12. If it's a standardized test, consider transferring all the answers from one section to the answer sheet at the same time. This can save time. Just

be careful: Make sure you're putting each answer in the right place.

13. If you're supposed to read a long passage and answer questions about it, read the questions *first.* That will tell you what you're looking for and *affect the way you read the passage.* If dates are asked for, circle all dates in the passage as you read. If you're looking for facts rather than conclusions, it will, again, change the way you read the passage. (When you first read the question, before you look at the answers, decide what you think the answer is. If your answer is one of the choices, bingo!)

14. The longest and/or most complicated answer to a question is often correct—the test maker has been forced to add qualifying clauses or phrases to make that answer complete and unequivocal.

15. Be suspicious of choices that seem obvious to a 2-year-old. Why would the teacher give you such a gimme? Maybe she's not, that trickster!

16. Don't give up on a question that, after one reading, seems hopelessly confusing or hard. Looking at it from another angle, restating it in your own words, drawing a picture, etc., may help you realize it's not as hard as you thought.

Analogies-study : succeed as eat : live

I may be a sick puppy, but I like analogies. In the heat of completing 30 of them on a test, I may have slight second thoughts, but I look upon them as incredible brain teasers. To help you figure out the right answer in an analogy, write it out or at least *think* it out. Suppose the question was:

POLICE : ARREST

(A) priest : church
(B) doctor : prescribe
(C) driver : sleep
(D) lawyer : court

What's the relationship between "police" and "arrest"? First of all, what parts of speech are "police" and "arrest" in this example? "Noun : verb."

The correct answer is going to have the same relationship. Two of the answers, (B) and (C), are "noun : verb." So we've eliminated two of the four already.

What is the relationship between "police" and "arrest"? "Arrest" is one thing police do as part of their job.

Which now seems correct? The doctor or the driver? If you substitute "doctor" and "prescribe" in the above sentence, doesn't that sound correct? But if you put "driver" and "sleep" in the same places, does it make sense? Not really. We assume that, at some point or other, all drivers sleep, but it isn't a part of their job.

Some samples for you to taste

Many of these basic principles apply to the other types of questions you'll find on an objective test. Matching one item with another, completing sentences, doing math problems, choosing the correct vocabulary word—all rely on:

1. Your prior knowledge gained from studying for this particular course.
2. All the reading, studying, and listening you've been doing for years.
3. Your common sense.
4. Your ability to eliminate as many as possible of the potential answers.

5. Paying close attention to and following directions.

Let's run through an example of another type of question, this one involving antonyms (even though they're gone, thankfully, from the SAT):

MAMMOTH:

(A) colossal
(B) minuscule
(C) perpendicular
(D) moderate

The test writer has thrown in (A) to see if you'll flub up and choose a synonym. Not exactly dirty pool, but a technique to watch for. Choice (C) is a kind of off-center joke. Some people think that, because it is so unusual, it must be right. Answer (D) is a variation on (A) in that it refers to size, but it's not the right size for the answer.

The correct answer is (B). Even if you didn't know what "minuscule" meant, you should have been able to figure out that "mini" is tiny or little or as close to the opposite of "mammoth" as you're going to get here.

Comprehension questions

This is the portion of the test where you find a short essay, followed by several questions. You are supposed to find the answers to those questions in the essay. Unlike the multiple-choice questions, where the answer is actually right in front of you, the answers to the essay questions may well be hidden in one fashion or another.

Not since 3rd grade have you had an essay question that asks, "How old was Thomas Jefferson when he first went to Bloomingdale's?" and, lo and behold, back in the essay it clearly says, "Thomas Jefferson was 17 when he visited Bloomingdale's for the first time." Unfortunately for you, those questions went out with notes that said, "Do you love me? Yes or No!" and recess.

You're lucky if you get questions like, "How old was Thomas Jefferson when he became President?" and the essay says, "Thomas Jefferson ascended to the office of the President 33 years after his first election as a member of the Virginia House of Burgesses in 1768."

Buried somewhere else in the essay will be something like, "Jefferson, born 33 years before the Declaration of Independence..." Because you should know that the Declaration of Independence was written in 1776, you can figure out he was born in 1743 and that he became president in 1801. The rest is history.

Don't confuse me with facts

Look at that example again. Did it ever say the year of Jefferson's birth or the year he became President? Nope. It gave you, in two different places, enough information to figure it out.

At the same time, those tricksters have thrown in enough dates and numbers to get people to write down "33" or "66" as the right answer. Also, they don't offer the information in strict chronological order—another way to mess you up.

This is where too little attention to detail can get you a wrong answer. Before you search for the answer, you need to decide what the *question* is.

Don't jump to conclusions so quickly that you grab the first number that you see. In fact, you can be pretty sure that any number that you see will *not* be the answer.

In the Jefferson example, you might have quickly scribbled down the following information just to get your bearings, and the correct answer:

1. 1776	2. 1768	3. 1801
−33	+33	−1743
1743 birth	1801 Prez	58

Here's the method I recommend for answering comprehension questions:

1. Read the questions first. Consider them clues to the puzzle. You'll be alerted to what the essay is about so you don't start cold.

2. Slowly read the essay, keeping in mind the questions you've just read. Don't underline too much, but do underline conjunctions that change the direction of the sentence: "nevertheless," "however," "although," "yet," etc. If you notice such a "shift" word, there is a good chance that this sentence will figure into one of the questions.

   For example, this sentence in the essay, "John Smith was the kind of writer who preferred writing over editing, *while* his wife, Lois, was interested in the latter over the former," might provide the answer to the question: "Did Lois Smith prefer writing or editing?" A too-careless glance back at the text will cause you to select "writing" as the answer.

3. Read the questions again. Then go back and forth, finding the answer to the first one, the second one, etc. Don't skip around unless the first question is an absolute stumper. If you jump around too much, you'll get confused and you won't answer any of the questions completely or correctly.

You're failing this test: True or false?

I think true-false tests are generally more insidious than multiple-choice, because the latter at least offers the correct answer, which you may pick out without knowing it's correct. That's the bad news.

The good news is that it's hard to beat 50-50 odds!

What can you do to increase your scores on true-false tests? Be more inclined to guess if you have to. After all, I encouraged you to guess on a multiple-choice test if you could eliminate enough wrong answers to get down to two, one of which is correct. Well, you're already there! So, unless you are being penalized for guessing, guess away! Even if you are being penalized, you may want to take a shot if you have the faintest clue of the correct answer.

What tricks do test makers incorporate in true-false tests? Here are three to watch out for:

1. Two parts (statements) that *are* true (or, at least, *may* be true), linked in such a way that the *whole* statement becomes false. Example: "Since many birds can fly, they use stones to grind their food." Many birds *do* fly, and birds *do* swallow stones to grind their food, but implying a *causal relationship* (the word "since") between the two clauses makes the *whole* statement false.

2. The longer and/or more complicated a statement in a true-false test, the less likely it's true, because every clause of it must be true (and there are so many chances for a single part of it to be false).

3. Few broad, general statements are true *without exception*. So always be on your guard when you see the words "all," "always," "no," "never," or other such absolutes. As long as you can think of a *single* example that proves such a statement false, then it *is* false. But be wary: There *are* true statements containing such absolutes; they are just rare.

Matching

Match the following countries with their capitals:

Thailand	Paris
Japan	Tokyo
France	Kuala Lumpur
Malaysia	Bangkok

Match the obvious ones first. Let's say you know Paris and Tokyo are the capitals of France and Japan, respectively. Look at the two remaining choices. Here is where common sense and good general knowledge will come in handy.

Because you probably get a lot of your world news from the radio and TV, you may well have heard the combos more than you've seen them. Go with the ones that "sound right." (In this case, Bangkok, Thailand and Kuala Lumpur, Malaysia.)

Sentence completions

Like many of the other kinds of problems, sentence completions can often be figured out by putting the question into context or into perspective. Here's an example:

"The hypnotist said to the man, 'You're very _____.' "

(A) sleepy   (D) ill
(B) rich   (E) busy
(C) ugly

Quick. What do hypnotists do? What do they say (at least in the movies)? It has to be (A). Now, at some time in the past three or four hundred years, a hypnotist has probably said all of the other words. He may also have said, "Do you know what Ronald Reagan's doing now?" That doesn't mean the other choices are *right*. We're looking for logic and common sense here.

Multiple-choice math

Process of elimination is important in finding the answers. There are some numbers to consider, also. For example, scan the problem below and see if you can figure out the answer without actually doing the math:

334 x 412 =

(A) 54,559
(B) 137,608
(C) 22,528
(D) 229,766

By performing one simple task, you can eliminate two of the possible answers. Multiply the last digits in each number (2 x 4). The answer must end in 8. So (A) and (D) have been eliminated...that fast!

Now, eyeball (B) and (C). Can you find the right answer quickly? Here you are doing educated guessing, known in math circles as "guesstimating." Look: 334 x 100 is 33,400. You should be able to do that without any tools. Therefore, (C) has to be wrong. You are left with (B).

Should you do the actual math to double-check your answer? I wouldn't. You are certain that (A) and (D) are wrong. Absolutely. You know that (C) is much too low. Mark (B) as the answer and move on.

Here are other ways to better your score on math tests:

☞ Try to figure out what is being asked, what principles are involved, what information is important and what's not. Don't let extraneous data throw you off track. Make sure you know the *kind* of answer you're seeking: Is it a speed, weight, angle, exponent, square root?

☞ Whenever you can, "translate" formulas and numbers into words. Estimate the answer before you even begin the actual calculation. At least you'll know the size of the ballpark you're playing in!

☞ Even if you're not particularly visual, pictures can sometimes help. Try translating a particularly vexing math problem into a drawing or diagram.

☞ Play around. There are often different paths to the same solution, or even equally valid solutions.

☞ When you are checking your calculations, try working *backwards*. I've found it an easier way to catch simple arithmetical errors.

☞ Try to write down all of your calculations—neatly. You'll be less likely to make a mistake if you take your time, and if you *do* make a mistake, it will be a lot easier to spot.

The importance of words

No matter how much you study principles and examples, you will be lost if the words used in the test are simply not in *your* vocabulary. I could make the point, of course, that without a sufficient vocabulary, you won't be able to keep up with the principles anyway. Like reading itself, building a workable vocabulary is absolutely essential to doing well on any kind of test, because you are more likely to understand the directions, questions, and possible answers.

Build your vocabulary as much as you can. Read good books. Listen to people who have large vocabularies. Write down words you don't know and become familiar with them. The more words you know, the better you can play the process of elimination game, and the better score you'll get. I highly recommend *Better Vocabulary in 30 Minutes a Day* by Edie Schwager (Career Press, 1996), for those of you who are word-challenged.

All of the above, none of the above

Some teachers have fallen in love with "all of the above" and "none of the above." You can't take one of their tests without those phrases appearing in every other question. *Hope* that you see "all of the above" as a potential answer to *every* question because *it gives you a much better chance to do better on the test* than your mastery of the material (or lack thereof) would normally warrant. Why? Because you don't have to be really sure that "all of the above" is correct to choose it. All you have to be is *pretty* sure that *two* answers are correct (and equally sure the others are not *necessarily* wrong). As long as there is—you feel—more than one correct answer, then "all of the above" must be the right choice!

Likewise, you don't have to be convinced that "none of the above" is the right answer, just *reasonably* sure that none of the other answers are absolutely correct.

Just be careful to read those instructions! If they say, "Choose the *best* answer" and you rapidly choose "(A) the Andes," you lose if (A) is merely *a* correct answer. "(E) all of the above" will still be the *best* answer if every *other* answer is *also* correct.

Here's a sample analysis to show you why you should love teachers infatuated with "all" and "none":

Which of the following authors won the Pulitzer Prize:

A. John Updike
B. N. Scott Momaday
C. Norman Mailer
D. All of the above
E. None of the above

Do you know for a fact that one of them *didn't* win? Yes? Then you *eliminate* (D) as a possibility. Do you know whether *any* of them won? If so, you eliminate (E). Do you know if *two* of them won? You may feel pretty confident that Updike and Mailer won, but not have any idea who Mr. Momaday is. *Doesn't matter*—once you know *two* won, (D) is the *only* possible answer.

A word about "easy" tests

Some people think "open book" tests are the easiest of all. They pray for them...at least until they see their first one.

These are the toughest tests of all, if only because even normally "nice" teachers feel no compunction whatsoever about making such tests as tough as a Marine drill instructor. *Heck, you can use your book!* That's like having a legal crib sheet, right? Worse yet, many open-book tests are also take-home tests, meaning you can use your notes (and any other books or tools you can think of).

Because you have to anticipate that there will be no easy questions, no matter how well you know that material, you need to do some preparation before you deal with this type of test:

- ☞ Mark important pages by turning down corners, using paper clips, or any other method that will help you quickly flip to important charts, tables, summaries, or illustrations.
- ☞ Write an index of the pages you've turned down so you know where to turn immediately for a specific chart, graph, table, etc.
- ☞ Summarize all important facts, formulas, etc., on a separate sheet.

☞ If you are also allowed to bring your notes or if it's a take-home test, write a brief index to your notes (general topics only) so you know where to find pertinent information.

Answer the questions you don't need the book for first, including those of which you're fairly sure and know where to check the answers in your book. Star the latter ones.

Then use the book. Check starred answers first and erase the stars once you have completed them. Then work on those questions for which you must rely fully on the book.

Although a take-home test is, by definition, an open-book test, it is the hardest of all. An open-book test in class simply can't last longer than the time allotted for the class. A take-home exam may give you a night or two, in some cases as long as a week, to complete.

Why are they so hard? You're *given* so much time because teachers expect that it will take you *longer* than the time available in class to finish. You may have to go well beyond your text(s) and notes even to get a handle on some of the questions, leading to some long nights at the library. Take any easy eight-hour tests lately? The longer you're given, the easier it is to procrastinate ("Heck, I've got another two nights!"), and we know where *that* leads.

There are only two good aspects to balance the scales. You've certainly been given the chance to "be all that you can be." No excuse for not doing a terrific job on a test with virtually no time limit. If you tend to freeze during a normal exam, you should have far less anxiety at home in comfortable surroundings.

CHAPTER 7

THE DAY OF THE EXAM: PSYCHING UP

Well, here you are. No longer are you thinking of the exam as being next month or next week or even tomorrow. You're sitting in the very room in the very chair and someone is heading your way with a test paper.

Margaret, lead the way

Right here, at the beginning of this chapter, let me tell you about my friend Margaret. She's going to help you get there—with a technique I call the Margaret Preview.

Margaret and her husband, Bob, lived in a large capital city in a Third World country. Because of his job, they had to attend a lot of receptions and dinners at other peoples' homes, but the streets of this particular city were not very well marked and the numbering system of the houses was not all that logical.

Bob and Margaret both had a thing about punctuality, so they devised a plan. Early on the day of the party, Margaret, armed with a city map and invitation, searched for the house or apartment. She didn't give up until she found it.

Thus, Bob and Margaret would arrive on time without having driven aimlessly around now-dark streets looking for a house or a whole neighborhood.

They could have been fashionably late for a party now and then. But you really don't want to be late for a test, do you?

If you're taking a test in a new surrounding, do the Margaret Preview. If it's in a different building or room, take a few minutes and find it. You don't want to discover 90 seconds before the bell that Room 1210A is in the *West* Tower and not immediately across the hall from Room 1211A in the *East* Tower where you are standing.

If it's off campus, check out the location a few days early. See how long it takes you (and adjust for weather, time of day, and day of the week). Where is the parking? Which door do you go in? Where's the nearest place to get a cup of coffee on the morning of the exam? Is there construction? Which streets are one way? Which exit do you take from the highway? Are there tolls?

The lifesaving bunch of stuff

Now that you're safely there, on time, what did you bring with you?

I used to make up what I called the Test Kit. Into my backpack went some pens or pencils (depending on what I needed for the test)—two or three of each; the book and workbooks associated with the test; my notes; a calculator, if allowed; a candy bar or other treat that would give me energy; photo ID and an entry card, if required.

By collecting all this mess in one place, I wouldn't be very likely to forget it. Also, if I did something dreadful like oversleep, I only had to grab the one thing that I had packed the night before and dash out the door.

You have enough to worry about the morning of a big test. Don't spend frantic minutes looking for something that you could have placed inside a backpack, briefcase, or large purse the night before.

Double your pleasure—sit alone

Unless you are already in an assigned seat, try to sit near the front so you will get the exam first and have some precious seconds at the end while the other papers are being passed to the front. It also places you near the teacher or proctor for easier access for questions.

Avoid sitting near someone who has a lot of noisy jewelry, is cracking or popping gum, or is too friendly with others in the immediate area. Be a hermit, in other words. Choose a quiet area.

Wear loose, comfortable clothes, the kind that you love, your favorite shirt or sweater or slacks. If you're left-handed, look for a left-handed desk. Check out the room for sunlight (too much or too little), lighting, heat and cold.

The Hoosier measuring system

Remember in the movie *Hoosiers* when the team that Gene Hackman was coaching made it to the state finals? The boys walked into the basketball arena and were overwhelmed by its size; it sure wasn't like the little gymnasiums they were used to playing in.

Coach was smart. He had them measure the basketball court. Whaddya know? It was exactly the same size as the one back in little Hickory. Point made. Point taken. They won, of course. (Oh, sorry, I thought you had seen the movie.) Pull a Gene Hackman move. Take a "measure" of the exam in front of you before you begin.

Go all the way

Begin at the beginning. Then move through to the end. No, I'm not talking about taking the exam. I'm talking about looking through the booklet, glancing at all the questions. If you have permission to go all the way through it, do that before you ever start. Just give yourself an overview of what lies ahead. That way you can spot the easier sections (and do them first) and get an idea of the point values assigned to each section.

You can also make sure your test is complete. Wouldn't it feel terrible to flash through the test, check your answers with minutes to spare, and *then* discover you missed that last essay question...which counts for 50 percent of your grade?

The art of war

There are three ways to attack a multiple-choice test:

1. Start at the first question and keep going until you reach the end, never leaving a question until you have either answered it fully or made an educated guess.
2. Answer the *easy* questions first—the ones you know the answers to without any thinking at all or those requiring the simplest calculations— then go back and do the harder ones.
3. Answer the *hardest* questions first, then go back and do the easy ones.

None of these three options is inherently right or wrong. Each may work for different individuals. (I'm assuming that these three approaches are all in the context of the test format. Weighted sections may well affect your strategy.)

The first approach is, in one sense, the quickest, in that no time is wasted reading through the whole test trying to pick out either the easiest or hardest questions. Presuming that you do not permit yourself to get stumped by any single question (so you spend an inordinate amount of time on it), it is probably the method most of you employ.

Remember, though, to leave questions that confuse you from the outset until the end and to allocate enough time to go back to those you haven't answered *and* to check thoroughly *all* of your answers.

The second approach ensures that you will maximize your right answers—you're putting off those that you find particularly vexing.

Many experts recommend this method because they maintain that answering so many questions one after another gives you immediate confidence to tackle the questions you're not sure about. If you find that you agree, then by all means use this strategy. However you may consider just *noting* the easy ones as you proofread the test. This takes less time and, to me, delivers the same "confidence boost."

The last approach is actually the one I used—I made it a point to do the very hardest questions first, then work my way "down" the difficulty ladder. (This means I often worked *backwards,* because many test makers and teachers make their tests progressively more difficult.)

It may sound like a strange strategy to you, so let me explain the psychology.

First of all, I figured if time pressure started getting to me toward the end of the test, I would rather be in a position to answer the easiest questions—and lots of them—in the limited time left than ones I really had to think about. After all, by the end of the test, my mind was simply not working as well as at the beginning!

That's the major benefit of the third approach: When I was most "up," most awake, most alert, I tackled the questions that required the most analysis, thinking, interpretation, etc. When I was most tired—near the end—I was answering the questions that were virtual "gimmes."

At the same time, I was also giving myself a *real* shot of confidence. As soon as I finished the first hard question, I already felt better. When I finished all of the hard ones, everything was downhill.

I would always, however, try to ensure adequate time to at least put down an answer for every question. Better to get one question wrong and complete three other answers than to get one right and leave three blank.

It is not the approach for everybody, but it may be right for you.

And don't fall into the "answer daze," that blank stare some students get when they can't think of an answer—for 10 minutes.

Do *some*thing. Better to move on and get that one question wrong than waste invaluable time doing nothing.

Ask questions immediately if you don't understand something. The proctor may not be able to say anything (or may not know anything to say), but it's worth a try.

If you get part of a question answered and you need to return to finish it, work out a little code for yourself. Put a symbol in the margin beside the problem that means "You're partly done here—come back to this one after you've done all the ones you can do."

Guess and guess again?

If you do guess at any of the objective questions and expect that your test paper will be returned to you, place a little dot or other symbol beside them. That way you will know how successful your guessing was. For example, suppose you guessed at 30 questions and got 22 of them right. That tells me your guesses are, for the most part, *educated* guesses, not wild stabs in the dark, and that you earned enough points to make it worthwhile, *even if you got penalized for missing eight others.* However, if you only got six right, review my comments on educated guessing. Something's not working for you.

When you think you have finished with a whole section, double-check to see if that's true. Make sure all the questions have been answered.

It's a long race—pace yourself

If you have 100 multiple-choice questions and you have 50 minutes allotted for that section, you don't have to be MIT material to figure that you should spend a maximum of 30 seconds on each answer. Check your progress two or three times during the 50 minutes.

Which reminds me: Don't depend on a wall clock to tell you the time. Bring your watch.

You say oral and I say aural

Listen up. When the teacher (or tape recorder) gives you a question, jot down the key words so that you can refer to them when you think up your answer.

Do the same thing if you are being given a dictation where you are expected to listen, then write down what you heard. Key words—the nouns and verbs—will help you "capture" the rest of the sentence.

If you don't understand the question (whether it's in a foreign language you're studying or in English), ask to have it repeated. Ask again if you still don't understand. Listen intently to everything.

For computer-scored tests

If you are required to color in a little rectangle to show which answer is correct so that a machine can score the results, mark the answer sheet very carefully. Stray pencil marks can be picked up by the computer, causing the wrong answer to be recorded. If you carefully filled in one box, only to change your mind later, completely, *completely* erase the first answer. If the computer picks up both markings, guess what happens? You don't get the point, even if one of the boxes is correct.

You deserve a break today

Take the breaks that are offered. You will benefit in the long run by going to the bathroom, getting a drink of water, eating a candy bar, or all of the above, rather than sitting there working through another algebraic equation.

Just as you needed the good sleep you got during the week, you'll need to be energized by the breaks. Besides, suppose you didn't move, and then, 20 minutes after the break, you've got to go the bathroom. Desperately. What if the proctor won't let you? Do you kill him and take the SAT while in prison at West Bubba, Arkansas? Or do you act smart and take the break when everyone else does?

While you're taking your test, you can perform some unobtrusive exercises at your desk that will make you feel refreshed. Try them right now. First, tense up your feet—squeeze them hard, then relax them, then squeeze them. Then do the same with the muscles in your calves, shoulders, hips, and abdomen. It's a pretty simple exercise but I find it energizes me when I am unable to get up and move around the room. Even moving the facial muscles helps. Do them looking down at your paper; otherwise your teacher will think you are having a coronary or making faces at her.

For my next trick

If you've just finished a big, big test, get out of town. Go to a movie or a party or something that will allow you to forget, for a few hours, that you have been keeping your nose to the grindstone for the past several days.

Go. Relax. Then go on to Chapter 8.

CHAPTER 8

POST-TEST: SURVIVAL AND REVIEW

"Winning isn't everything, but wanting to win is."
                    —Vince Lombardi (1913-1970)

"Winning is everything."

                                        —your mother

No, it's not. But you and I can understand what Mom's talking about, right? It's nice to win, whether it's a noontime intramural basketball game or getting an A on an exam.

Don't you agree that it feels even better to "win" when the exam has been tough, when it's been challenging and difficult, than when it was one of Mr. Bibble's easy unit tests.

Vince got it right. Wanting to win is important. Otherwise, why would you study so hard and give up so much for so long?

Now that you've done the studying and taken the test, you want to know the results.

Let's assume you did well. Congratulations! But no matter how many points you earned, reviewing the test is a vitally important exercise in preparing yourself for the next test—and for taking a hard look at the way you study.

If you take a standardized test and have the chance to get a copy of the exam—and your own answers—do so. It's unlikely you'll find they made any mistakes in the scoring of the exam, but it will be good exercise for you to review what you got right and what you didn't while the test is reasonably fresh in your mind.

The emphasis in this chapter, however, is on the tests you take from teachers. Most will review the overall results of the test with the class on the day they are returned. First of all, you want to make sure the answers that you missed are truly incorrect. Teachers make mistakes. I know that comes as a shock.

Don't become a nuisance by challenging everything in class, waving your hand and saying, in a pleading voice, "But, but, Mr. Squeezicks! I meant to say George Washington Carver instead of George Washington!"

Concentrate on the answers that are clearly marked wrong. Even if you're semi-alert, you should be able to grab a couple of extra points, points that might move you up another letter grade.

If the question really was ambiguous and your answer could arguably be as correct as the one the teacher chose, go ahead and make a pitch. This will be especially effective if a few others in the class chose the same answer. There *is* strength in numbers.

Your chances will be a lot better if you keep the discussion on a diplomatic level, of course, rather than getting snotty or snide. Teachers can get defensive sometimes.

Let's suppose you got the answer wrong, fair and square. Most likely, you got it wrong for one of these reasons:

You made a careless mistake

1. You wrote down the wrong letter or number. You knew the answer was (A), but, in your haste, you wrote down (B).

2. Similarly, you filled in the wrong box in the answer sheet. You see the mistake now. You vow not to do it again. (Good. That's the first step on the road to recovery.)

3. You left out a whole section of the test because you didn't turn the page, or you "thought" you had done it or...

4. You wrote in such a scribbled fashion or crammed the words together so much that the teacher pulled an "I can't read it so it's wrong" deal on your test and gave you no credit. (I'm on his side. Get your act—and your penmanship—together.)

5. You misread the directions. You missed the slightly important word "not," so you provided the exact opposite of what you should have.

6. You guessed wildly without even reading the options and ignored the fact that points would be deducted for wrong answers, so you got fewer points than if you had left the answer sheet blank for those questions.

You didn't know the material

1. You didn't read all the assignments, or get a complete set of class notes, or find out answers to questions you had about some of the material.

2. You attended class, took notes, and read the assignments, but you didn't understand what the
   topic was all about.

3. You needed to know a lot of facts—dates, names,
   events, causes and effects—and you didn't.

Your personal life got in the way

1. You brought into the test your worries that the
   person you're dating is going to dump you, that
   your parents are fighting again, that your kids
   are heading to reform school if you don't do
   something right now or...whatever.

2. You had a horrible cold, a terrible headache, or
   you got too little or too much sleep.

Next time I'll know better

Don't beat up on yourself too much. Do take the time to
evaluate how you did—the bad and the good. Maybe you
always hated essay questions but this time you did well.
It's as important to evaluate why you *were* successful as
why you *weren't*.

In that case, maybe you learned a lot from your study
group. Maybe your teacher gave you some good advice.
Maybe you read that section of this book first and it helped
you (I like that choice). Maybe you're picking up reading
and comprehension skills from a combination of factors.
Think back over what you may have done differently this
time. Give yourself a lot of the credit. After all, you took
the test all by yourself. Pat-on-the-back time!

The worrisome part is the "careless mistake" area, yet
it's probably the easiest to correct. Take a vow that you
won't do such silly things again. It's especially annoying
when you had the right answer and you simply circled the

wrong one. Next time, pay a little closer attention to what you're doing and pace yourself so you can double-check your work.

There's no substitute for knowledge

If you go into the test knowing only half the material, don't expect to get above the 50-percent mark. Doing well on a test, as I've been telling you all along, is a combination of knowing how to take the test and knowing the stuff that goes into the answers.

If you can't seem to get prepared, maybe you'd better go back and reread those earlier chapters. Get to class, get your work organized, manage your time, read the book, do your homework, the whole *shtick*.

Now's the time to see where the teacher got the questions that made up the test. What percentage of the test came from the lectures? From the book? From handouts?

It is unlikely that you're going to get an A in every class you take, but you can get the best grade possible. Even in classes that, for whatever reason, are way, way over your head, you can at least pass. In most cases, you're going to do a lot better than that.

Ask questions. Ask questions during class. Ask questions when you meet with your teacher. Join a study group and ask questions. Ask questions when the test results are being discussed.

Keep it all in perspective

What nerve you have! A personal life, you say? Isn't Chemistry 104 or American government more important?

Of course not. But turn the personal motor off now and then and spend time with your friends down at the Continental Congress.

Yes, we all have colds and sore feet and heartbreaks. That is life, after all. But we can compartmentalize the parts of our life now and then without going overboard with it. Remember the Imelda Marcos Theory.

Let's try that one again, shall we?

If you really messed up the test, sit down with your teacher and discuss the reasons (having done your self-evaluation, based on the areas mentioned in this chapter).

Ask if you can take another test—you may not be able to get any credit for it, but you'll impress him and he will look more kindly upon you when it comes time to enter your final grade on the official form.

Retaking "bad" tests is a good idea for another reason. Unless you just completely messed up in getting the right answers matched to the right questions, you probably performed so poorly because you didn't know the material well enough the first time.

Now you are giving yourself a second chance to learn material that will no doubt appear on future tests, and—this may come as a real shock—*you might actually need to know this information for some reason in your future life.*

A satisfactory completion of the retake will give you that boost of self-confidence that got stomped on when you got a bad grade the first time. "Hey," you're saying to the Test Demons, "I can do this!"

But don't miss the test entirely (unless you're on your death bed, of course) or you'll face the wrath of Mrs. Khan—the make-up exam. Think a lot of teachers look forward to creating an entirely new test *just for you?* That they're going to make it *easier* than the test you missed? Or that they'll spend *less time* with your test at home than the weekend they had to grade 30? Think you want to stay far away from Mrs. Khan's make-up tests?

Good answer.

Come with me now to the inner sanctum

I've been talking to you about what you can and should do. Now, let's take a peek in the next chapter at this whole test business from the teacher's point of view. C'mon, he won't bite.

CHAPTER 9

HOW TEACHERS MAKE UP TESTS

"Examinations are formidable even to the best prepared, for the greatest fool may ask more than the wisest man can answer."
—Charles Caleb Colton (1780?-1832)

Apparently, Mr. Colton had just flunked his midterm. You've got one advantage over Colton: You're going to read this chapter and learn how the "greatest fools" make up those tests. I'm sorry to say that some teachers look upon tests as ways to beat down challenges to their authority ("I'll show them who knows this stuff!") or as punishment ("That'll teach them not to love English lit!"), but fortunately the key word here is "some." Let's look at how a *typical* teacher makes up a test.

I'm just an average kind of guy

If students (who have studied and made a valid attempt to do well on the test) earn a grade from "excellent" to "good" to "average" (that is, A to B to C), this tells them where they stand and the *teacher* where he stands, too.

If the test results show everyone getting an A or everyone getting Ds and Fs (after honest attempts to do well), the teacher has messed up.

On tests, the majority of students will get Bs and Cs, with a small number getting As and Ds. There should be an even smaller number of Fs, "rewards" for those who truly don't have a clue or who don't care.

Any test is evaluating the teacher, too. He or she has an obligation to give you information, help you understand it, make assignments that have some validity, and lead you progressively through a series of learning exercises.

The test should reflect your understanding of this body of knowledge. And although the burden is on you to do the work and learn the material, there is an additional burden on the teacher to make sure everyone (except those who don't care) is actually *learning.*

The wise teacher provides several opportunities during the semester to "test" how well you are learning. Quizzes (scheduled and surprise ones), papers, reports, projects, tests on units, chapters or whole books, oral reports, etc. All of this should add up to your evaluation—your grade.

Some teachers just love one type of question. Some are true-false freaks; others push the multiple-choice/short answer combo. If old tests, former students, the teacher's own comments on the test coming up, and your own personal experience tell you this is true, you might as well study for that kind of test. You still have to know the material, of course. It's just that you may need to remind yourself that you are going to have to deal with it in a particular fashion.

The best teachers use a combination of test questions to find out what you know. Frankly, some of them hate grading essay questions, so they rarely use them.

Why do teachers choose essay questions?

1. They are quicker and easier to prepare.
2. They may be preferred when a group is small and the test will not be reused.
3. They are used to explore students' attitudes rather than measure their achievements.
4. They are used to encourage and reward the development of the students' skill in writing.
5. They are suitable when it's important for the students to explain or describe.
6. They are more suitable to some material. You're likely to have more essay questions in English and history than you are in the sciences.

Teachers use objective questions because:

1. They are preferred when the group is large and the test may be reused.
2. They are more efficient when highly reliable test scores must be obtained quickly.
3. They are more suitable for covering a larger amount of content in the same amount of time.
4. They are easier for the teacher to give an impartial grade. Every student has to write down "C" to get number 22 correct.
5. They are easier for some teachers to create.
6. They may be used when students need to demonstrate or show.

A thousand points of right

At the time the teacher decides what kinds of questions she will ask and determines what each question will cover, she must also assign a point value to each question.

She will assign higher point values to questions dealing with material that has been emphasized in lectures, class discussions, and readings. She'll also assign more points to areas requiring more time and attention.

Think about it: You've never taken a test where each true-false question was worth 20 points and the long essay was worth five. She will clearly show the points possible for each section and/or question so you can decide how to spend your time.

Teachers have checklists, too

The teacher has selected the material to be covered. She's told you, at least in general terms, what the test will cover. She has decided on the format, assigned points, and written the questions, then double-checked to make sure she has included everything she wanted to include.

She has made sure the questions are different from those on previous tests, as she suspects that some of you will look at them, hoping she'll use the same questions.

She has set up the test in a format so there is no confusion, made sure it is free of typos, and checked her questions and answers to make sure they're not ambiguous.

Should we give her a passing grade?

The "test" for her comes when she sits down to grade what you've done. If half the students completely messed up one of the questions—but messed it up in the same way—she has to admit that the directions were not clearly written. She may even decide to throw out the question.

If she consistently finds that even her best students only complete half of her tests, she *should* conclude she made the test too long or too complicated. And she *should* shorten or simplify future ones. (And, of course, you *should* get an A just for showing up.)

A key word that the teacher should remember when making up or grading a test is "reasonable." What is the *reasonable* number of questions students should be expected to answer in 45 minutes? What should a teacher *reasonably* expect students to know after two weeks of a complicated course?

You can learn to fake sincerity

No, you can't. I just said that to keep your attention. Let me leave you with this thought about your relationship with your teachers: Teachers like students (and give them better grades) if they show genuine interest in the subject and the class. You don't have to be a teacher's pet or Geek of the Month, but if you like what you're learning, show it.

If you've decided that you love chemistry nearly as much as public speaking and major leg cramps, don't feel it necessary to tell your teacher. He *loves* this stuff. He goes to conventions *with other chemistry teachers*. He spends his weekends reading books like *50 Ways to Make Milkshakes with Hydrochloric Acid.* Just endure.

Fill in the blank so you won't go blank

I'll leave you with one more thing—the item I referred to in Chapter 4. On the next page is the form I've designed to help you sort out what you've got to do when, where, and how. Photocopy it, then fill in the blanks.

There. I've said it. I'm done. You're just getting started.

Don't ever say again, "She gave me a C!" No, *she* didn't. You give yourself the grades you deserve, the grades you earn by either studying or goofing off. So what grade are you going to give yourself next time?

Pre-test organizer

Class:_____**Teacher:**_____
Test date:_____ **Time:** From_____ to_____
Place:_____
Special instructions to myself (take calculator, dictionary, etc.):_____

_____

Materials I need to study for this test (check all needed):

- ❑ Book
- ❑ Workbook
- ❑ Class notes
- ❑ Handouts
- ❑ Tapes/videos
- ❑ Old tests
- ❑ Other_____

Format of the test will be (write the number of T/F, essays, etc., and total points for each section):

_____
_____
_____
_____
_____

Study group meetings (times, places):
1. _____
2. _____
3. _____
4. _____
5. _____

Material to be covered:
Indicate topics, sources, and amount of review (light or heavy) required. Check box when review is completed.

Topic	Sources	Review
_____	_____	☐ ____
_____	_____	☐ ____
_____	_____	☐ ____
_____	_____	☐ ____
_____	_____	☐ ____
_____	_____	☐ ____
_____	_____	☐ ____

After the test:
Grade I expected_____Grade I received_____
What did I do that helped me?_____
_____
_____
_____
_____
_____

What else should I have done?_____
_____
_____
_____
_____
_____
_____
_____

INDEX

ADD, 232-239
ADHD, 232, 233
Analogies, 404-406
Anxiety Professionals, 346
Asking questions in class,
    256, 260
Assignments, 266
Attention Deficit Disorder,
    see ADD

Binders, 268-270
Body language, 259
Breaks, 37, 49, 423-424

Card catalog, 99
Careless mistakes on tests,
    427
Class notes, 254-290
    and asking questions,
    260, 268, 274
    and class format, 273-274
    assignments, 266
    and distractions, 256,
    257
    and knowledge of

teacher, 265-266
    and listening, 255,
    270-272
    and preparing required
    materials. 268-270
    and selective listening,
    271-272
    and tape recorders,
    260-262
    and teachers' styles,
    274-276
    and verbal clues, 258
    and what you don't know,
    273
    binder system, 268-270
    mapping, 285, 286, 290
    nonverbal clues, 259
    practice exercise, 282-283
    reviewing, 277
    successful strategies,
    264-277
Classes
    afterwards, 288-289
    choosing, 51-52

format, 273-274
hands-on, 274
lecture, 273
participation, 31,
  287-288
questions, 287
scheduling, 52
seminar, 273
Clues in textbooks,
  292-295
Color-coding, 230, 362
Comic novel, 282-283
Competition, 346
Comprehension questions,
  406-408
Computer, 103-119
  buying, 105-107
  going online, 109-118
  hardware, 103
  Internet, 118-119
  skills, 29
  software, 108-109
Correcting a test, 426
Concept tree, 314
Cramming, 365, 366

Daily Schedule, 214-215,
  219, 240, 243, 359-360,
  369
Deadlines, 356-357
Dewey Decimal System,
  95-96
Distractions, 183-184, 227,
  238, 256, 257

Effective note-taking,
  247-251, 300
Eliminating answers,
  400-402

Essay tests, 388-396
  and lack of time,
    393-394
  and length, 391
  and organization,
    389-392
  and outlining, 392
  and proofreading, 393
  and reviewing answers,
    393
  common instructional
    verbs, 394-396
  how to approach, 389-391
  layout of answers, 392
  materials for, 389
  when lost, 391
  writing too much, 394

Flashcards, 382
For Entrepreneurs Only,
  235
Foreign language texts, 67

Goal pyramid, 42-43
Goal-setting, 43-44,
  237-238

Habits, 35-37
Harrell, Wilson, 235
Hartmann, Thom, 232,
  235, 236, 237
Hoosier Measuring
  System, 418-419
Hyperactivity, 232

Imelda Marcos Theory,
  347
Inverted Pyramid Theory,
  380-382

Kids, studying with, 198-199

Library, 92-102
  card catalog, 99
  Dewey Decimal
  Classification System, 95-96
  Internet, 98
  Library of Congress
  System, 96-97, 98
  New York Public Library, 94-95
  newspaper indexes, 99
  organization, 93-94, 95-98
  periodical indexes, 99
  personal, 85-91
  research, 100-102
  skills, 28-29
  U.S. Documents monthly catalog, 100
  vertical file, 100
Listening, 254-263, 270-272
Listening skills, 255, 262
Luhan, Mable Dodge, 301

Mapping, 285, 286, 290
Margaret Preview, 416-417
Matching tests, 410
Math tests, 411-412
Memory, 26-27
Motivation, 41-45
  extrinsic, 41-42
  intrinsic, 41-42
  rewards, 44-45

Multiple-choice tests, 404-405

Nonverbal clues, 259
Note-taking, 30, 374-376
  and ADD, 262-263
  and binder system, 268-270
  and control of time, 250
  and mapping, 285-286, 290
  and shorthand, 278-290
  and skimming texts, 292-295
  effective, 247-251, 300
  equipment, 252-253
  for oral reports, 317-323
  in class, 30, 278-290
  in the library, 30, 92-102
  pitfalls of poor, 248-249
  practice exercises, 282-284, 301-308
  preparing requirements, 252-253
  textbook, 30, 291-297, 316
  vocabulary lists, 315
Notes, 374-376
  abbreviating, 278-290
  poor, 248-249

Objective tests, 397-415
Old exams, 382-383
Open book tests, 414-415
Oral reports, 147-150
Outlines, 129, 136-138

Parkinson's Law, 352
Perfection, 48-49
Periodical indexes, 99
Pop quizzes, 372
Practice tests, 348
Pre-Test Organizer, 381,
437-438
Primary sources, 308-309
Prioritizing, 202, 213
Priority Task Sheet,
213-215, 218, 238, 240,
242,
Priority Tasks This Week,
355, 357, 359, 368
Project Board, 204-209,
212-213

Reading, 26-27, 56-91,
376-379
aesthetic, 60, 67-68
appendicies, 58
bibliograpy, 58
comprehension, 69-73,
296
critical, 60
end-of chapter
summaries, 293
fiction, 67, 85
for detail, 62-63
foreign language texts,
67
glossary, 58
index, 58
introduction, 57
pleasure, 60, 67-68
preface, 57
quick reference, 60
recall, 75

recognition, 76
remembering, 73-74,
76-85
retention, 74-75
skimming and scanning,
60-61, 294-295
speed, 69, 71-72
subheads, 59, 60, 61
table of contents, 57
technical texts, 63-67,
296-297
Research,
Retention, 26-27
Reviewing,
answers, 393
notes, 267-268
Rewards, 44-45, 238
Ritalin, 232

SAT, 384-387
Scan, 60-61
Selective listening,
271-272
Self-competition, 346
Self-discipline, 45, 364
Sentence completion tests,
410
Shorthand, 278-290
Skim, 60-62
Stress, 347
Study clock, 363-364
Study environment, 59,
180-194, 221
checklist, 200
Study group(s), 195-197,
275
Study skills, 23-33
Study time, 186, 352-369,

Studying
 and staying focused, 49
 fighting
  tiredness/boredom, 50
 with small kids, 198-199
Subject areas, evaluation,
 55

Tape recorder, 260-262
Teachers, 383-384
Technical texts, 63-67,
 296-297
Term plan, 201-211
Term-Planning Calendar,
 206-207, 210-211, 212,
 240, 241, 355, 357, 359
Test anxiety, 343-351
Tests
 "all of the above,"
  413-414
 analogies, 404-406
 and elimination, 400-402
 and exercise, 423-424
 and guessing, 399-400
 and pressure, 349-351
 and stress, 350
 and teachers, 426,
  432-436
 and time management,
  352-369
 and vocabulary, 412-413
 and weighted sections,
  398
 anxiety, 343-351
 careless mistakes on, 427
 comprehension
  questions, 406-408
 computer-scored, 423

 correcting, 426
 cramming, 365, 366
 day of, 416-424
 directions, 397-398
 essay, 388-396
 how teachers make up,
  432-438
 matching, 410
 math, 411-412
 multiple-choice, 403-404
 "none of the above,"
  413-414
 objective tests, 397-415
 open book, 414-415
 pop quizzes, 372
 preparation for, 32
 relative importance of,
  347-349
 SAT, 384-387
 sentence completion, 410
 standardized, 384-387
 study schedule for,
  364-366
 studying with kids,
  198-199
 true/false, 408-409
 weighted sections, 398
Textbook(s)
 as primary sources,
  308-309
 foreign language, 67
 notes from, 298-309
 reading ahead in,
  276-277
 technical, 63-37, 296-297
Time,
 and quilt, 168
 and time traps, 166, 188

as currency, 157
natural approach to, 158
problems with, 157
Time line, 313
Time management, 23-43,
27-28
a trial run, 178
adapting system, 176-177
and ADD, 237-239
and anticipating
opportunities, 167
and choices, 161
and color-coding, 230,
362
and commuting, 225-226
and flexibility, 161, 174,
229
and freedom, 167
and goals, 229
and interruptions, 364
and planning, 159,
162-172
and prioritizing, 166, 213
and rewards, 44-45, 238
and schedules, 229
and scheduling, 215-216
and study environment,
221
and studying smarter,
170
and the big picture, 169
as a liberating tool, 173
doing consistently,
177-178
hitting the wall, 221
long-term benefits of,
170-171
myths of, 173-175

peak performance period,
186
questions to ask about
routine, 358
realities of, 176-178
rewards of, 163-172
short-term benefits of,
166
tips for succeeding at,
220-231
to-do list, 213
Time traps, 166, 188
To-do list, 213, 353, 360
True/false tests, 408-409

U.S. Documents monthly
catalog, 100
Verbal clues, 258
Verbatim notes
Vertical file, 100
Vocabulary lists, 315

Weighting, 398
Writing papers, 31-32,
120-150
basic rules, 121-122
bibliography cards,
130-136
citing online information,
132-133
documentation, 141-142
editing, 146
final draft, 147
first draft, 138-143
footnotes, 142-143
lateness, 123-124
library research,128,
129-136, 143

note cards, 125, 134-139,
149
note-taking, 134-136
old papers, 124-125
organizational
approaches, 125
outline, 136-138
presentation, 123-124
proofreading, 146-147
second draft, 143-146

teacher's
instructions, 122-123
temporary outline, 129
temporary thesis,
128-129
topic, 126-128
work schedule, 126
writer's block, 140-141

"Your Starting Point"
chart, 24-25